Lecture Notes in Computer Science 13171

More information about this subseries at https://link.springer.com/bookseries/7409

Asbjørn Følstad · Theo Araujo ·
Symeon Papadopoulos · Effie L.-C. Law ·
Ewa Luger · Morten Goodwin ·
Petter Bae Brandtzaeg (Eds.)

Chatbot Research and Design

5th International Workshop, CONVERSATIONS 2021
Virtual Event, November 23–24, 2021
Revised Selected Papers

Editors
Asbjørn Følstad (iD)
SINTEF
Oslo, Norway

Theo Araujo (iD)
VU Amsterdam
Amsterdam, The Netherlands

Symeon Papadopoulos (iD)
CERTH-ITI
Thessaloniki, Greece

Effie L.-C. Law (iD)
Durham University
Durham, UK

Ewa Luger (iD)
University of Edinburgh
Edinburgh, UK

Morten Goodwin (iD)
Center for Artificial Intelligence Research
University of Agder
Kristiansand, Norway

Petter Bae Brandtzaeg (iD)
University of Oslo
Oslo, Norway

ISSN 0302-9743   ISSN 1611-3349 (electronic)
Lecture Notes in Computer Science
ISBN 978-3-030-94889-4   ISBN 978-3-030-94890-0 (eBook)
https://doi.org/10.1007/978-3-030-94890-0

LNCS Sublibrary: SL3 – Information Systems and Applications, incl. Internet/Web, and HCI

This Springer imprint is published by the registered company Springer Nature Switzerland AG
The registered company address is: Gewerbestrasse 11, 6330 Cham, Switzerland

Preface

Introduction

Driven by the interest of commercial and public sector service providers, chatbots are increasingly available as a user interface to information and services. Application areas span from customer service and marketing on the one hand, to education, coaching, and therapy on the other. Chatbots are also used as a channel for information support regarding the COVID-19 pandemic by health authorities worldwide. The increased interest in open domain chatbots, motivated by advances in natural language processing and large language models, as well as strengthened capabilities of social or relational chatbots contribute to making the scope of interest for chatbot applications truly broad. In response to the current interest in chatbots, as well as the variety of chatbot application areas, chatbot research is a growing academic field involving a wide range of disciplines.

The CONVERSATIONS workshop series was established to serve as a venue for sharing and collaboration across researchers and disciplines identifying with the field of chatbot research. Here, researchers and practitioners have enjoyed a yearly meeting place, starting with the initial workshop organized as a full day event under the International Conference on Internet Science, INSCI 2017. Since 2019, the CONVERSATIONS workshop has been organized as a two-day stand-alone event for cross-disciplinary sharing and collaboration, involving researchers and practitioners from the humanities, social sciences, management, design, technology research, and human-computer interaction.

Across the CONVERSATIONS workshop series, some key directions for chatbot research have emerged. The continued development and improvement of chatbot applications clearly require research on enabling technologies, platforms, and systems. Successful uptake and use of chatbots also require new knowledge on user needs and motivations, chatbot user experience, and conversational design, as well as ethical considerations and social implications. There is also emerging interest in how to design for collaboration and service provision in networks of users and chatbots.

This year's workshop, CONVERSATIONS 2021, was the fifth event in the series. The workshop was arranged as an online event due to the COVID-19 pandemic. It was hosted during November 23–24, 2021, by the University of Oslo in collaboration with SINTEF, the University of Amsterdam, the Centre for Research and Technology Hellas, Durham University, the University of Edinburgh, and the University of Agder. About 180 participants from 31 countries attended the workshop.

Paper Invitation, Review, and Revision

We developed the workshop Call for Papers based on key research directions identified over the workshop series. The Call for Papers was distributed to the network of researchers and practitioners associated with the workshop series as well as relevant general mailing lists within fields such as human-computer interaction, information retrieval, communication research, and information systems research. Three submission categories were allowed for the workshop: full papers, position papers, and groupwork proposals. In total, we received 35 submissions: 25 full papers, five position papers, and two groupwork proposals. All submitted full papers and position papers were subject to a rigorous double-blind review process. Each paper was reviewed by three independent reviewers drawn from the Program Committee. The review process of each submission was led by one of the seven workshop organizers, i.e., each led three to five reviewer processes. Acceptance decisions were made in a dedicated organizers' meeting. Submissions authored by a workshop organizer were reviewed and decided without involvement of, and blind to, the authoring organizer.

Twelve submissions were accepted as full papers – one without changes, two after minor revision, and nine after major revision. Revisions were accepted after a final control for compliance with reviewer change requests and, when needed, additional revisions were requested. The acceptance rate for full papers was 48%.

Workshop Outcomes

The workshop program spanned two days and included two keynote speakers, one groupwork, and five paper sessions.

The workshop keynote speakers were Roger K. Moore, University of Sheffield, and Ana Paiva, University of Lisbon. In his talk, Moore provided an overview of research on embodied and disembodied conversational agents and discussed research themes common to both. Paiva, in her talk, presented research advances and discussed challenges regarding interaction in groups of humans and agents.

The workshop groupwork was organized by Giuseppe Aceto and Federica Tazzi, Assist Digital, and involved a collaborative exercise applying a speculative design approach to identify challenges and opportunities in future chatbots.

The paper sessions were constituted of full papers and position papers organized in five topical clusters. As these proceedings only include the accepted full papers, here these are organized in three themes: chatbot user insight, chatbots supporting collaboration and social interaction, and chatbot UX and design.

The first theme, chatbot user insight, includes four papers on studies that provide insight into users' chatbot perceptions or preferences, addressing a varied set of application domains. De Cicco et al. present a study on chatbot user acceptance, applying an adapted technology acceptance model to understand the factors that impact intention to use in the retail domain. Koebel et al. provide insight from domain experts to support the design of chatbot applications to support older adults with cognitive impairments. Félix and Ribeiro summarize findings from co-creation sessions to enable the design of improved dialogues in chatbots for cancer patients. Hobert presents findings from a longitudinal study of a chatbot for supporting students during a university course in computer programming, identifying student needs and preferences based on their chatbot interactions.

The second theme, chatbots supporting collaboration and social interaction, concerns how chatbots may support collaboration and how to design for social interaction in chatbots. Taule et al. present a study on how chatbots supporting human resource management are taken up as part of the organizational interplay involving human resource professionals, the chatbot, and the organization at large. Alves et al. contribute the design and study of a chatbot to support newcomer participants in open-source software projects. Yildiz et al. propose an approach for flexibly integrating social practices in chatbot interaction, and Lobo et al. suggested how a cognitive frames model may be applied to support chatbot adaptation to social context.

The third theme, chatbot UX and design, addresses different approaches to strengthen chatbot UX through the design of chatbot interaction or appearance. Chaves and Gerosa present a study on user perceptions of variation in conversational register, with implications for conversational design in chatbots. Kamoen et al. investigate different designs for a voting advice chatbot, and how these impact user experience as well as the benefit of the chatbot interaction to the user. Mooshammer and Etzrodt, in a study of relevance for the design of voice interaction, address how gender-neutral voices impact user experience. Finally, Pawlik provides a study on the effect of gendered anthropomorphic design clues on performance expectancy, effort expectancy, social influence and, ultimately, behavioral intention.

Three papers were nominated for the CONVERSATIONS best paper award. These papers were those with the highest reviewer scores, excluding any organizer authored papers. From the three highest scoring papers, the best paper was selected by the workshop organizers. The award for the CONVERSATIONS 2021 best paper was given to Sandra Mooshammer and Katrin Etzrodt for their paper "Social Research with Gender-Neutral Voices in Chatbots – The Generation and Evaluation of Artificial Gender-Neutral Voices with Praat and Google WaveNet". The other best paper nominees were Maria Inês Lobo, Diogo Rato, Rui Prada, and Frank Dignum for their paper "Socially Aware Interactions: From Dialogue Trees to Natural Language Dialogue Systems", and Eren Yildiz, Suna Bensch, and Frank Dignum for their paper "Incorporating Social Practices in Dialogue Systems".

The engaging paper sessions, keynote talks, and groupwork, along with a record number of participants, enabled CONVERSATIONS 2021 to fill its purpose as a multidisciplinary venue for sharing and collaboration for chatbot researchers and practitioners. These post-workshop proceedings are a key result of the workshop, as these make the content of the workshop available for a broader audience, to support future chatbot research. As organizers, we already look forward to the next CONVERSATIONS, to be held in 2022.

November 2021

Asbjørn Følstad
Theo Araujo
Symeon Papadopoulos
Effie L.-C. Law
Ewa Luger
Morten Goodwin
Petter Bae Brandtzaeg

Organization

General Chairs/Workshop Organizers

Asbjørn Følstad   SINTEF, Norway
Theo Araujo   University of Amsterdam, The Netherlands
Symeon Papadopoulos   Centre for Research and Technology Hellas, Greece
Effie L.-C. Law   Durham University, UK
Ewa Luger   University of Edinburgh, UK
Morten Goodwin   University of Agder, Norway
Petter Bae Brandtzaeg   University of Oslo and SINTEF, Norway

Program Committee

Alexander Mädche   Karlsruhe Institute of Technology, Germany
Amela Karahasanovic   SINTEF, Norway
Ana Paula Chaves   Federal University of Technology – Paraná, Brazil
Carolin Ischen   University of Amsterdam, The Netherlands
Christian Löw   University of Vienna, Austria
Christine Liebrecht   Tilburg University, The Netherlands
David Kuboň   Charles University, Czech Republic
Despoina Chatzakou   Centre for Research and Technology Hellas, Greece
Eleni Metheniti   CLLE-CNRS and IRIT-CNRS, France
Fabio Catania   Politecnico di Milano, Italy
Frank Dignum   Umeå University, Sweden
Fréjus Laleye   CEA, France
Frode Guribye   University of Bergen, Norway
Gaël de Chalendar   CEA, France
Guy Laban   University of Glasgow, UK
Jasper Feine   Karlsruhe Institute of Technology, Germany
Jo Dugstad Wake   NORCE and University of Bergen, Norway
Jo Herstad   University of Oslo, Norway
Konstantinos Boletsis   SINTEF, Norway
Lea Reis   University of Bamberg, Germany
Leigh Clark   Swansea University, UK
Marcos Baez   Claude Bernard University Lyon 1, France
Margot van der Goot   University of Amsterdam, The Netherlands

Marita Skjuve   SINTEF, Norway
Raphael Meyer von Wolff   University of Göttingen, Germany
Rricha Jalota   Saarland University, Germany
Sebastian Hobert   University of Göttingen, Germany
Stefan Morana   Saarland University, Germany
Stefan Schaffer   DFKI – German Research Center for Artificial
                                     Intelligence, Germany
Sviatlana Höhn   University of Luxembourg, Luxembourg
Ulrich Gnewuch   Karlsruhe Institute of Technology, Germany
Zia Uddin   SINTEF, Norway

Contents

Chatbot UX and Design

Chatbot User Insight

Understanding Users' Acceptance of Chatbots: An Extended TAM Approach

Roberta De Cicco[1,2](✉) ⓘ, Serena Iacobucci[1,2] ⓘ, Antonio Aquino[1] ⓘ, Francesca Romana Alparone[1] ⓘ, and Riccardo Palumbo[1,2] ⓘ

[1] Department of Neuroscience, Imaging and Clinical Sciences, University of Chieti-Pescara, Chieti, Italy
roberta.decicco@unich.it
[2] CAST, Center for Advanced Studies and Technology, University of Chieti-Pescara, Chieti, Italy

Abstract. Chatbots represent a viable interaction layer between online retailers and customers, however, when it comes to online purchases in the form of conversational commerce, customers' resistance could turn out to be a big challenge for marketers. This study provides a deeper understanding of how consumers perceive chatbots and their intention to use them for online purchases. Based on an extended Technology Acceptance Model, the study examines whether and how the original TAM's exogenous constructs combined with trust, compatibility, and perceived enjoyment predict a positive attitude and, consequently, a higher intention to use chatbots for online shopping. A total of 208 respondents participated in an online survey and Structural Equation Modeling (SEM-PLS) was applied to test the hypotheses. Moreover, a qualitative textual analysis of participants' answers was performed to dig deeper into users' motives for developing positive, neutral/ambivalent, or negative attitudes toward the chatbot. In doing so, the study provides useful information to online businesses in electronic retail activities, as the results highlight the importance of designing chatbots that fit both consumer's cognitive needs and affective desires.

Keywords: Chatbots · Conversational commerce · TAM · Compatibility · Trust · Perceived enjoyment · Textual analysis

1 Introduction

In their 2016 Annual Conferences, the world's Tech Giants - Facebook, Google, and Microsoft - announced the launch of their own bot platforms. This announcement motivated a new generation of virtual assistants, specially designed to interact with users through instant messaging apps: chatbots [10]. This news represented a big boost to conversational commerce which allows consumers to make purchases over platforms like Facebook Messenger [18]. Since their launch, an increasing number of firms have started employing chatbots to deliver automated customer support, content, interactive experiences, and potentially more convenient and personal ways to access content and

© Springer Nature Switzerland AG 2022
A. Følstad et al. (Eds.): CONVERSATIONS 2021, LNCS 13171, pp. 3–22, 2022.
https://doi.org/10.1007/978-3-030-94890-0_1

services [5] as — through the messaging platforms — chatbots are able to respond with structured multimodal messages [59]. It comes as no surprise that, according to Research and Markets, the chatbot market size is projected to grow from $2.6 billion in 2019 to $9.4 billion by 2024. In fact, retail and e-commerce market segments are projected to grow at the highest compound annual growth rate, owing to the increasing request to provide customers with a consistent omnichannel experience [36]. However, although being a promising marketing channel, the full potential of chatbots is still not realized, in part due to challenges associated with changing user needs and motivations [5]. Past studies have already started addressing the importance of chatbots for business purposes [e.g. 2, 14]. Still, further research is required to understand the process by which chatbots enhance customers' experience in the online retailing context.

From a business perspective, ensuring a proper chatbot design is the key for avoiding marketing pitfalls. We believe a key element for a successful implementation of chatbots for online purchases relies on the understanding of the determinants of consumers' attitudes and intention to use them. The Technology Acceptance Model is considered an adequate starting point in providing a good and affordable way of gathering information about individuals' perception of a technology and determining behavioural intention for technology usage [47]. Studies applying TAM have been carried out with different research purposes, subjects, systems and tasks with diverse research methodologies and under different environments such as online retailing [e.g. 8, 22]. There is no shortage of studies applying TAM to chatbot acceptance, such as Rese et al. [44], Zarouali et al. [59], Araujo and Casais [1], Kasilingam [28] who respectively extended TAM with determinants such as enjoyment, affect, perceived risk, and trust. In this line, to respond to the call for studies enhancing knowledge on the variables that count most in the interaction with shopping chatbots, we contribute to the existing body of knowledge on technology acceptance for chatbots in retail by integrating TAM [11] with three context-specific factors of high relevance to online retail and human-chatbot interactions: compatibility, trust, and enjoyment. While some of the above-mentioned constructs have been mostly individually addressed also in other studies of chatbot acceptance [e.g. 44, 59], our study investigates these constructs as part of a single model to verify the validity of the relationships proposed by TAM in a chatbot shopping context and to better understand the role of the added constructs into this model. The final aim is to provide a deep understanding of the aspects beyond the key TAM variables that could assist managers and practitioners in their aim to implement an efficient and widely accepted service.

Furthermore, we address the need for triangulation-based methodological approaches, introducing a qualitative textual analysis of participants' answers to open-ended questions related to their attitude. Our qualitative findings, although preliminary, provide a deeper look into users' motives for chatbots acceptance or rejection, and allow us to examine and polish such motives with a greater level of sophistication compared to what would have emerged from a pure quantitative approach. Digging deeper into textual data, we were able to spot otherwise disregarded potential implications, thus underlining how mixed methods could help us expand the evidence base in Chatbot research.

2 Theoretical Framework and Hypotheses Development

2.1 TAM

TAM [12] is a widely adopted theory in information systems research as well as in other fields [31] for the study of the determinants of individuals' technology usage and acceptance. Studies applying TAM have been carried out with different research purposes, subjects, systems, tasks, and methodologies. Recent research involves online shopping in the form of mobile commerce such as Instagram commerce, Facebook commerce [6] and chatbots [1, 44]. TAM is considered a flexible, parsimonious, and widely applicable theory to examine technology use [47]. To increase the understanding of research phenomenon, relevant contextual constructs are usually incorporated depending on the technology of interest to offer more complete and conclusive findings [25]. Given these premises, we consider the TAM as an appropriate starting point in determining behavioral intention. However, although TAM can be considered a good model to understand the adoption of a new technology, given the intrinsically interactive and innovative feature of chatbots as well as the objective (conversational commerce), following the need to add context-specific factors that could capture some criticality of online purchasing through conversational platforms, further elaborate on TAM, by integrating three additional and reasoned predictors: compatibility, trust, and perceived enjoyment. Following Shi et al. [50], the study spotlights compatibility as an essential innovation characteristic in omnichannel customer experiences, serving as an underlying mechanism through which interactions with chatbots impact their usage intention for online purchases. Second, due to the still low diffusion and the lack of familiarity with conversational commerce, it is hard for customers to judge whether making purchases through chatbot is safe and trustworthy, which makes trust a further factor in determining the chatbot usage intention. Finally, when shopping via websites, consumers' enjoyment partially stems from balancing the utilitarian benefits of saving time and effort [29, 32] with the process of personally browsing for information about products and transactions through an active, first-person experience. Thus, the potential impact of the presence of virtual salespersons on such perception of enjoinment is key for an all-encompassing assessment of attitudes and purchasing behavioral intents in the chatbot domain [14]. The extension of the original model has here been designed to overcome some limits and critics regarding the absence of contextual factors and measures intrinsically depending on the individual personality and experience (compatibility and trust) or feelings and emotions (perceived enjoyment) [21] that TAM has been put through over the years [20]. We believe the present study helps fill this gap by empirically testing an enriched TAM including a set of variables whose relationships have never been tested together before in a structural equation model approach to understand what variables contribute most to explaining the intention to use chatbots. TAM consists of four principal constructs predicting actual usage: Perceived Ease Of Use (PEOU), Perceived Usefulness (PU), Attitude, and Intention to use. PU and PEOU are the two key exogenous constructs, attitude and intention are key endogenous factors. PEOU is defined as *"the degree to which a person believes that using a particular system would be free of effort"* ([11] p. 320), where the effort represents the finite resources people can allocate to the activities they are dealing with. Studies in different domains, such as mobile commerce [9], and virtual reality [35], confirm that PEOU positively affects PU. The rationale is that if a technology is perceived ease to use, users may operate with minimal effort and stress during the same amount of time and therefore perceive the technology to be more useful [52]. Research also confirmed the effect of PEOU on consumer attitudes toward the adoption of new technologies such as mobile apps [40]. Generally, in online commerce both PEOU and PU positively influence consumer attitude which in turn affects usage intention [41, 53]. In the original TAM's PU is defined as *"the degree to which a person believes that using a particular system would enhance his or her job performance"* ([11] p. 320). By adapting PU in an online shopping context, a reasonable definition is given by Ha and Stoel [22] who believe that this represents the final outcome resulting from a chain of shopping activities [22]. PU is an extrinsic motivation [44]: chatbot's users are searching for furniture and want to obtain product ideas. The model also assumes that users perceiving positive consequences of using a specific technology develop a positive attitude toward using the technology. Studies confirmed the positive relation between PU and attitude toward e-commerce [33] and more specifically, e-commerce through mobile applications (i.e. mobile commerce [9]). As TAM suggests, besides a positive effect on attitude, PU also directly affects behavioral intentions. Amongst others, the effect of PU on intention to use was found in video-on-demand services [42] and mobile wireless technology adoption [29]. Another important connection in TAM is between attitude and behavioral intention. This part of the model, which has its roots in the Theory of Reasoned Action (TRA) [17] suggests that a favorable experience generates a positive attitude, which enhances customers' future intentions. Attitude refers to a person's feeling toward a specific object or behavior. This is supposed to enhance behavioral intention, that is, the subjective probability that a person will engage in a certain behavior [17]. Among others, research confirms attitude is a significant predictor of intention to use information technologies [52], online shopping [7], and mobile commerce [9].

2.2 Compatibility, Trust, and Perceived Enjoyment

Compatibility, one of the constructs at the heart of Rogers' Innovation Diffusion Theory, refers to the degree to which a technology is consistent with users' existing beliefs, habits, present and prior experiences [46]. Research suggests that integrating TAM with other acceptance and diffusion theories improves its predictive and explanatory power [8]. Online purchasing via chatbots represents an important innovation within the broader framework of shopping modes. Compatibility could help explain how well such innovation fits potential adopters' lifestyle, needs, and shopping preference and give significant insights on how this could affect crucial variables like perceived usefulness, attitude, and intention. Previous studies found a positive link between compatibility and people's adoption of new information technology [49]. Compatibility turns out to be especially relevant for technology innovations [58], since high compatibility of a technology speeds up its adoption. Specifically, researchers found that compatibility has a direct positive effect on perceived usefulness [38], attitude twd the technology [8], and intention to use [49].

McKnight and Chervany [37] define trust as the extent to which one believes that the new technology usage is reliable and credible. Beliefs about trust are a key factor influencing consumer acceptance of online shopping [22]. Generally, the more consumers trust a certain technology, the less they are worried about using it for shopping. Trust has always played a crucial role in the business-to-consumer (B2C) relationships, and with the emergence of virtual marketplaces, such role has become even more relevant and demanding, as consumers operate in a more abstract and opaque space. Empirical studies incorporated trust into TAM confirming its role as an antecedent of attitude [3, 33]. Bashir and Madhavaiah [3] confirmed that trust is one of the most critical factors of Internet banking. Generally, users perceive a lower level of trust when they are explicitly disclosed about the virtual identity [13]. Thus, whether customers trust chatbots constitute critical issues in understanding behavior, especially if we consider that some consumers do not trust chatbots to provide them with the same level of service as humans would.

TAM is dominated by variables reflecting rational and cognitive processes, as the authors recognized that these variables should have a heavier weight than affective processes in predicting intention to use. However, previous research suggests that consumers adopt new technologies not just to enhance performance but also as sources of enjoyment [13]. Many studies conceptualize such hedonic motivation as 'perceived enjoyment' [57] which is considered a good predictor of information technology acceptance [53]. In the present study, perceived enjoyment can be referred to the extent to which the shopping experience with the chatbot is perceived to be enjoyable. Research identifies perceived enjoyment as a significant positive predictor of attitude [15, 36], thus although positive cognitive attributes are important factors to develop a favorable predisposition toward new technologies or new applications of an existing technology, as posited in Van der Heijden [54], the hedonic nature of a system is still a relevant boundary condition to the validity of acceptance models.

2.3 Hypotheses

The following hypotheses are based on the literature review in the preceding sections:
H1. Perceived ease of use is positively related to perceived usefulness
H2. Perceived ease of use is positively related to and attitude toward using the chatbot
H3. Perceived Usefulness is positively related to attitude toward the using chatbot
H4. Perceived Usefulness is positively related to intention to use
H5. Compatibility is positively related to perceived usefulness
H6. Compatibility is positively related to attitude toward using the chatbot
H7. Compatibility is positively related to intention to use
H8. Trust is positively related to attitude toward using the chatbot
H9. Perceived enjoyment is positively related to attitude toward using the chatbot
H10. Attitude toward using the chatbot is positively related to intention to use

3   Research Method

3.1   Measurement Development, Procedure and Data Collection

To test the research hypotheses, a survey was administered to measure the constructs in the model. The first part was designed to acquire demographic information and gain insights on gender, age, use of messaging apps, and online shopping experience; the second part consisted of statements regarding the constructs of interest. Previous research was reviewed to ensure that a comprehensive list of measures was included and a seven-point Likert-scale was used to determine the extent to which a participant strongly *disagrees* (1) or *agrees* (7) with all the statements. The list of items is reported in the Appendix. Data for this study were collected via an online survey shared on social networks. After participants gave their explicit consent to voluntarily take part in the study, they were instructed to interact with the chatbot and look for information about office and home furniture and then virtually buy a desired product. The time for completing the task and the survey was about 15 min. During the dialogues, users answered the chatbot's questions, and this, in turn, provided product recommendations based on consumers' answers (Fig. 1). Chatfuel, one of the leading platforms for developing chatbots, was used to create the chatbot. After participants completed the task, they were readdressed to the questionnaire. 233 participants completed the questionnaire. 25 participants were discarded since they did not meet the requirements to take part in the study, that is being of full age and possessing a Facebook account. The final sample included 208 participants (Mage = 24.06, SD = 5.2), 94 males (45.19%) and 114 females (54.81%). The survey recorded respondents' online shopping behavior and chatbot experience. 63.0% of the respondents indicated that they buy less than once on a monthly basis. 45.2% had never used a chatbot before. 47.6% had never used it to look for information and 79.3 to make online purchases. These data witness the low penetration of chatbots for online shopping.

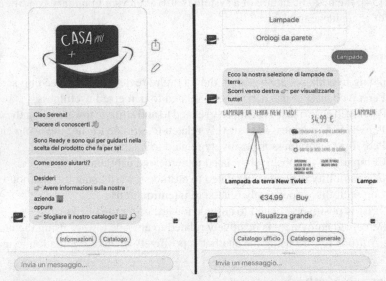

Note: The chatbot firstly introduces itself and asks the user if he/she wants to read some information on the Company or just flick through the catalogue. After the user clicks on catalogue he/she is showed the options to choose between the catalogue for home or for office. The available products are waste baskets, lamps and wall clocks.

Fig. 1. Example of the interaction with the chatbot

4 Data Analysis and Results

4.1 Partial Least Square (PLS) Path Modeling

Structural Equation Modeling (SEM) using the Partial Least Square (PLS) technique was applied in the current study to test the hypotheses. PLS-SEM is used in various fields of academics, including consumer behavior as it provides less contradictory results than regression analysis in terms of detecting mediation effects [43]. Moreover, when the research objective is to explore theoretical extensions of established theories, this approach provides higher reliability in causal explanations and overcomes the apparent dichotomy between explanation and prediction, which is the basis for developing managerial implications [24]. The PLS is usually analyzed and interpreted in two stages: firstly, by assessing the reliability and validity of the measurement model; and secondly, by assessing the structural model through interpreting the path coefficients. The following sections discuss the results of these two stages.

4.2 Measurement Model (Construct Validity)

The outer model was assessed through the validity and reliability of the measurement scales to ensure psychometric properties. Validity was based on both convergent and discriminant validity. Convergent validity was evaluated through the strength and significance of the loadings. The results of the initial measurement model showed that four items (PEOU 3, PEOU5, PU2, and PE2) were problematic due to low factor loadings, so they were removed for subsequent analysis in line with Ha and Stoel [22]. The results of the final outer model indicate that all the 25 remaining indicators had loadings exceeding the satisfactory level of >0.7 [61]. Reliability and validity tests were conducted to ensure that the measurements provided sufficient coverage of the investigative questions. Cronbach's Alpha assessed the consistency of the items measuring a particular concept. According to Saunders et al. [48], a value of 0.7 and above indicates that the items in the scale are measuring the same variable of interest. All the variables fulfilled the requirements for internal consistency, item loading, AVE, and Composite Reliability (See Table 1).

To assess discriminant validity, Fornell Larcker criterion-Latent Variable Correlations and Cross loading (Discriminant Validity) were considered [19]. As shown in Table 2, the diagonals represent the square roots of AVE and the off-diagonals represent the correlations. The diagonal values are higher than off-diagonals, thus meaning that discriminant validity exists according to Fornell Larcker criterion. Likewise, loadings for each item (bold values in Table 3), were above the recommended value of 0.5 and higher than all its cross-loadings showing that discriminant validity.

The amount of variance explained by R^2 provides an indication of the model fit as well as the predictive ability of the endogenous variables [23]. According to Hair et al. [24], the minimum level for an individual R^2 should be greater than a minimum acceptable level of 0.10. As reported in Fig. 2, the R^2 values of all endogenous variables 'Perceived Usefulness', 'Attitudes toward the chatbot' and 'Behavioral Intention to Use' were higher than the threshold (56.2%, 79.8%, and 77.6% respectively). Overall, the model is valid and proves to be a valuable approach to examine the significance of the paths associated with the variables.

Table 1. Construct validity

Research construct	Item	Item loading	AVE	CR	α
Perceived ease of use	PEOU1	0.839	.712	.937	.919
	PEOU2	0.828			
	PEOU3	0.887			
	PEOU4	0.791			
	PEOU5	0.804			
	PEOU6	0.908			
Perceived usefulness	PU1	0.907	.797	.959	.949
	PU2	0.828			
	PU3	0.885			
	PU4	0.926			
	PU5	0.878			
	PU6	0.927			
Perceived enjoyment	PE1	0.955	.907	.967	.949
	PE2	0.955			
	PE3	0.947			
Trust	T1	0.896	.735	.893	.819
	T2	0.867			
	T3	0.807			
Compatibility	C1	0.924	.855	.947	.916
	C2	0.917			
	C3	0.933			
Att. TWD using the chatbot	A1	0.914	.853	.959	.942
	A2	0.941			
	A3	0.906			
	A4	0.932			
Intention to use	BI1	0.939	.881	.937	.865
	BI2	0.938			

4.3 Structural Model

Once established the measurement model, we assessed the structural relationship. Before the assessment of path coefficient, multicollinearity was inspected, and no issues were found as an examination of the variance inflation factors (VIF) indicated that the values were lower than the threshold of 5.0 [45]. As shown in Table 4, the bootstrap procedure revealed that PEOU is positively related to PU, nevertheless it is not significantly related to Attitude. In this case, we only found a slight tendency toward significance. PU is

Table 2. Discriminant validity – latent variable correlations

	PEOU	PU	PE	TRUST	COMP	ATT	INT
PEOU	**.844**						
PU	.663	**.893**					
PE	.476	.674	**.952**				
TRUST	.476	.432	.504	**.857**			
COMP	.507	.638	.742	.572	**.925**		
ATT	.608	.757	.809	.615	.776	**.924**	
INT	.495	.666	.727	.571	.837	.822	**939**

positively related to Attitude, but not Intention to use. Compatibility is positively related to PU, Attitude and Intention. Trust and attitude are positively and significantly related, as well as PE and Attitude are. Finally, as expected, attitude is positively related to Intention to use the chatbot. Table 4 highlights the hypotheses and shows the path coefficient among the latent variables and bootstrap critical ratios. As specified by Hair et al. [23], a bootstrap T-Statistics at 95% confidence interval using 5000 samples was assessed to determine the stability of the estimates (acceptable values above 1.96).

4.4 Content Analysis of Consumers' Attitudes Toward the Chatbot

To further investigate what contributes to shaping participants' attitudes toward the chatbot, the relative items were followed by an open-ended question that asked participants to motivate their scores. The qualitative analysis of participants' answers, consisting in a thematic synthesis, was guided by the work of Löfgren [34] and followed the guidelines for Framing and Interpreting Qualitative data in Management and Business Research [16]. Two researchers independently read the available textual data, labelled markers and recurring patterns that would denote positive, negative or ambivalent/neutral sentiment. Scores across raters were compared and, when divergent, a third researcher expressed their opinion on the perceived tone. This procedure allowed us to split the sample into three broad sentiment categories: positive (N = 92); neutral or ambivalent (N = 11) and negative (N = 98). Seven answers were excluded as participants wrote random text. Answers were then iteratively read, and coders were instructed to compare their annotations and highlight the main themes raised from participants in different subgroups. To remain as unbiased and open-minded as possible [27], a third researcher was included when discussing the subcategories emerged, resulting in the scenario illustrated below.

Positive Sentiment. The majority (69) of the positive evaluations were motivated by Chatbots' "Efficiency and ease of use", with typical answers stating that *"Chatbots allow you to save time and if you have any questions, you just press a simple button and get the answer without having to wait"*. The second topic emerging from positive evaluations (8) is "Information Relevance and Availability", with participants reporting that Chatbots not only *"(…) let you access much more information"*, but also reduce the

Table 3. Cross loadings (discriminant validity)

	PEOU	PU	PE	TRUST	COMP	ATT	INT
PEOU1	**0.839**	0.507	0.338	0.387	0.385	0.461	0.359
PEOU2	**0.828**	0.472	0.358	0.374	0.358	0.450	0.358
PEOU3	**0.887**	0.596	0.355	0.389	0.396	0.483	0.374
PEOU4	**0.791**	0.631	0.540	0.466	0.538	0.568	0.538
PEOU5	**0.804**	0.530	0.388	0.374	0.443	0.523	0.440
PEOU6	**0.908**	0.590	0.399	0.404	0.422	0.566	0.408
PU1	0.669	**0.907**	0.558	0.340	0.542	0.661	0.568
PU2	0.457	**0.828**	0.580	0.404	0.542	0.596	0.549
PU3	0.605	**0.885**	0.580	0.381	0.521	0.657	0.545
PU4	0.550	**0.926**	0.652	0.408	0.634	0.724	0.657
PU5	0.633	**0.878**	0.561	0.337	0.516	0.615	0.553
PU6	0.630	**0.927**	0.670	0.440	0.648	0.777	0.679
PE1	0.466	0.641	**0.955**	0.493	0.700	0.789	0.691
PE2	0.438	0.626	**0.955**	0.451	0.649	0.749	0.658
PE3	0.455	0.659	**0.947**	0.493	0.770	0.771	0.727
T1	0.471	0.401	0.470	**0.896**	0.523	0.573	0.548
T2	0.426	0.312	0.308	**0.867**	0.407	0.459	0.396
T3	0.325	0.387	0.496	**0.807**	0.526	0.537	0.506
C1	0.504	0.646	0.729	0.557	**0.924**	0.749	0.759
C2	0.461	0.516	0.653	0.506	**0.917**	0.662	0.738
C3	0.443	0.602	0.675	0.522	**0.933**	0.737	0.822
A1	0.591	0.709	0.684	0.607	0.735	**0.914**	0.777
A2	0.560	0.713	0.775	0.595	0.752	**0.941**	0.810
A3	0.568	0.692	0.720	0.537	0.658	**0.906**	0.708
A4	0.527	0.681	0.809	0.530	0.718	**0.932**	0.737
BI1	0.519	0.688	0.703	0.610	0.754	0.815	**0.939**
BI2	0.409	0.562	0.661	0.460	0.818	0.727	**0.938**

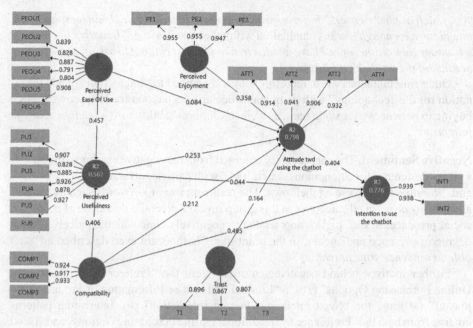

Fig. 2. PLS Algorithm results with R^2

Table 4. Structural relationships and hypotheses testing

H	Path	Path coefficient	Standard error	T-statistics	P value	Decision
H1	PEOU - > PU	0.457	0.060	7.583	.000	Supported
H2	PEOU - > A	0.084	0.057	1.473	.070	NS
H3	PU - > A	0.253	0.062	4.084	.000	Supported
H4	PU - > BI	0.044	0.045	0.982	.163	NS
H5	C - > PU	0.406	0.055	7.350	.000	Supported
H6	C - > A	0.212	0.062	3.410	.000	Supported
H7	C - > BI	0.495	0.065	7.655	.000	Supported
H8	T - > A	0.164	0.049	3.369	.000	Supported
H9	PE - > A	0.358	0.064	5.618	.000	Supported
H10	A - > BI	0.404	0.070	5.798	.000	Supported

time needed by "(…) *showcasing only relevant details*" and providing further ones that can be accessed "(…) *with just one click and without waiting for customer service nor manually browsing the website*".

A smaller subgroup of 5 participants was labeled as "Only for Specific Purposes Users" as, although being extremely positive about the technology, they specified that they deemed it suitable for purchases that do not require to go very deep into details,

"(…) *such as phone covers, or accessories in general that don't need much explanation, one picture is enough*", or in combination with other sources, e.g. *"Usually I like to have a broader look online, once I have an idea in mind I use a chatbot to ask for some further details on the product and just buy it"*.

Other miscellaneous worth reporting topics are linked to "Interactivity" and "Fascination for the Technology" with participants declaring a passion for interactive, lifelike buying experiences over static ones, as well as Chatbots' ability to "(…) *mimic real-life purchases"*.

Negative Sentiment. The core category emerged from the negative sentiment group was a clear "Preference for autonomous search" (44), with participants stating that they *"like"* and *"are able to"* browse on their own. The recurrent use of keywords such as *"alone"* and *"on my own"* in all categories in this group reveal a potential downside of perceived social presence. In fact, participants tended to negatively connotate the perceived great degree of presence and agency, to the point that Chatbots are even described as "(…) *able to influence your purchases"*.

Further motives behind negative sentiment were the "Preference for Traditional Online Purchasing Options" (16), a "Limited Amount of Information or Products Displayed" (10) and the "Need for human-human interaction" (9). Interesting patterns emerge from both the "Preference for Traditional Online Purchasing Options" and "Need for human-human interaction" categories, as they denote how participants with negative scores were evaluating the Chatbot as an alternative for physical store shopping and Human-Customer Service rather than as an alternative to online purchases. In fact, participants' negative responses were not motivated by the Chatbot's inability to perform its task compared to traditional eCommerce Purchases (e.g. proceed to check-out), but rather by highlighting that *"Interacting with humans is far way better than interacting with machines"* and that Chatbots "(…) *cannot replicate an experience that entails the human intuition"*. As confirmed by these sparse examples of speciesism [45], that emerged from other answers in this subset as well (e.g. *"It is unethical to promote robots that will be taking over human jobs"*), it is possible that participants in their answers were not evaluating the technology *per se*, but rather incorporating a general negative attitude toward AI as a whole, specifically when comparing their performances with those of human assistants.

Finally, smaller subgroups report a "Lack of trust" (3), not only related to privacy concerns (e.g. *"I don't feel my data are protected")* but also toward the technology as a whole (e.g. *"It is too early to trust Chatbots"*), as well as poor functionality, both in terms of "Technical Issues" and "Chatbot's lack of understanding", even when they succeeded in completing the simulated purchase.

Neutral Sentiment. Coherently with the expectations, participants in the subgroup tap from both positive and negative motives and report that, despite Chatbots' being "Efficient and Easy to Use" (9) and satisfying their "Openness to New Technological Experiences" (2), they have "Limited Amount of Information or Products Displayed" (4) and still cannot completely make up for the "Need for human-human interaction" (4). The main patterns that refrain ambivalent participants from fully appreciating Chatbots are the following. First, unlike participants in the positive subgroup - they rarely acknowledge or realize that Chatbots could work well in different contexts, such as those where there is a limited choice available, or the purchase-decision making process has already taken place. As happened in the negative subgroup, participants with neutral scores tend to perceive Chatbots as substitutes, and not as complementary tools for eCommerce stores, alleging that not enough information can be accessed (e.g. *"Certainly easy and quick in the wide web, but it cannot display all items and items' information available"*). Secondly, as for participants in the negative subgroup - ambivalent users tend to contrast Chatbots with human-assisted service for purchasing rather than with websites (e.g. *"Easy to buy, but it's not safe as with a real human being"*).

5   Discussions and Implications

Given the increasing chatbot adoption by online retailers, this study offers a significant contribution to research studying human-chatbot interactions in the context of online retailing. Specifically, in the wake of those studies that applied TAM to investigate chatbots acceptance, this study advances the state of the art in acceptance literature on shopping chatbots [44, 59] by highlighting the role of both utilitarian and hedonic factors and further identifying compatibility as an additional key predictor of perceived usefulness, attitude, and intention to use.

Results − in line with Fishbein and Ajzen's Theory of Reasoned Action [17] − show that user intention to adopt a chatbot for online shopping is predicted by a powerful mediator, that is users' attitude toward using it. Consistently with prior research [53] results also prove compatibility to be a strong positive predictor of perceived usefulness, attitude, and most important, intention to use. Interestingly, in line with Araujo and Casais's [1] study on shopping-assistant chatbots, this relation has even a larger path coefficient than the attitude-intention relation, thus providing a better understanding of the variables needing a major focus. It is important for companies to measure the extent to which mobile messenger chatbots are perceived compatible with consumers' believes, lifestyle, needs and online shopping behavior by gathering user information and characteristics to incorporate their preferences into chatbots and ensure that consumers consider chatbots compatible with the way they like to purchase (for instance, by aligning the conversational style to the user's one, or learn about customers' time preferences for online shipping do deliver around-the-clock service and highlight specific products that they may be interested). As in the original TAM [11] and consistently with the literature on e-commerce systems [22, 33], virtual stores [8] and even chatbots [59], perceived usefulness positively predicts the attitude toward using the chatbot. However, unlike the original model, in this specific case, individuals do not directly associate utility to intentions as perceived usefulness does not significantly influence the intention to use chatbots. This result is in contrast with Rese et al.'s [44] study on chatbots acceptance. The level to which individuals believe that interacting with the chatbot will help them gain their performance, i.e. shopping goal, here does not represent a significant factor. These results might be explained by the fact that participants were not particularly identified with the simulated purchase and the consequently simulated monetary expense, which could also explain the limited effect of trust on attitude compared to compatibility and perceived enjoyment. This result, in line with other studies on other emerging technologies [8], may suggest that utility has a remarkable influence on behavioral intention mainly in mandatory systems and less in voluntary contexts. On the other hand, in line with Kim and Garrison [30], perceived ease of use strongly influences perceived usefulness, thus suggesting that if chatbots are difficult to use and confusing, it is less likely that users will experience a convenient interaction and this, in turn, will cause a worse evaluation of the technology. This means that those systems requiring little or no effort and that can minimize mental anxiety in their use are more likely to enhance e-shoppers' perceived utility, make the purchasing experience and the shopping task with the chatbot more pleasant. The study confirms the controversial results about the impact of perceived ease of use on attitude toward IT technologies [54]. As shown by the PLS path modelling, the relation between perceived ease of use and attitude, although slight tending, is not statistically significant. This result supports Zarouali et al.'s [59] findings in predicting consumer responses to a chatbots on Facebook. So, as in Van der Heijden [54, 55], it is reasonable to believe that perceived ease of use is a 'threshold' variable, meaning that once a certain evaluation level is reached, the variable no longer contributes to a favorable attitude. In few words, being the chatbot embedded in the messenger platform which users are certainly familiar with (as confirmed by the content analysis, with participants reporting "speed and ease of use as main motivation for their positive evaluation), appeared to be such easy-going while offering efficient online purchasing facilities, that probably PEOU reached threshold levels in most of the respondents' minds and this could explain why their evaluation did not generate any effect on their attitudes toward the chatbot. Finally, in line with the literature about the variables that best account for the online context and conforming to studies on chatbots where enjoyment was integrated to TAM to measure acceptance [28–50], this study underlines the considerable importance of enjoyment as a determinant of attitude toward using chatbots for online shopping. Looking more closely at the path coefficients, perceived enjoyment has the strongest relation with this attitude, even higher than perceived usefulness, thus indicating that consumers seem to place a greater value on the hedonic and affective dimension when using this system for their online shopping.

5.1 Theoretical Implications

This study investigates human-chatbot interactions in the context of online retailing through the lens of TAM [11]. The model was here revised with the integration of new constructs as further predictors of chatbot acceptance for online shopping to overcome the limit of adopting the original model that, alone, would not have caught important determinants of the adoption of the chatbot for online purchases.

Our results help to understand the relationships occurring among the seven constructs and to identify those variables that have a major impact on attitude toward using the chatbot (i.e. compatibility, enjoyment, and usefulness) and on the intention to use it (i.e. attitude and compatibility). Taken together, our findings complement technology acceptance literature, showing that the theoretical underpinnings of the TAM may be fruitfully combined with trust, compatibility, and perceived enjoyment to predict consumers' attitude and intention to use chatbots for online shopping [22]. Overall, our findings also complement the literature on human-chatbots interaction in the business domain suggesting that chatbots showing features that fit consumers' lifestyles, that convey characteristics related to amusement, fun as well as reliability are the most effective to be used in the online shopping context.

5.2 Practical Implications

Overall, our findings provide several practical contributions for marketers dealing with how to benefit from this new online commerce trend [4]. Practitioners should consider enabling a more engaging conversational style with pictures, emoticons, and GIFs to entertain the user (especially the younger cohorts). Similarly, boosting trust and confidence in purchasing when using these conversational systems should be a key objective for marketers. In this regard, when introducing themselves, chatbots could provide some statements reassuring the user about the safety of the transaction and the sensitive information disclosed, and the possibility to interact with a real human being in case of failure. The chatbot should undoubtedly offer a useful service but even more demanding is the need for the chatbot to fit the users' lifestyle and the way they usually make online purchases, as confirmed by the thematic analysis that showed how almost the majority of negative sentiment is motivated by the preference to browse for information autonomously or to purchase via more traditional tools, such as company website. This is particularly relevant when the aim involves addressing more promising target groups. Finally, we note that manually coded sentiment measures, in 62 out of 208 cases, showed a different evaluation if confronted with the self-reported explicit scores. Although no apparent directional pattern emerged from this change-of-mind (i.e. participants almost equally shifted from positive to negative (or neutral) scores and vice versa) we believe that this could be a potentially relevant insight for practitioners. With more and more companies implementing post-chat surveys that require users not only to rate their previous interaction (e.g. via a star-rating systems), but also to back it up with textual explanation, further studies are needed to clarify whether asking participants to motivate their answers could mitigate emotional, impulsive guts responses and make sure to obtain a more accurate, reasoned feedback.

6 Limits and Future Research

Although this study provides interesting insights into the factors affecting the intention to use chatbots for online shopping, it is not free from some limitations. The sample is limited mainly to a younger cohort, older or less digitally proficient audiences could provide different results. Although the study was carried out in a realistic and ecological environment, consistent with what consumers normally do in their day-to-day lives, because this study focuses on intentions and not actual use, future research could collect usage and purchase data from real companies to verify whether intentions truly lead to actual behavior. Another potential limitation of the study is the simulated purchase situation. Even though this method has shown good results in studies on online shopping [51], future research could offer credits that allow participants to truly complete the transaction. Future studies may consider additional constructs in the model such as perceived risk, resistance toward the technology, or social presence.

Moreover, as emerged from our qualitative analysis, future studies are called to disentangle the dynamics between participants' perception of the limited information accessible via Chatbots (e.g. in terms of product reviews and characteristics) and the reported skepticism toward the authenticity of Chatbot-mediated content. These apparently contradictory issues raised by participants open interesting research opportunities on how enriching Chatbots with further information available around offered products and services might hamper rather than necessarily increase users' attitudes, depending on the perceived reliability and genuineness of such information. Finally, summing up the main topics emerged from our brief qualitative analysis, we raise the need to better investigate how to a) frame Chatbots as complementary tools along the whole online purchase funnel; b) reassure that Chatbots leverage similarities with human-human interaction in order to improve the purchasing flow in already automated purchases, but are not necessarily substitutes of human-human interactions; c) disambiguate and define specific context and products where the limited information displayable in typical conversational interfaces does not hamper users' purchase intention.

Appendix

Construct/items	Loadings	M(SD)
Perceived Ease of Use (Davis 1989) [12]		5.51(.99)
1. Is it easy to understand how the chatbot works?	0.839	
2. Is it easy to remember how to easily interact with the chatbot?	0.828	
3. Is it frustrating to use the chatbot to shop online? R*	0.479	
4. Is the interaction with the chatbot clear and comprehensible?	0.887	
5. Does the interaction with the chatbot require an excessive mental effort? R*	0.473	
6. Is it easy to find the information you are looking for with the chatbot?	0.791	
7. Do you think you could easily become skilled using the ch. for online shopping?	0.804	
8. Do you find the messenger chatbot overall easy to use?	0.908	
Perceived Usefulness (Davis 1989) [12]		4.83(1.29)
1. Does the chatbot facilitate the online shopping experience?	0.907	
2. Is the chatbot effective for online shopping?*	0.516	
3. Does the ch. allow users to have a higher control on the online shopping process?	0.828	
4. Does the chatbot provide support to the online shopping experience?	0.885	
5. Does the chatbot improve the online shopping experience?	0.926	
6. Does the chatbot speed up the online shopping experience?	0.878	
7. Do you find the chatbot overall useful for online shopping?	0.927	
Compatibility (Hsu et al. 2007) [26]		3.98(1.74)
1. Using a chatbot for online shopping is compatible with all aspects of life-style	0.924	

(continued)

(*continued*)

Construct/items	Loadings	M(SD)
2. I think using a ch. for online shopping fits well with the way I like to shop online	0.917	
3. Using a chatbot for online shopping fits into my life-style	0.933	
Trust (Van Pinxteren et al. 2019) [56]		4.63(1.43)
1. I feel like the chabot has my best interest at heart	0.896	
2. The chatbot provides accurate information	0.867	
3. I feel I can rely on the chatbot to do what was supposed to do	0.807	
PERCEIVED ENJOYMENT (Moon and Kim 2001) [39]		3.93(1.56)
1. Using the chatbot gives enjoyment to me while shopping online	0.955	
2. Using the chatbot keeps me engaged while shopping online *	0.446	
3. Using the chatbot gives fun to me while shopping online	0.955	
4. Using the chatbot stimulates my curiosity while shopping online	0.947	
ATTITUDE (Manis and Choi 2018) [35]		4.64(1.45)
1. My overall impression of using chatbot for online shopping is good	0.914	
2. My overall impression of using chatbot for online shopping is positive	0.941	
3. My overall impression of using chatbot for online shopping is satisfactory	0.906	
4. My overall impression of using chatbot for online shopping is favorable	0.932	
INTENTION TO USE (Caprara and Barbaranelli) [7]		3.89(1.73)
1. I would probably use the chatbot for online shopping in the next 6 months	0.939	
2. I plan to use the chatbot for online shopping in the next 6 months	0.938	

Note. R = reversed items. * denotes items that were removed from CFA.

References

1. Araújo, T., Casais, B.: Customer acceptance of shopping-assistant chatbots. In: Marketing and Smart Technologies, pp. 278–287. Springer, Singapore (2020). https://doi.org/10.1007/978-981-33-4183-8
2. Araújo, T.: Living up to the chatbot hype: the influence of anthropomorphic design cues and communicative agency framing on conversational agent and company perceptions. Comput. Hum. Behav. **85**, 183–189 (2018)
3. Bashir, I., Madhavaiah, C.: Consumer attitude and behavioural intention toward Internet banking adoption in India. J. Indian Bus. Res. **2**, 67–102 (2015)
4. BigCommerce.: The World of Chatbots: Customer Service, Business Automation & Scalability (2019). https://www.bigcommerce.com/blog/chatbots/#transitioning-into-and-also-out-of-chatbots. Accessed 6 May 2021

5. Brandtzaeg, P.B., Følstad, A.: Chatbots: changing user needs and motivations. Interactions **25**(5), 38–43 (2018)
6. Brusch, I., Rappel, N.: Exploring the acceptance of instant shopping–an empirical analysis of the determinants of user intention. J. Retail. Consum. Serv. **54**, 101936 (2019)
7. Caprara, G.V., Barbaranelli, C.: Capi di governo, telefonini, bagni schiuma. In: Cortina, R. (ed.), pp. 268–2000. Milano, Italy (2000)
8. Chen, L., Gillenson, L., Sherrell, L.: Enticing online consumers: an extended technology acceptance perspective. Inf. Manag. **39**(8), 709–719 (2002)
9. Chi, T.: Understanding Chinese consumer adoption of apparel mobile commerce: an extended TAM approach. J. Retail. Consum. Serv **44**, 274–284 (2018)
10. Dale, R.: The return of the chatbots. Nat. Lang. Eng. **22**(5), 811–817 (2016)
11. Davis, F.D.: Perceived usefulness, perceived ease of use and user acceptance of information technology. MIS Q. **13**(3), 319–340 (1989)
12. Davis, F.D., Bagozzi, R.P., Warshaw, P.R.: User acceptance of computer technology: a comparison of two theoretical models. Manag. Sci. **35**(8), 982–1003 (1989)
13. De Cicco, R., Palumbo, R.: Should a Chatbot disclose itself? Implications for an online conversational retailer. In: International Workshop on Chatbot Research and Design, pp. 3–15. Springer, Cham (2020). https://doi.org/10.1007/978-3-030-68288-0
14. De Cicco, R., e Silva, S.C., Alparone, F.R.: Millennials' attitude toward chatbots: an experimental study in a social relationship perspective. Int. J. Retail Distrib. Manag. **48**(11), 1213–1233 (2020)
15. Dickinger, A., Arami, M., Meyer, D.: The role of perceived enjoyment and social norm in the adoption of technology with network externalities. Eur. J. Inf. Syst. **17**(1), 4–11 (2008)
16. Easterby-Smith, M., Jaspersen, L.J., Thorpe, R., Valizade, D.: Management and Business Research, 5th edn. Sage, London (2021)
17. Fishbein, M., Ajzen, I.: Misconceptions about the Fishbein model: reflections on a study by Songer-Nocks. J. Exp. Soc. Psychol. **12**, 579–584 (1976)
18. Forbes: Will 2019 Be The Breakout Year For Conversational Commerce In The U.S.? (2019). www.forbes.com/sites/forbestechcouncil/2019/05/07/will-2019-be-the-breakout-year-for-conversational-commerce-in-the-u-s/#26985dfa4ac9. Accessed 13 Mar 2021
19. Fornell, C., Bookstein, F.L.: Two structural equation models: LISREL and PLS applied to consumer exit-voice theory. J. Mark. Res. **19**(4), 440–452 (1982)
20. Goodhue, D.L.: Comment on Benbasat and Barki's "Quo Vadis TAM" article. J. Assoc. Inf. Syst. **8**(4), 15 (2007)
21. Ha, I., Yoon, Y., Choi, M.: Determinants of adoption of mobile games under mobile broadband wireless access environment. Inf. Manag. **44**(3), 276–286 (2007)
22. Ha, S., Stoel, L.: Consumer e-shopping acceptance: antecedents in a technology acceptance model. J. Bus. Res. **62**(5), 565–571 (2009)
23. Hair Jr, J.F., Hult, G.T.M., Ringle, C., Sarstedt, M.: A primer on Partial Least Squares Structural Equation Modeling (PLS-SEM). Sage, Thousand Oaks (2016)
24. Hair Jr, J.F., Sarstedt, M., Ringle, C.M., Gudergan, S.P.: Advanced Issues in Partial Least Squares Structural Equation Modeling. Sage, Thousand Oaks (2017)
25. Hong, W., Chan, F.K., Thong, J.Y., Chasalow, L.C., Dhillon, G.: A framework and guidelines for context-specific theorizing in information systems research. Inf. Syst. Res. **25**(1), 111–136 (2014)
26. Hsu, C.L., Lu, H.P., Hsu, H.H.: Adoption of the mobile Internet: an empirical study of multimedia message service (MMS). Omega **35**(6), 715–726 (2007)
27. Jones, C., Hayter, M., Jomeen, J.: Understanding asexual identity as a means to facilitate culturally competent care: a systematic literature review. J. Clin. Nurs. **26**(23–24), 3811–3831 (2017)

28. Kasilingam, D.L.: Understanding the attitude and intention to use smartphone chatbots for shopping. Technol. Soc. **62**, 101280 (2020)
29. Kim, J., Fiore, A.M., Lee, H.H.: Influences of online store perception, shopping enjoyment, and shopping involvement on consumer patronage behavior towards an online retailer. J. Retail. Consum. Serv. **14**(2), 95–107 (2007)
30. Kim, S., Garrison, G.: Investigating mobile wireless technology adoption: an extension of the technology acceptance model. Inf. Syst. Front. **11**(3), 323–333 (2009)
31. King, W.R., He, J.: A meta-analysis of the technology acceptance model. Inf. Manag. **43**(6), 740–755 (2006)
32. Koufaris, M., Kambil, A., LaBarbera, P.: A: Consumer behavior in web-based commerce: an empirical study. Int. J. Electron. Commer. **6**(2), 115–138 (2001)
33. Li, R., Chung, T.L.D., Fiore, A.M.: Factors affecting current users' attitude toward e-auctions in China: an extended TAM study. J. Retail. Consum. Serv. **34**, 19–29 (2017)
34. Löfgren, K.: Qualitative analysis of interview data: a step-by-step guide. Video file. Accessed 29 Aug 2021
35. Manis, K.T., Choi, D.: The virtual reality hardware acceptance model (VR-HAM): extending and individuating the technology acceptance model (TAM) for virtual reality hardware. J. Bus. Res. **100**, 503–513 (2019)
36. Markets Insider: Global Chatbot market anticipated to reach $9.4 billion by 2024 - robust opportunities to arise in retail & eCommerce (2019). https://markets.businessinsider.com/news/stocks/global-chatbot-market-anticipated-to-reach-9-4-billion-by-2024-robust-opportunities-to-arise-in-retail-ecommerce-1028759508. Accessed 2 May 2021
37. McKnight, D.H., Chervany, N.L.: What trust means in e-commerce customer relationships: an interdisciplinary conceptual typology. Int. J. Electron. Commer. **6**(2), 35–59 (2001)
38. Min, S., So, K.K.F., Jeong, M.: Consumer adoption of the Uber mobile application: Insights from diffusion of innovation theory and technology acceptance model. J. Travel Tour. Mark. **36**(7), 770–783 (2019)
39. Moon, J.W., Kim, Y.G.: Extending the TAM for a World-Wide-Web context. Inf. Manag. **38**(4), 217–230 (2001)
40. Munoz-Leiva, F., Climent-Climent, S., Liébana-Cabanillas, F.: Determinants of intention to use the mobile banking apps: an extension of the classic TAM model. Span. J. Mark **21**(1), 25–38 (2017)
41. Nassuora, A.B.: Understanding factors affecting the adoption of m-commerce by consumers. J. Appl. Sci. **13**(6), 913–918 (2013)
42. Pereira, R., Tam, C.: Impact of enjoyment on the usage continuance intention of video-on-demand services. Inf. Manag. **58**, 103501 (2021)
43. Ramli, N.A., Latan, H., Nartea, G.V.: Why should PLS-SEM be used rather than regression? Evidence from the capital structure perspective. In: Avkiran, N.K., Ringle, C.M. (eds.) Partial Least Squares Structural Equation Modeling. ISORMS, vol. 267, pp. 171–209. Springer, Cham (2018). https://doi.org/10.1007/978-3-319-71691-6_6
44. Rese, A., Ganster, L., Baier, D.: Chatbots in retailers' customer communication: how to measure their acceptance? J. Retail. Consum. Serv. **56**, 102176 (2020)
45. Rezaei, S.: Segmenting consumer decision-making styles (CDMS) toward marketing practice: a partial least squares (PLS) path modeling approach. J. Retail. Consum. Serv. **22**, 1–15 (2015)
46. Rogers, E.M.: Diffusion of Innovations, 4th edn. Free Press, New York (1995)
47. Sagnier, C., Loup-Escande, E., Lourdeaux, D., Thouvenin, I., Valléry, G.: User acceptance of virtual reality: an extended technology acceptance model. Int. J. Hum.-Comput. Interact. **36**(11), 993–1007 (2020)
48. Saunders, M., Lewis, P., Thornhill, A.: Research Methods for Business Students. Pearson Education, New York (2009)

49. Schmidthuber, L., Maresch, D., Ginner, M.: Disruptive technologies and abundance in the service sector-toward a refined technology acceptance model. Technol. Forecast. Soc. Change **155**, 119328 (2020)

50. Shi, S., Wang, Y., Chen, X., Zhang, Q.: Conceptualization of omnichannel customer experience and its impact on shopping intention: a mixed-method approach. Int. J. Inf. Manage. **50**, 325–336 (2020)

51. Smith, C.L., Hantula, D.A.: Pricing effects on foraging in a simulated Internet shopping mall. J. Econ. Psychol. **24**(5), 653–674 (2003)

52. Sun, J., Chi, T.: Key factors influencing the adoption of apparel mobile commerce: an empirical study of Chinese consumers. J. Text. Inst. **109**(6), 785–797 (2018)

53. Sun, Y., Bhattacherjee, A., Ma, Q.: Extending technology usage to work settings: the role of perceived work compatibility in ERP implementation. Inf. Manag. **46**(6), 351–356 (2009)

54. Van der Heijden, H.: Factors influencing the usage of websites: the case of a generic portal in The Netherlands. Inf. Manag. **40**(6), 541–549 (2003)

55. Van der Heijden, H.: User acceptance of hedonic information systems. MIS Q. **28**, 695–704 (2004)

56. Van Pinxteren, M.M., Wetzels, R.W., Rüger, J., Pluymaekers, M., Wetzels, M.: Trust in humanoid robots: implications for services marketing. J. Serv. Mark **33**(4), 507–518 (2019)

57. Venkatesh, V., Thong, J.Y., Xu, X.: Consumer acceptance and use of information technology: extending the unified theory of acceptance and use of technology. MIS Q. **36**, 157–178 (2012)

58. Vijayasarathy, L.R.: Predicting consumer intentions to use on-line shopping: the case for an augmented technology acceptance model. Inf. Manag. **41**(6), 747–762 (2004)

59. Zarouali, B., Van den Broeck, E., Walrave, M., Poels, K.: Predicting consumer responses to a chatbot on Facebook. Cyberpsychology Behav. Soc. Netw. **21**(8), 491–497 (2018)

60. Zhang, Y.: A study of corporate reputation's influence on customer loyalty based on PLS-SEM model. Int. Bus. Res **2**(3), 28–35 (2009)

Expert Insights for Designing Conversational User Interfaces as Virtual Assistants and Companions for Older Adults with Cognitive Impairments

Kathrin Koebel[1] , Martin Lacayo[1] , Madhumitha Murali[1],
Ioannis Tarnanas[2] , and Arzu Çöltekin[1(✉)]

[1] Institute of Interactive Technologies, University of Applied Sciences and Arts Northwestern Switzerland FHNW, Brugg-Windisch 5210, Switzerland
arzu.coltekin@fhnw.ch
[2] Altoida Inc., Houston, TX 77027, USA

Abstract. In this paper, with the overarching goal to make new technologies more useful and usable to older adults, we examine the benefits and shortcoming of conversational user interfaces (CUIs) for older adults, including those with mild cognitive impairment, and dementia-family diseases. We focus on virtual assistants and companions, and approach the question based on in-depth expert interviews we have conducted with eight experts who have first hand insights from working with older adults in varying settings combined with evidence in empirical studies and meta analyses we found in the literature. These rare expert insights suggest that CUIs have considerable merit as virtual assistants and companions, i.e., more advantages than disadvantages for this specific demographic group, but they need to be designed carefully to function. Based on a qualitative evaluation, we outline specific design recommendations we gathered based on the literature and the featured interviews.

Keywords: CUI · Chatbots · User acceptance · Cognitive training and interventions · Dementia · Alzheimer's

1 Introduction and Background

Globally, the number of people over 60 is nearly one billion today [2]. This number has doubled since 1980, and it is predicted to double again in 2050 [2]. These demographic trends are also reflected in the increasing number of cognitive disorders such as in dementia family diseases, i.e., according to the international federation of Alzheimer and dementia associations, "every 3 s, someone in the world develops dementia" [1]. Taking these aging and cognition facts along with how rapidly technology evolved in the last decades and continues to evolve, as

Supported by Innosuisse grant 39337.1 IP-ICT.

well as the well-documented age-related accessibility issues to technology solutions [3,19], a pressing need emerges to optimize technologies for older adults. These technologies govern our lives, and making them accessible for older adults would mean helping people function independently as long as possible.

In this paper, we focus on a specific computational solution that is becoming viable in recent years due to the advances in machine learning supported natural language processing (NLP): Conversational user interfaces (CUIs). Boradly, CUIs aspire to mimic human-human interaction by means of adding verbal abilities (text or speech) as an interaction modality when humans interact with machines, often in combination with others such as manual or gesture-based interactions [4,5]. As most technologies, CUIs are under-studied for older adults and even less so for older adults with cognitive impairments. This is an important research gap: It is well documented that spatial memory is impaired with aging [9], and thus CUIs are promising complementary interaction methods that might compensate against this impairment.

Furthermore, CUIs could potentially provide a sense of companionship to those who suffer from age-related cognitive decline or cognitive impairments because people around them might find it difficult to keep up a conversation with less and less coherence in speech with advancing dementia [8]. In this paper, we focus on the specific question of if CUIs might be particularly useful for older adults, especially those with cognitive impairments, via a concise review of the literature and interviews we conducted with a selected group of experts who work with cognitive aging. Our objective is to obtain and offer a better understanding how to design CUIs, specifically, virtual assistants and companions, especially those on the cognitive impairment spectrum. Our approach is motivated by the fact that those with cognitive impairments might also suffer from poor metacognition, people who work with them (the experts we interviewed) will have important insights that they may not be able to communicate.

1.1   Related Work

Even in healthy-aging, humans experience a decline in physical, perceptual, motor and cognitive abilities [9], which are inevitably amplified if the person has a cognitive impairment. These abilities all matter in human computer interaction (HCI) research and applications, but software systems are not always optimized to take the weakening abilities into account. Digital technologies are rarely tested with (or adapted to the needs of) older age groups, even though optimizing technological solutions to cognitive aging is becoming entirely possible: Advances in digital health solutions and availability of personal mobile devices offer exciting new opportunities to assess and *monitor* a person's cognitive state and abilities fairly easily, and even predict cognitive impairment [6,7]. Once we are able to assess a person's cognitive state reliably, we can optimize interfaces and interactions, and design cognitive interventions accordingly.

It is important to remember that cognitive health interventions for older adults target some of the most vulnerable people. Because these interventions are sensitive, many people are involved in the care pipeline which can be costly, and logistically difficult to deliver. Leveraging digital technologies, especially those based on smartphones which are already relatively commonplace, is an obvious approach to address this shortfall. However, issues of design effectiveness, particularly in the areas of usability, desirability, and adherence appear to be forming barriers to adoption [10,17].

Even though digital cognitive interventions and training paradigms are subject to much debate with contradictory outcomes [10,11], this line of thinking has been pursued successfully to some degree with visuospatial interfaces [12–14]. Based on such earlier work, we believe addition of a CUI as virtual assistants of companions can be a scalable solution to engage older adults and patients, which can infer the context and intent of their messages, and provide personalized feedback in a natural way minimizing additional cognitive demands. Computerized cognitive therapies (CCT) are typically provided through structured top-down interfaces, i.e., without a CUI, as evidenced by a lack of studies on CUIs for older adults [29]. However, when CCT are designed and applied properly [11,17,20], they are effective, and in some cases could be delivered via a CUI. For example, Khosla and Chu [15] designed multi-question quizzes to instill a sense of usefulness, increase self-confidence, and build resilience for accepting cognitive decline. A similar approach could be adapted to a CUI. In this vein, for example, Sansen et al. [26] proposed a robotic companion for the older adults to engage them in conversations, Laban et al. [5] similarly discussed social robots for supporting post-traumatic stress disorder, while Ho et al. [16] demonstrated that the emotional response to a CUI can be (depending on the application and design) comparable to interacting with a human, and at times might even be superior to it.

It appears, however, some HCI approaches and design decisions may be overall more usable and desirable, and may lead to higher adherence levels than others in our context with older adults [10,17]. If a specific design choice leads to higher adherence to physical of cognitive exercises, this can have implications in the context of health and behavioral change; for example, increased adherence may have an even greater impact than improved treatments [18]. Even though new technologies can be challenging to learn and use effectively for older adults [19], it has been shown that chatbots and messaging applications, even in the form of simple text exchanges, are highly effective in encouraging behavioral changes, and especially in increasing treatment adherence [20], where the *framing* of the message is of high importance [21]. The benefits of simple text messaging have been demonstrated in various domains, e.g., antiretroviral treatment for HIV/AIDS [22], and medication after coronary heart disease [23]. It appears that the simplicity and familiarity of messaging platform renders them easier to use than other applications [24]. It is also possible that relatively simple CUIs (as virtual assistants) can help keep track of a patient's medications, motivate them to follow their schedule, inform them about side effects, or simply enable them to search for information that they need.

At the moment, it is clear for technical, medical, and legal reasons that CUIs cannot; and arguably should not, attempt to replace healthcare personnel and real human contact, but they can be of great value in assisting patients, monitoring their vitals (e.g., medication, sleep, diet, etc.) and alert professionals when necessary, relieving some of the demands on medical professionals and caregivers [25]. They can also be of value as they can keep company and entertain [15,16], similarly as how humans find engaging online content that fits their own tastes, but delivered in a more proactive, verbally driven manner to those who may not be able to follow the latest trends online.

In sum, CUIs might offer high levels of usability and usefulness for people with cognitive decline or impairments, and given that verbal communication is deeply embedded in human nature, this is not surprising. In this vein, a specific type of conversation, i.e., the solicitation of stories from a user's own life appear to help exercise their speech and memory capabilities, and stands out as an especially promising approach for cognitive interventions [26]. Such an approach, if recorded, also builds knowledge about the individual, thus can eventually afford personalizing the dialog facilitated by a CUI, and, non-verbal communication could be a part of an animated onscreen or augmented reality assistant. However, *how* these CUIs are designed is critically important. Previous research demonstrates that incorporating gamification and personalized interactions can further improve adherence to chatbots, thus to the goals of underlying software, such as a prescribed cognitive training, e.g., by displaying customized reminders, encouraging messages, by enabling chat for keeping the users company, and adding careful use of playfulness to entertain them [27,28]. These measures can go a long way in ensuring user uptake, engagement and retention, and they *can* be provided by artificial intelligence (AI) powered CUIs especially if we can personalize the CUI based on individual observations over time.

Given the above, we believe CUIs as virtual assistant/companion apps are promising and viable solutions to make digital health applications more accessible (usable, learnable, and thus desirable) for older adults, and may have value especially for those with age-related cognitive decline or impairments. We specifically focus on mild cognitive impairment (MCI), which can be seen in post-operative cognitive dysfunction (POCD), and/or early stages of dementia-family diseases such as Alzheimer's disease (AD). Although empirical evidence is only accumulating at this point in time, there are promising signs that CUIs may increase adherence (a well-known, unsolved behavioral problem) of older adults to helpful software such as e-coaches and other cognitive and/or physical training interventions, keep them company and entertain them when social interactions are hindered by e.g., cognitive issues, and simply be more usable for older adults. We present more specific arguments and our findings below, after outlining our methodology.

2   Methods

We chose to interview experts instead of the patients themselves, mainly because metacognition also gets difficult with cognitive impairment, therefore it might not be straightforward to interview people in varying brain health conditions. Experts who work with them, and directly observe them, thus, are an extremely valuable source of information. Although we interviewed a small number of people (n = 8), each of them have years (taken together, 119 years) of experience working with older adults with varying cognitive health conditions. These experts can imagine the implications of placing a CUI in front of a patient in a much more grounded way than most of us who develop software, and thus the interviews provide us with rare and unique insights from their encounters with older adults.

2.1 Participants

We conducted semi-structured interviews with eight aging and cognition experts (age range 25–55) in various domains that represent clinical, day-to-day care, and research perspectives. An overview of the professional expertise (domains, years) of our participants can be found in the Table 1 below.

Table 1. Professional background of the experts we interviewed.

#	Background (experience in years)
E1	Neuroscientist, cognitive training, brain disorders (13)
E2	Neuroscientist, brain injuries, geriatric rehabilitation (16)
E3	Neuroscientist, cerebrovascular and neurodegenerative markers of AD (9)
E4	Psychologist, dynamics of healthy aging (15)
E5	Neurologist, brain health and computational biomarkers (21)
E6	Developer of computer games for older people (19)
E7	General practitioner, including experience with older patients (20)
E8	Nurse with work experience in a dementia ward (6)

2.2 Materials

We conducted the interviews remotely using a video conferencing app (Zoom). An informed consent document was prepared on an online word editing software (Google docs) and delivered electronically by email before the interviews. No other specific software or hardware was needed besides a computer with an Internet connection.

2.3 Procedure and Analysis

We recruited the experts from our professional network based on their publications, conference presence and activities in other areas that had a focus on older adults both healthy-aging and those with brain-health issues, and scheduled the sessions by email. An informed consent form was delivered in the same email for them read before joining the session. Once they joined the session, they gave their consent verbally in recorded video. The interview duration was about one hour (50 mins, with a 10 min buffer). Since the interview was semi-structured, we asked all our interviewees the same questions. A selection of these questions are presented in the Table 2 below. We also allowed them time to offer insights based on what the conversation inspired, or if there were important issues we did not think to ask. Participants were not monetarily compensated, and sessions were recorded based on their consent for internal use. We then transcribed the recordings selectively based on an audio content analysis, i.e., we identified the relevant keywords and themes that were mentioned by the interviewees using an inductive approach. We open-coded the interview data qualitatively broadly following the discourse analysis methods [36]. We analyzed the words, phrases and sentences in the interviews to capture the main messages within the verbal data. We then summarized the feedback into categories in a close-coding session, grouping the open-coded themes. Two researchers from the authoring team were involved in the coding process, which resulted in dozens of codes which was reduced to 30 codes covering the most repeated/emphasized words (role, friend, companion, assistant, caregiver, coach, personality, adaptive, personalized, individual, loneliness, social, patient, comforting, neutral, non-patronizing, agreeable, ACT, empower, animate, encourage, suggest, acceptance, feedback, self-reflect, stories, exercise, dancing, routine, adherence) and grouped under 5 overarching themes (level of expertise, emotional intelligence, personalization, practical features, user acceptance). The analysis was presented and discussed by the authoring team in internal meetings. Below, We detail the most important findings in relation to these themes, embedded with a literature review, in a narrative summary.

Table 2. Example questions used in the interviews. Each category had 3-10 questions some of which involved rating on a 6-point Likert scale. Open comments were always invited. Full list of questions are available upon request.

Introduction, briefing	Interviewee's domains of expertise, experience with CUIs, inviting them to think about their interactions with MCI patients
Potential and usefulness of CUIs	Do you think a CUI would be of use for a patient with MCI? [yes/no, why]
Personality of the CUI	What characteristics should the 'personality' of the CUI possess, particularly with regard to the target population (seniors, POCD/MCI/AD patients)?
Capabilities of the CUI	On what topics should the user be able to chat with the CUI? What should the CUI NOT do? (actions or topics to be avoided)
Habit building	What type messages would foster good habits? (specific examples) What should the CUI NOT do? (actions or topics to be avoided)
Usability, UX, user acceptance	What interaction paradigms would enhance the CUI's usability? What features might help that the patient will enjoy or look forward to using the app without getting bored or too "stressed"?
MCI, POCD, AD patients	Problems for POCD/MCI/AD patients that a CUI could help? Requirements that are specific to this group?
Wrap up final comments	If you were designing a CUI assistant/companion app, functionalities and content would you prioritize? Can you recap your vision of a personal assistant for MCI patients?

3   Results: Pros and Cons of CUIs for Older Adults

Although CUIs as virtual coaches or cognitive training apps are shown to help increase human well-being different domains and might be more usable for older adults than other interfaces [24, 29], there are also valid arguments against them. Some of these arguments focus on technological factors e.g., limits in a CUI's operational capacity, others on psychological matters e.g., lack of user acceptance. Below we highlight concerns as well as opportunities pointed out in previous research and in our expert interviews, based a narrative that contains our own position embedded in it.

3.1   CUI's Level of Expertise

Even though there is evidence that AI can outperform physicians in certain tasks (e.g., diagnostics benefit quantitatively comparing large data), people trust human counterparts more than digital solutions [30]. Our experts [E1–8] observed that current CUIs can come off unnatural as they cannot properly interpret emotional and non-verbal components of human interactions. Importantly, the domain is loaded with ethical and legal questions which are still mostly open. For example, should humans always be aware that they are talking to a machine? Who would be responsible for the mistakes an algorithm would make? An in-depth treatment of these questions are beyond the scope of this paper, however, a carefully designed *helper* CUI, i.e., an assistant or companion, can provide a relatively uncomplicated and cost-effective solution with unique strengths. Several experts [E3, E7] commented that due to its constant availability, a CUI can continuously monitor and analyze conversation content, thus pick up subtle changes much earlier than a physician using traditional methods capturing patient data at a particular moment in time, and the data produced by a CUI may be considerably richer than other that of other apps if it improves adherence.

3.2   CUI's Emotional Intelligence/Importance of Personalization

Many current CUIs are based on decision tree models, and thus can only interact with the user based on predefined questions and answers. Those can be perceived as incompetent, boring, rigid, impersonal, and can frustrate users. However, there may be a positive side to this simplicity [E7]: A structured, somewhat predictable conversation can support patients with cognitive issues such as mild cognitive impairment (MCI), Alzheimer's disease (AD) or postoperative cognitive dysfunction (POCD), as structure and repetition can make them feel secure. For example, E7 said:

> *"Structure is exactly what people need. They like to hold on to structure [...] I can imagine that even someone with [only] slight cognitive deficits would like structure, because structure means security [...], what you ultimately strive for. So I see a benefit."*

Also importantly, our expert interviews revealed that many older adults with cognitive issues might be embarrassed by their condition, and may be more willing to ask and accept help from an anonymous, machine-like device than from a human. It has indeed been demonstrated that in some cases (e.g., depressive disorder), the use of chatbots result in a higher rating of therapeutic alliance between patient-and-chatbot than between patient and clinician [31]. Future CUIs based on machine learning (ML) and AI will be smarter than their counterparts today, especially given the unprecedented progress in natural language processing (NLP). These next generation CUIs will understand a user's context, behavior patterns and preferences, thus can tailor content and timing of prescribed interventions or necessary assistance in a personalized manner. An ideal CUI should be configured to be discreet and respect user's privacy, automatically adapt to the user's needs and mood (e.g., through sentiment detection) as this might give a stronger feeling of being understood and increase adherence [E2], *and* offer options to manually adjust settings. This would enable both user-driven personalization (i.e., user configured) and an AI-driven one (i.e., AI learns and proposes or imposes adaptive changes). Personalization is also relevant to caregivers and family members (not only the older adults and MCI/AD patients) as the CUI can be configured to facilitate the communication in a customized manner as well as learn the communication patterns of the caregivers and family members with the older adults around them and lead to insights into a patient's experience. In our interviews, experts expressed contrasting views on what level of personal rapport between patient and chatbot is desired: some believe that emotional connection strengthens adherence to interventions [E4], while others expressed concerns about emotionally loaded conversations, as a machine is likely not able to respond to human emotions appropriately, which can lead to frustration and other negative emotions in the human counterpart [E6, E7, E8]. This is also an ethical quagmire in terms of human connection. For example, one of the experts said:

> *"[...] when you talk about a caregiver and friend, an emotional and social component comes into the game, the chatbot cannot do that. It would even be pathological if someone said "The chatbot is my friend". It must never become a friend, it would already draw or entail a part of the social isolation." [E7].*

Similarly, E6 stated that:

> *"From an ethical perspective, chatbot should not pretend to be a human, it has to be clear that the user is interacting with a computer [...] user should agree if he/she wants to get "manipulated/deceived" with such a device as long as he/she can still decide for themselves" [E6].*

3.3   Most Promising CUI Features as Expressed by Experts

In our expert interviews, functionalities such as *encouraging* patients, *reminding* them of tasks such as following prescriptions and exercises, and *animating* or *nudging* them to engage in activities stood out as the most promising features. Below we elaborate on a few of these.

First and foremost, *encouraging patients*, and *rewarding* them for their efforts was mentioned by all experts. It is crucial though that messages are not too repetitive nor patronizing, and a variety of sincere and specific motivational messages and compliments are configured, worded to reassure and foster a sense of self-efficacy. Similarly, acceptance commitment therapy (ACT) messages have great potential, which have improved treatment outcomes in various chronic conditions [32], and lend themselves well for digital interventions. **Secondly**, several experts [E2, E3, E6, E8] mentioned integrating *social features* as human interactions can feel much more authentic and rewarding than e.g., a compliment given by a chatbot. Also, psychological mechanisms involved in interaction with machines can be complex; e.g., a simple algorithmic rewards in computer games can be addictive (as in gambling), and people can 'humanize' robots and software, and feel affection or attachment for them. The key is designing an *appropriate* reward system, and for that, it is important to understand what motivates the individual user [33]. Additionally, for many chronic health issues, adherence to prescribed protocols (e.g., medication, exercise, nutrition, cognitive interventions) appears to be a difficult problem. In the context of older adults' adherence to digital interventions, we must also consider memory lapses. Experts expressed that even the simple, customizable *reminder* functionalities aligned to a patient's daily routines (to support building new habits) bear great potential. It is important that the user does not feel *controlled* by the bot in general, nor this feature in particular, as negative feelings can lead to a decline in user acceptance. The **third** highly recommended CUI feature is to *animate* or *nudge* patients (plus caregivers, family members) to e.g., contact others, play an active game, go for a walk or initiate dancing. Such prompts could be aligned to some predefined targets (e.g., social engagement, cognitive training, physical activities) and the degree of challenge should adapt to the user's current social, mental and physical fitness level, context and capabilities. Combining physical and cognitive exercises (as in exergames and multi-domain training) have positive effects as well [34], and experts posited that adding social components in such interventions may have an even greater effect [E3, E6]. Plus, explaining why a particular activity is beneficial also increases adherence [E4, E5, E8]. These insights overlap substantially with a recent meta analysis study [29].

3.4 Factors of User Acceptance

User acceptance of CUIs surfaced as an important theme in our interviews, for which practical, social and psychological reasons were mentioned. Several experts mentioned the technology acceptance models (TAM) [35]. Specifically, a *senior* TAM (STAM) adaptation [37] (see Fig. 1), which specifies similar variables and system characteristics, e.g., facilitating conditions and social influence impact perceived usefulness and ease of use, and lead to user acceptance (or rejection). On the practical side, adoption of new technologies, including smartphones, is generally lower in older adults [19]. User interfaces are not customized to the

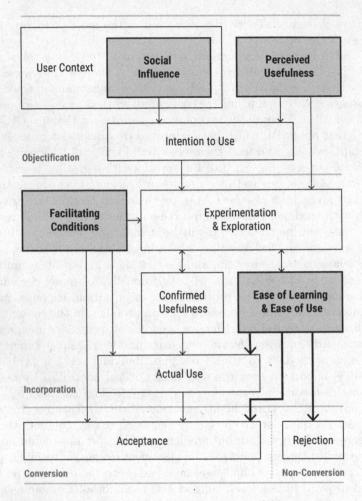

Fig. 1. Senior technology acceptance & adoption model (STAM) by Renaud and Van Biljon [37]. Figure redrawn and emphasis added by the authors.

specific needs of this demographic group, making operation of applications and devices unnecessarily difficult for older adults, especially for those with cognitive impairments. CUIs aimed at older adults should be subjected to high usability standards, and tested in carefully designed experiments.

Privacy and security issues may also require special attention with older adults to prevent exploitation, specifically of people in more vulnerable states (e.g., MCI, AD, POCD). Less tech-savvy users may not feel confident about configuring a device listening to them, and speech can contain sensitive information. Evidently, there are large individual differences in technology competence depending on e.g., level of education [38]), type of technology [20], incentive [39], or if it enhances engagement with family [E2]. Furthermore, social context and subjective norms are important aspects for older adults' acceptance of CUIs as assistants of companions. Many questions are raised in this context from various social and cultural groups: Is it respectful and dignified that a patient is cared for or treated by a CUI? To what degree can a chatbot help against the issue of loneliness that many older adults experience? Is it (un)ethical if the chatbot would provide a (fake) sense of companionship to a patient? While some resist such technology-driven solutions due to their potentially deceptive nature, others, who are more optimistic about technology, may encourage its use and be early adopters themselves. Linked to these issues, some experts consider loneliness as one of the biggest problems of MCI patents [E3, E8], for which CUIs *can* help, i.e., they might not only assist and entertain, but also reinforce social contact with other humans.

Another dimension of user acceptance of any technology is its perceived usefulness. In the case of CUIs for people with cognitive deficiencies, this starts with psychological aspects, notably that patients must first of all *accept* their need for support [E8]. Some patients try to mask the cognitive decline and reject interventions, others (mainly advanced AD) may not be aware of their condition and thus may not cooperate. CUIs (or machines in general) offer great potential in these situations as they can support patients in an unobtrusive manner, bypassing some of the social anxieties cognitive impairments can cause. If patients feel empowered through the CUI, if it increases their independence and if it helps them to better achieve their goals, acceptance will certainly increase. Experts recommend framing interventions around one's personal well-being [E1], patients should be explained why CUIs in general and specific exercises in particular are beneficial for them [E4, E5, E8]. Also feedback mechanisms add value, as this supports self-reflection and offers a sense availability to the patient. Also, CUIs do not get impatient, they are never tired or under stress, which brings up the question of how the 'personality' of a CUI should be designed to increase user acceptance. In response to this question, experts mentioned attributes such as *friendly, helpful, patient, empathetic, comforting, reassuring, encouraging*, and *motivating*, but all emphasized the importance of personalization, and fine-tuning for cultural differences.

If patients *like* the personality of the CUI, they are likely to feel more comfortable than if they did not, and their anxiety levels might thus be reduced [E3]. This is extremely important, as anxiety can have negative impacts on treatment outcomes. Empathetic CUIs that display a positive tenor can increase adherence [40], however, CUI's messaging should not downplay severeness of a patient's condition [E3], rather, CUI should offer coping strategies that support the patient as well as the caregivers and family members in dealing with the condition. Last but not least, we cannot overstate the importance of usability when designing CUIs for this target group. Aging can come with reduced visual ability, hearing difficulties, decrease of fine motor skills, attention and memory glitches and consequently, a decline in learning speed. All experts emphasized carefully considering structure, language, UI and interaction design (Table 3), which also appear in related literature [41].

Table 3. Practical advice by our experts concerning ease of use of CUI/chatbot.

Content and structure	To accelerate adaptation, the CUI must be clearly structured and self explanatory, not overloaded with many features or sensory stimuli, and should not intimidate the user.
Language	Messages must be simple and unambiguous, complex syntax should be avoided and the wording should never make the patient feel 'talked down' or unintelligent.
Interface and interaction design	Beyond the obvious (e.g., large font and target size, high contrast), the application should be characterized by high fault tolerance (for touch and voice interaction).
Voice	Although voice interaction causes less friction than a visuospatial interface, a combination of text and voice might increase intelligibility for patients with visual or hearing impairments

While CUIs are considered more intuitive and manageable than visuospatial interfaces by many, it is important to remember that e.g., voice interfaces have their own unique usability challenges. For example, privacy issues arise when other people can hear the conversation, thus, an option to switch to headphones and to another interaction modality should be provided. Also, patients might speak a lesser-studied language or dialect, use or pronounce words in unexpected ways, have a soft voice, and as such, the CUI needs to be trained for the individual user's speech patterns. Another issue is that the speech might be directed to someone else, thus unintended conversations might be initiated and generate confusion. More pragmatically, if the patients *depend* on the CUI and do have have access to it because they lost their device or forget to charge it etc., it is important have built-in monitoring functions and prompts that prevent serious negative side effects. All these concerns requires that the CUI should be able to learn and adapt, otherwise they will not live up to their potential.

4   Discussion and Conclusions

Given that there are signs of promising digital cognitive assessments running on a smartphone or a tablet that enable precise, sensitive and long-term monitoring of human cognitive health [6,7], it is more imaginable now than ever that we can deliver timely digital interventions that might help ease patients' troubles, keep them company and possibly protect their cognitive reserve. Such digital interventions, however, seem to be out of reach for many older adults due to a new form of digital divide [42] ignited by lack of usability stemming from an awareness and understanding of barriers to technology adoption among older age groups. Motivated by filling this gap, specifically, the current lack of understanding and awareness of the needs of patients with cognitive impairments, and to eventually find ways to optimize technology solutions for them and their caregivers/family members, we interviewed eight experts who worked with older patients, each in a different capacity.

Usability concerns when designing for older adults are discussed in related research communities, however, arguably, not much of this knowledge is implemented in practice given the low levels of technology adoption among older adults. Importantly, psychological aspects, for example, embarrassment people feel about having a cognitive impairment is rarely taken into account. Such feelings are very common due to stigma around dementia, and affect people's behavior deeply. When software are designed by technologists without psychological insights, important mishaps can occur, e.g., a CUI might make the patient uncomfortable because it would have the wrong tone, reveal too much to others, or might create high cognitive load, preventing technology acceptance and use. In this vein, a key finding in our interviews was that CUIs can be desirable for people with cognitive impairments given that they might allow bypassing social anxieties (feeling embarrassed about the condition), if *message framing* is right. Message framing appears to be of utmost importance not only to prevent a CUI from belittling or patronizing the users; but to reduce anxiety, motivate, encourage and reward them. While personalized and sophisticated systems can increase benefits in monitoring and managing the disease, even simple text based solutions, if message framing is right, offer important benefits and should be exploited. For this ACT messaging seems to be a promising concrete lead to explore. On the other hand, for CUI apps aiming at behavior change, details matter: CUI should encourage the patient but should not mislead them, it should offer rewards but do not overdo it not to lead a negative, addiction-like behavior, it should explain the user why and exactly how the suggested behaviors will improve their lives. As such, these observations stimulate dozens of new research questions to find the right message framing both those that are generalizable, and those that are personalized for individual cases with the help of AI-based solutions. Another important insight, also well documented in the literature, is that in connection to feeling the stigma as well as struggling with processing information, people with cognitive impairments tend to withdraw, and loneliness is a major issue. Such social isolation leads to much needed stimulation for the brain and affects people's motivation to fight the disease, creating a negative loop: they withdraw because of the disease, disease gets worse because they withdraw. This line of thinking brings up the companion apps. Virtual companions that provide (proactive) stimulation -from simply entertaining the user to prompting/nudging towards social behavior- may have much value in protecting cognitive reserve. A successful CUI, however, must present the right 'personality. It appears that the level of realism creates a host of issues. If the CUI is too mechanical, people may be reluctant to trust it (humans still trust humans more than machines), but if it is too realistic, it might generate a false sense of friendship which does not exist. If the patient perceives the CUI as a friend (to replace a real friend), it might have negative consequences in terms of already impoverished human connections, and it might upset the user when the friend does not come through. Thus, the level of realism is a very important factor and must be delicately designed, specifically challenging to get it right for people with cognitive impairments not to add further to their confusion. Perhaps a solution to this is to enable social features integrated within the CUI app to ensure connections to other humans are regularly provided. Similarly as the behavior change related notes above, the companion apps are also in their early days and more experiments are needed to find the most effective solutions that pose no harm to the patients. Simpler CUIs, i.e., the assistants rather than companions, are less complicated as they would most likely increase effectiveness of people in following any prescribed medical procedure, e.g., before and after surgery, following an exercise plan at home, or taking one's medication timely, and in the right doses, etc. In all cases, even in the simplest for of assistance, though it is necessary to remember that speech can contain sensitive, private information and there is not only a risk of making people uncomfortable but can open up a risk of exploitation. Security and privacy, again, especially given the vulnerabilities of this group, should be taken very seriously.

We believe this qualitative evaluation, coupled with quantitative evidence in literature from empirical studies gives us unique insights in designing CUIs, especially for older adults. Based on consolidating results from the literature and the expert interviews, we are convinced that CUIs –given that they are designed with a user-centric approach, personalized as much as possible, and any hearing loss issues are accounted for– may be a very good interaction alternative that is well suited for older adults, especially for those with cognitive impairments such as MCI, POCD or AD. Whether as assistants or companions, carefully designed CUIs that are adjusted to users' context and needs are useful, and can become effective means to increase adherence to cognitive training and lifestyle interventions for this demographic group. However, we believe that user acceptance of a CUI will increase, only if the design is adjusted specifically for this demographic groups (healthy-aging adults, MCI, POCD and AD patients), making the benefits of the CUI apparent for the user, and as the interface is personalized over time, we expect that a CUI will be easier to use than a visuospatial interface for this age group. While the messages we take from these interviews are largely positive with specific design recommendations, it is important to remember that a qualitative interview with only eight experts might not reflect the global reality. Our observations in this paper thus should be taken as a starting point for design recommendations and be validated with the target user group for the goals of each CUI implementation. Similarly, we plan to follow the key ideas in this paper with a series of CUI prototypes, and user experiments for better understanding the limitations of CUIs and specific CUI designs.

References

1. Numbers of people with dementia. Alzheimer's Disease International (ADI) (2021). https://www.alzint.org/about/dementia-facts-figures/dementia-statistics/
2. United Nations: World Population Ageing Highlights, pp. 1–40. New York (2017)
3. Czaja, S.J.: Current findings and issues in technology and aging. J. Appl. Gerontol. **40**(5), 463–465 (2021)

4. Huesser, C., et al.: Gesture interaction in virtual reality. In: Ardito, C, et al. (eds.) Human-Computer Interaction – INTERACT 2021. INTERACT 2021. LNCS, vol. 12934. Springer, Cham (2021). https://doi.org/10.1007/978-3-030-85607-6

5. Laban, G., et al.: Tell me more! assessing interactions with social robots from speech. Paladyn, J. Behav. Robot. **12**(1), 136–159 (2021)

6. Meier, I.B., et al.: Using a digital neuro signature to measure longitudinal individual-level change in Alzheimer's disease: the Altoida large cohort study. Nat. Partner J. (NPJ) Digit. Med. **4**(1), 1–9 (2021)

7. Buegler, M., et al.: Digital biomarker-based individualized prognosis for people at risk of dementia. Alzheimer's Demen. Diagn. Assess. Dis. Monit. **12**(1), e12073 (2020)

8. Dijkstra, K., et al.: Conversational coherence: discourse analysis of older adults with and without dementia. J. Neurolinguist, **17**(4), 263–283 (2004)

9. Park, D.C., et al.: Models of visuospatial and verbal memory across the adult life span. Psychol. Aging **17**(2), 299 (2002)

10. Souders, D.J., et al.: Evidence for narrow transfer after short-term cognitive training in older adults. Front. Aging Neurosci. **9**, 41 (2017)

11. Lampit, A., et al.: Computerized cognitive training in cognitively healthy older adults: a systematic review and meta-analysis of effect modifiers. PLoS Med. **11**(11), e1001756 (2014)

12. Hill, N.T., et al.: Computerized cognitive training in older adults with mild cognitive impairment or dementia: a systematic review and meta-analysis. Am. J. Psychiatr. **174**(4), 329–340 (2017)

13. Lokka, I.E., et al.: Virtual environments as memory training devices in navigational tasks for older adults. Sci. Rep. **8**(1), 1–15 (2018)

14. Lokka, I.E., Çöltekin, A.: Perspective switch and spatial knowledge acquisition: effects of age, mental rotation ability and visuospatial memory capacity on route learning in virtual environments with different levels of realism. Cartogr. Geogr. Inf. Sci. **47**(1), 14–27 (2020)

15. Khosla, R., Chu, M.-T.: Embodying care in Matilda: an affective communication robot for emotional wellbeing of older people in Australian residential care facilities. ACM Trans. Manag. Inf. Syst. (TMIS) **4**(4), 1–33 (2013)

16. Ho, A., et al.: Psychological, relational, and emotional effects of self-disclosure after conversations with a chatbot. J. Commun. **68**(4), 712–733 (2018)

17. Valenzuela, T., et al.: Adherence to technology-based exercise programs in older adults: a systematic review. J. Geriatr. Phys. Therapy **41**(1), 49–61 (2018)

18. Sabaté, E., et al.: Adherence to Long-term Therapies: Evidence for Action. World Health Organization (2003)

19. Leung, R., et al.: How older adults learn to use mobile devices: survey and field investigations. ACM Trans. Access. Comput. **4**(3), 1–33 (2012)

20. Mohadisdudis, H.M., Ali, N.M.: A study of smartphone usage and barriers among the elderly. In: 3rd International Conference on User Science and Engineering (i-USEr), pp. 109–114 (2014)

21. Harrell, E.R., et al.: Investigating message framing to improve adherence to technology-based cognitive interventions. Psychol. Aging **36**, 974–982 (2021)

22. Pop-Eleches, C., et al.: Mobile phone technologies improve adherence to antiretroviral treatment in a resource-limited setting: a randomized controlled trial of text message reminders. AIDS **25**(6), 825 (2011)

23. Park, L.G., et al.: A text messaging intervention to promote medication adherence for patients with coronary heart disease: a randomized controlled trial. Patient Educ. Counsel. pp. 261–268 (2014)

24. Sarkar, S., Sivashankar, P., Seshadri, H.: Mobile SMS reminders for increasing medication adherence. Int. J. Pharm. Sci. Rev. Res. **32**, 228–237 (2015)
25. Fadhil, A.: A conversational Interface to improve medication adherence: towards AI support in patient's treatment. arXiv preprint arXiv:1803.09844 (2018)
26. Sansen, H., et al.: The Roberta ironside project: a dialog capable humanoid personal assistant in a wheelchair for dependent persons. In: 2nd International Conference on Advanced Technology for Signal and Image Processing, pp. 381–386 (2016)
27. Fadhil, A., Gabrielli, S.: Addressing challenges in promoting healthy lifestyles: the al-chatbot approach. In: Proceedings of the 11th EAI International Conference on Pervasive Computing Technologies for Healthcare, pp. 261–265 (2017)
28. Robinson, N.L., et al.: Social robots with gamification principles to increase long-term user interaction. In: Proceedings of the 31st Australian Conference on Human-Computer-Interaction, pp. 359–363 (2019)
29. El Kamali, M., et al.: Virtual coaches for older adults' wellbeing: a systematic review. IEEE Access **8**, 101884–101902 (2020)
30. Seymour, M., et al.: Facing the artificial: understanding affinity, trustworthiness, and preference for more realistic digital humans. In: Proceedings of the 53rd Hawaii International Conference on System Sciences HICSS-53 (2020)
31. Bickmore, T.W., et al.: Response to a relational agent by hospital patients with depressive symptoms. Interact. Comput. **22**(4), 289–298 (2010)
32. Anthony, C.A., et al.: ACT delivered via a mobile phone messaging robot to decrease postoperative opioid use in patients with orthopedic trauma. J. Med. Internet Res. **22**(7), 1–14 (2020)
33. Traver, K., Sargent, B.K.: The Healthiest You. Simon and Schuster, New York City (2011)
34. Gavelin, H.M., et al.: Combined physical and cognitive training for older adults with and without cognitive impairment: a systematic review and network meta-analysis of randomized controlled trials. Ageing Res. Rev. **66**, 101232 (2020)
35. Davis, F.D.: A technology acceptance model for empirically testing new end-user information systems: theory results. Ph.D. Dissertation. Massachusetts Institute of Technology (1985)
36. Talja, S.: Analyzing qualitative interview data: the discourse analytic method. Libr. Inf. Sci. Res. **21**(4), 459–477 (1999)
37. Renaud, K., Van Biljon, J.: Predicting technology acceptance and adoption by the elderly: a qualitative study. In: Proceedings of the 2008 Annual Research Conference of the South African Inst of Computer Scientists, pp. 210–219 (2008)
38. Kivipelto, M., et al.: The Finnish geriatric intervention study to prevent cognitive impairment and disability (FINGER): study design and progress. Alzheimer's Demen. **9**(6), 657–665 (2013)
39. Berkowsky, R.W., et al.: Factors predicting decisions about technology adoption among older adults. Innov. Aging **1**(3) (2017)
40. De Gennaro, M., et al.: Effectiveness of an empathic chatbot in combating adverse effects of social exclusion on mood. Front. Psychol. **10**, 3061 (2020)
41. Darvishy, A., Seifert, A.: Altersgerechte Webseitengestaltung: Grundlagen und Empfehlungen (2013)
42. Elena-Bucea, A., et al.: Assessing the role of age, education, gender and income on the digital divide: evidence for the European Union. Inf. Syst. Front. **23**(4), 1007–1021 (2021)

Understanding People's Expectations When Designing a Chatbot for Cancer Patients

Beatriz Félix[✉] and Jorge Ribeiro

Fraunhofer Portugal AICOS, Porto, Portugal
{beatriz.felix,jorge.ribeiro}@fraunhofer.pt

Abstract. With the overall increase of cancer patients, there is a growing demand for better healthcare services, more patient-centred care, and more user-centred eHealth tools. Chatbots are great tools to bridge communications between health providers and patients and have already been used with success in healthcare.

In the present study, we set out to explore how people perceive a cancer chatbot and to understand preferences and expectations concerning the communication between a chatbot and newly diagnosed cancer patients. The insights from the remote co-creation sessions will enable us to design better chatbot dialogues, with human-like characteristics, that communicate with appropriate content and tone of voice.

Keywords: Chatbots · Co-design · Conversational agents · Cancer patients · Healthcare

1 Introduction

Cancer is expected to affect one in three people in the next two decades. According to the World Health Organization (WHO), 19.3 million people were diagnosed with cancer in 2020 and this number is expected to increase to 30.2 million in 2040[1]. These growing numbers will strain the current health systems, leading to increasing demand for more efficient communication channels between patients and healthcare providers. eHealth systems are being used with success to improve health management and patient involvement [42]. Moreover, healthcare systems are moving to more patient-centred care. Patients increasingly seek more control over their health and to do so they need to be well informed [2].

Cancer patients undergo treatments and long-term care in hospitals. Providing them with reliable information facilitates decision-making and treatment adherence, which may have an overall effect on the progression of the disease [1]. The lack of reliable information about the disease, treatments or symptoms is one of the most common unmet needs of an oncology patient [16]. Consequently,

---

[1] Cancer Fact Sheets: https://gco.iarc.fr/tomorrow/en/dataviz/isotype.

© Springer Nature Switzerland AG 2022
A. Følstad et al. (Eds.): CONVERSATIONS 2021, LNCS 13171, pp. 39–54, 2022.
https://doi.org/10.1007/978-3-030-94890-0_3

user-friendly tools should be created to empower cancer patients by addressing their concerns.

Conversation is one of the preferred coping mechanisms used by cancer patients [36] but engaging in a conversation with them can be challenging. According to Brandtzaeg and Følstad [8], people have a predisposition to adhere to behaviours that mimic human-to-human interaction. However, knowing they are interacting with a robot, they feel more at ease to ask questions they might not otherwise feel comfortable asking a healthcare professional [6,11]. Conversation has been recognized to facilitate the success of certain healthcare interventions. Talking through the process, receiving information and understanding procedures helps boost patients' confidence [20]. Chatbots offer an interface that simulates human-like conversations through text or speech by using artificial intelligence (AI) algorithms and natural language [41], and have been used with success to facilitate communication in healthcare [21]. Knowing there is always an accessible connection, with a short timespan between questions and answers, motivates users to engage in conversations and makes virtual agents a feasible tool to hold users' attention [19]. Moreover, we found that not much research has been carried out to understand how users prefer to communicate with health services.

The aim of this work was to explore how to design a conversational agent targeted at recently diagnosed cancer patients to support them and their caregivers during the onboarding process at a hospital. For this purpose, we conducted three remote co-creation sessions with people without cancer and asked the participants to put themselves in the position of cancer patients. The goal was to understand people's preferences and expectations with regards to communication with a healthcare chatbot. The contribution of this work lies in the understanding of how to design a conversational agent in the healthcare field that caters to the needs of cancer patients.

2   Background

2.1   Chatbots for Cancer Patients

Chatbots in healthcare have been emerging during recent years. Healthcare services have been using these systems to improve communication between patients and their institutions, designing them with different purposes such as diagnosis, prevention and therapy [21].

In the oncology field, chatbots are assisting patients in three main areas: mental health, follow-up, and self-management. Regarding mental health, chatbots like Vivibot [15] and VIK [7,9] are helping cancer patients deal with the disease and its associated stress and anxiety. Chatbots are helping collect patients' data in follow-up by patients, either for studies [30] or after treatments and surgeries [32]. The self-management area focuses on helping patients with more practical questions on the illness and with self care [6,22].

All of these studies focus on the adoption and engagement of these chatbots by the patients, while studies that seek to find what patients actually look for in a chatbot are very limited.

2.2 Attribution of Human Characteristics to Chatbots

When discussing the use of chatbots, one of the key questions is whether they should have human characteristics such as gender, race or even personality. Anthropomorphism is the attribution of human traits to non-human entities and is used in conversational agents to make them more accessible and familiar to users [33, 39]. Trust is one of the most discussed personality traits regarding bots, especially from the designer's point of view. According to McDuff and Czerwinski [26], people are not willing to trust a machine with important decision-making in spite of the fact that the machine performs certain tasks, such as planning and numeric analysis, better than humans. Rapp et al. [35] states the chatbot's ability to interpret users' requests correctly and reply with useful information in a human-like manner, which helps users gain more trust in the machine. Empathy is also a very important trait for users. This sentiment can be two-fold: the feeling of concern for other people's emotions or the emotional response deriving from other's emotions [35]. Having unrealistic expectations of the bots and their intelligence can lead to frustration when patients feel their concerns are not understood and addressed [18].

Research has shown that it is possible to design these systems with emotional intelligence and human traits to render them more trustworthy and reliable to users. There is, however, no simple and effective universal rule. According to Hwang et al. [17], by studying dialogues between humans and the interaction between a human and a chatbot, we can create a personality with the help of linguistic markers. The choice of words and linguistic patterns can reveal a great deal about a person's emotional state. Therefore, if the designer can match the linguistics of the user to the chatbot's persona, it is more likely that the user will create an emotional connection with the system and consequently establish more rapport. Kate Moran [27] presents a framework of four dimensions based on 4 primary tones of voice. With this, Moran [28] concluded that the tone of voice affects user perception of the brands.

Regarding the use of emojis in health services, Fadhil et al. [13] noticed low engagement in conversations about the user's condition as opposed to when the topic was mental health. Smestad and Volden [39] studied the importance of personality in a chatbot and concluded that people interacted more with the chatbot with a pleasant personality and not so much with the chatbot that did not express emotions. Additionally, Thies et al. [40] concluded that personality type depends on the kind of interaction the user seeks with the bot. Finally, Lucas et al. [25] achieved positive results when using chatbots in a clinical context. Under similar circumstances, people showed more willingness to dialogue with machines than with other humans.

2.3   Participatory Design in Chatbots

Participatory design, more commonly known as co-design, is a study methodology maxim of "knowing by doing", that is, the manner in which people perform their tasks and how they can be studied to enhance them [3]. Through group interactions, participants are provided with tools and techniques to design a solution by bringing in their expertise and sharing their knowledge with the designers [4].

Co-design has been used in the design of chatbots to increase their value and bring them closer to their users [47]. This methodology has been used to design several chatbots in different areas such as social integration [10], education [31], to combat online harassment in young adults [31], or to promote life skills [14].

In healthcare, [29] and [38] promote the use of participatory design for designing chatbots. This methodology has been used by [5], who used workshops to create journeys and sketch their own ideas for possible solutions for a chatbot that would coach adolescents with special health needs through transitions of care. Easton et al. [12] used their workshops to choose from several chatbot's personalities, from their appearance to sound and format. They also designed scripts and performed adapted wizard of oz experiences. Xu et al. [46] explained how the stakeholders of an app for caregivers with atopic dermatitis helped in the creation of the user's interface and in determining the knowledge of the chatbot.

Another topic worth mentioning is the selection of personality traits by participants in the design of chatbots. Through different activities, [10,12,34,39] these authors address the chatbot's personality and discuss how the chosen traits influence the way users perceive the chatbot.

3   Methodology

In preparation for the co-creation sessions, we developed exploratory research to determine the main problems and concerns of patients and workers at the Portuguese Oncology Institute - IPO-Porto. We started by conducting semi-structured, individual, interviews with twelve participants - four administrative workers from the institution, five patients and three caregivers. We asked participants to share their personal experiences and introduced the idea of having a conversational agent to help them in their journey. We concluded that the chatbot should be targeted at new cancer patients and their process. Patients tend to feel most disoriented and confused at the beginning, where they mentioned the need for additional help. While many mentioned their expectations in terms of the chatbot's knowledge, participants did not disclose what they imagined the chatbot to be. The insights from this initial work were used to design the activities of the co-creation sessions.

3.1   Participants

In total, eight people participated in this study, of which five were female and three were male. The participants were selected by convenience sampling. Since cancer incidence is higher in patients over 50, we aimed to recruit older participants and people who had had some contact with cancer patients. However, we were unable to recruit enough participants who met all the requirements and included additional participants outside these criteria. Participants were, on average, 46.25 years old, six of whom were over 42. Six participants had, or have had, a close relative or friend with cancer. Only one participant worked in healthcare as a nurse. Regarding chatbot experience, only half the participants (4) knew the term 'chatbot'. However, when the term was explained and a few examples were given, 50% of participants said they had never used one, 25% used a chatbot once and the other 25% use chatbots once a month.

3.2   Study Design

Due to the COVID pandemic, the co-creation sessions were carried out online. A total of three co-creation sessions were conducted. The participants were asked to participate in a video call on the Microsoft Teams[2] platform and while on the call they were asked to access a link to the MURAL[3] app. The consent forms were e-mailed to the participants prior to the session along with a short questionnaire with demographic requests and questions about their experience with chatbots. All of the activities were conducted in this web application. The video call was recorded for additional analysis. The sessions were held with two to three participants per session with an approximate duration of 50 min. Initially, the participants were explained the purpose of the research and, in particular, the purposes of the session. Afterwards, the platform was explained and a tutorial was presented on how to work with the different tools in MURAL. Prior to the co-creation sessions, a test session was performed with two persons under the circumstances described above to validate the protocol. Data from the test session was not used in this analysis.

The co-creation session consisted of three activities:

Activity 1. Intended to understand what participants imagined behind the chatbot. Inspired by the activities performed by Easton et al. [12] and Khasnabish et al. [23], we wanted to explore the features of the chatbot and we tried to get users to explain the importance of the chosen traits. We also discussed how participants imagined the chatbot's personality [43]. At first, they would individually pick a set of characteristics, either psychological or physical, to describe the chatbot. The participants were asked to write down words or sentences on post-its and, in addition, had the opportunity to pick pictures or icons to assist with their ideas. After five minutes, the participants were asked to stop the activity and the moderator initiated a brainstorming session to understand the reason behind those choices. With this exercise, we sought to understand the

---

[2] https://www.microsoft.com/pt-pt/microsoft-teams/group-chat-software.
[3] MURAL is a digital work space for visual collaboration where participants can interact with each other: https://www.mural.co/.

most important characteristics in a chatbot for cancer patients and what made participants feel more comfortable while talking to the conversational agent.

Activity 2. Aimed to look into the participants' approach to the chatbot. We also wanted to get training phrases for the chatbot framework, similar to [44], on the roleplay activity performed in their study. Because the co-creation sessions were carried out remotely, we had to adapt the exercise. Participants were given three different scenarios and were asked, based on the scenarios, how they would ask the chatbot for help. They proceeded to write down their responses individually.

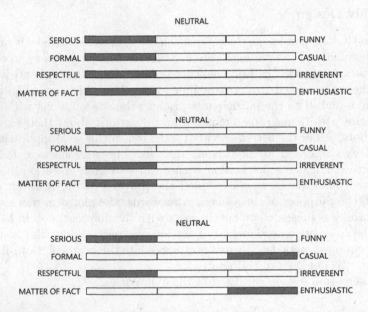

Fig. 1. Tones of voice created for the co-creation sessions. Adapted from [27]

Activity 3. Aimed to understand the preferred tone-of-voice in a chatbot for cancer patients. We were inspired by Kucherbaev et al. [24] and Khasnabish et al. [23], and carried out an adaption of their roleplay exercise. Since the number of participants was small and, in most sessions, made up of odd numbers, we created eight chatbot mockups with different discourses. The dialogues were created based on Kate Moran's framework of four dimensions of the tone of voice [27]. Three types of tones were created as presented in Fig. 1. To these three tones, we added variants such as emojis or predefined answer options. Finally, we added one more chatbot dialogue that had no introductory message, with the user initiating the dialogue. Participants had to choose the two chatbots they liked most and the two they liked least by putting green circles (for the ones they preferred) or red circles (for the ones they disliked), as can be observed in Fig. 3. When the voting was completed, we initiated a brainstorming session, inspired by Wiratunga et al. [44], where the moderator asked questions on the reasons behind the voting to better explore their points of view on the chatbot's user interface.

4   Results and Discussion

In our study, we found that participants preferred a chatbot with human characteristics, that mimics a human and does not have robot-like features. Similarly, Brandtzaeg and Følstad [8] mentioned that people feel more at ease with human-like systems. Smestad and Volden [39] studied the importance of personality in a chatbot and concluded that users were more satisfied with the chatbot with the most pleasant personality as opposed to the one that did not mimic human traits. The dialogue and chatbot's introduction to users were also discussed in these activities. According to Rozga et al. [37], the chatbot must present itself as a robot to let users know upfront who they are dialoguing with. However, contrary to what was expected from [6,11,25], participants felt more comfortable when the chatbot did not mention, directly that it was a robot. With respect to the dialogue, we discovered that users prefer a more formal and respectful tone of voice, similar to [45], and also in agreement with the findings from [28]. It is very important for the participants that the chatbot understands their requests correctly and answers in a non-condescending manner, which is highly desirable with these types of systems, in line with the findings by Rapp et al. [35]. The same author mentions that human-like behaviours increase users' trust, which is consistent with the insights from our study. Additionally, participants were not pleased with the use of emojis, stating they were not essential and can be misinterpreted as playful, which is consistent with the work of Fadhil et al. [13].

In their work [34], Potts et al. found that participants preferred a mid-thirties female or gender-neutral chatbot. In our study, most participants chose female avatars to represent the virtual assistant as well. However, when discussing this answer, participants mentioned that it was not intentional, thus further research is needed. Moreover, contrary to other co-designed chatbots [10,14,43], in our study, participants found it unnecessary to attribute a name to the chatbot.

While we focus on cancer patients, we believe that these findings could be especially useful for the design of chatbots for patients with long-term illnesses, or even for healthcare in general. Patients with long-term illnesses like cancer receive a large amount of information and must deal with a turmoil of emotions that can influence their decision-making process. A chatbot can help these patients navigate through the onboarding at the hospital, as well as access and manage information during their journey.

4.1   Activity 1

Participants were asked the following question: "What do you imagine behind the chatbot?". Different perspectives were brought up. Most participants imagined

how they wanted the chatbot to be while others, who had a more technological background, already had a mental model of the chatbot, both in terms of
development and operation modes.

The responses were then divided into five categories, as presented in Table 1:
avatars, speech-related, knowledge, psychological traits, and other traits that did
not fit the psychological realm but are related to physical and personality traits.

Participants were presented with three types of **avatars**: human-like, robots,
and the institution's logo. Additionally, they had the opportunity to choose an
avatar beyond the options presented. Participants were more prone to choose a
human-like avatar as opposed to robots or the logo - the latter with one vote
each. The reasons given are related to a feeling of comfort. P3: *"I know it's a
computer-based system, however, I feel more comfortable thinking there is a person behind it (...)"*. Even though they were aware it is a computer-based system,
they preferred to imagine it as a human being with human characteristics. We
found that the avatars of healthcare professionals were preferred due to having
"knowledge of the disease" (P7) and being *"the right fit to help them"* (P2).
Four of the six participants who chose the human avatars stated that gender did
not matter and that their choice was based on the avatar they liked the most
or the first they saw. But two participants justified their choice. P3, male, chose
the female avatar explaining he would place more trust in a female character,
probably because of a maternal affinity, as opposed to P4, female, who chose the
male avatar due to male objectiveness. These opinions can be related to previous
experiences and, although most participants selected a female avatar, according
to the results we cannot reach any conclusions regarding the choice of avatars
based on gender. Moreover, other participants, with more technical background,
had some difficulties in overlooking their previous knowledge and experiences
and creating empathy with the presented human-like avatars, P5: *"I am aware it
is a computer-based system that we are interacting with, but that system was created by programmers from the institution and the information that the program
will have available and the interaction it will carry out will be in representation
of the institution (...)"*.

Considering **speech**, we found that people prefer simple, explanatory, and
clear language. They underscored being able to *"talk to anyone"* (P3), meaning
the bot should not use medical jargon but, rather, explain what certain terms
mean. All participants were Portuguese speakers and, as such, they find it important that the chatbot speak the same language and not English, the universal
language for computer-based systems. In the Portuguese language, there is a
clear distinction between the 2nd person singular and the 3rd person singular,
the latter being more formal/respectful and preferred for this system. P1: *"Always
formal, in my opinion, this can all be done being formal. (...) There needs to
be a certain formality."*. They want the chatbot to be friendly, such as calling
them by their name, but also keeping a respectful distance. Another aspect that
was mentioned was the oral speech. Many participants stated they would prefer
a bot with oral speech to understand emotions through different tones in the
voice. This is a validation of the findings from the interviews, where participants

Table 1. Characteristics presented by participants in activity 1.

Speech related	Psychological traits	Knowledge	Other traits
Amiable speech	Calm	Detailed information	Always answer, even if it takes time
Call people by their name but with formal speech	Calming	Expert on the subject	Available
Clarity	Cold	FAQs	Average height
Clear and efficient communication	Considerate	Have alternatives if it doesn't know the answer	Clarifier
Concise	Cooperative	Information from institution's staff	Feeling heard
Explanatory	Fond	Not being vague	Lets people be at ease
Have a formal speech	Friendly	Programmed answers	Middle age
Knows how to talk with any person	Gentle	Relevant information	Resolutive
Multilingual	Good listener	Solutions	Uncomplicated
Portuguese speaker	Interested	Useful	
Preferred oral speech over written speech because it has intonation and it's easier to tell if it is more friendly	Kind	Who knows how to accommodate	
Simple conversation	Not intimidating	Who knows how to answer to what was asked	
Simplicity	Polite		
Talk in the third person (in Portuguese)	Receptive		
To not speak with medical terms without explanation			

mentioned that the speech should allow everyone to understand and, preferably, they would like to choose between written and oral communication.

Considering the **knowledge** of the chatbot, all participants considered it should have extensive knowledge on the disease and everything related to it, but the aspect they focused on most was the way the bot presents the information. Participants emphasized the bot should offer precise answers, and not state everything about that subject. P7: *"Smart as in it knows how to answer the question I asked and nothing less. (...) It needs to know, should know, that's why it is a robot: it is prepared to always have an answer."* The information presented should be helpful, detailed, and relevant. Having their questions properly answered is of great importance to the participants and it matches the findings by [35].

Regarding the **chatbot's traits**, some adjectives were presented. They characterized the bot as *"caring"* (P2) and *"interested in the patient"* (P4). It should be a good listener and always offer a kind word. They presented many human characteristics which match the findings from [33, 35, 39]. P4: *"(...) to get as close to a human as possible, with the following characteristics: be thoughtful, know how to accommodate and give a word of hope (...)"*. People feel more comfortable talking if the other side is responsive and takes into consideration/validates their feelings. Some interesting findings were the use of physical traits. One participant mentioned the age and height of the person behind the chatbot and said he was looking for someone who would not intimidate him and would make him feel more at ease to share his concerns. P3: *"If I imagine I'm talking to a person that's much taller than me, maybe I won't feel as comfortable. (...) If they are average height, we're looking at each eye-to-eye, and the conversation might run better"*.

4.2   Activity 2

In this activity, we were looking to understand how participants initiate the conversation with the bot. Although participants suggested in the first activity that the chatbot should have human-like qualities, most of the questions presented in this activity were more detached than if the participant was speaking to a person. The majority did not greet the bot and only three of eight participants used "please" and "thank you" in their questions, as can be observed in Fig. 2. The results obtained are to be used as intents in the building of the chatbot.

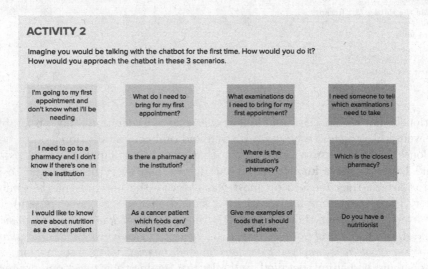

Fig. 2. Example of activity 2 on MURAL

4.3   Activity 3

Different themes emerged during the discussions of this activity such as tone of voice, the name of the chatbot, the use of emojis, and the attribution of human traits to the chatbot.

According to the participants' votes, the **tone of voice** preferred was a combination of serious, respectful, casual and matter-of-fact. Enthusiasm was also appreciated, especially the bot that sent an additional message reminding them of things they had not asked but the bot felt were important. Participants found it very reassuring and that it *"transmitted a sense of interest that everything runs smoothly"* (P3). These results are in line with those found by [28] which showed that people prefer a more empathetic form of speech from a healthcare institution. The speech that gathered the most dislikes was the one with no introduction. This made participants feel it was not listening and showed a lack of availability as they, as users, want to feel heard and understood.

It is a common practice in chatbot design to **introduce the bot** by mentioning that the participants are speaking to a robot [37]. People want this information so they can manage their expectations accordingly and, in some

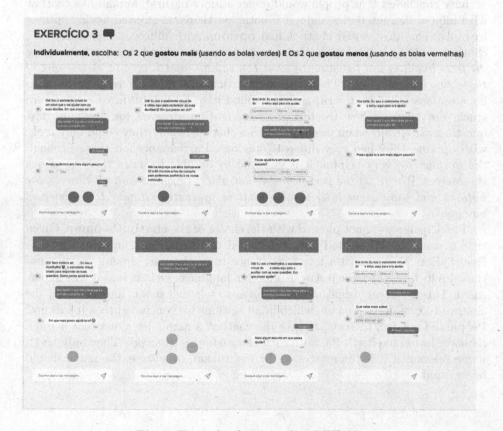

Fig. 3. Example of activity 3 on MURAL

cases, make them feel more at ease [6,11,25]. However, we were unable to confirm this statement, and our results diverge from this theory: participants in all three sessions mentioned that they did not like when the chatbot presented itself as a robot using that term. The reasoning is that, although they know they are talking to a machine, they prefer not to be informed of such. P1: *"Even though I know there is a robot on the other side, I would rather not be informed of it."* They prefer that it introduce itself as a virtual agent or a virtual assistant, which indirectly informs them that they are chatting with a bot. P8: *"When it says "I'm the virtual assistant", we already know it's a robot".*

According to [13], participants, the majority of which were under 30 years old, were welcoming of **emojis** when discussing mental health and private information, but not when discussing daily activity or other information. However, in this study emojis were not at all appreciated. Only one participant out of eight said she enjoyed having the emojis because it *"breaks the ice"* (P4). The majority stated they did not vote for that chatbot due to the emojis and some considered that using emojis was *"too playful"* (P3). Interestingly, participants also showed concern that not using emojis might not please other users.

As opposed to what would be expected given that the results from the first activity concluded that people would prefer a more natural, human-like chatbot with human characteristics and not robotic, participants enjoyed having options to reply. The most voted chatbot had **options** with different topics that the chatbot could be helpful with. Only one participant disliked this chatbot, saying *"it feels like it is not listening to what I'm saying, and I have to choose one of those five options"* (P4). The remaining participants were extremely pleased to have options other than writing. They found it to be helpful in case they were stuck, not knowing how to start the conversation, or even for "yes" or "no" questions. However, when presented with a chatbot where they could only reply with options, they had very different opinions. Participants felt that, although the options are very helpful, it is essential to be able to write their questions themselves. P7: *"(...) the person might not able to express himself through the options and want something besides what is presented. It might be easier in writing.".*

Participants were not pleased with the choice of the **chatbot's name**. Given that it was a health-related bot, we decided to introduce it, in some cases, as HealthyBot. This caused a lot of resistance from the participants. Some mentioned reluctance because it was in a foreign language. Others said it was impersonal. This led to an insightful discussion as to whether it was important for the chatbot to even have a name, which in all sessions we concluded that it was not. People did not feel the need to give the chatbot a name, let alone that it use a name to introduce itself. P3: *"Just virtual assistant is enough".* They only find a name relevant if it is the mascot of the institution, otherwise, the name should be omitted.

5   Limitations of the Study

This was a small, qualitative study performed with predominantly well-educated participants of Portuguese nationality. One of our main limitations was the fact that we could not conduct the co-creation sessions with actual cancer patients or caregivers. Nevertheless, we believe that these findings will help us design better chatbots for healthcare.

6   Conclusion and Future Work

The aim of this study was to create a chatbot to help cancer patients navigate the onboarding process at the hospital. In this paper, we described the co-creation sessions in detail, as well as the major findings from these sessions. The insights from the co-creation sessions enabled us to better understand people's expectations and preferences with regards to the tone of voice, content, and human characterization of the chatbot. Our goal was to contribute to the community with our insights regarding the design of chatbots for cancer patients, as well as the use and adaptation of remote tools in the co-creation process.

For future work, we would like to proceed with the design of the chatbot, incorporating all of the findings from both the interviews and the co-creation sessions. Additionally, we would like to consider the possibility of adapting the conversational agent into a voicebot, allowing users to choose between texting or speaking, something that was mentioned during the sessions. We also believe the co-creation sessions should be carried out with actual cancer patients, to further validate the results found.

References

1. Abrahamson, K.: Dealing with cancer-related distress. Am. J. Nurs. 110(4), 67–69 (2010)
2. Akeel, A.U., Mundy, D.: Re-thinking technology and its growing role in enabling patient empowerment. Health Inform. J. 25(4), 1278–1289 (2019). https://doi.org/10.1177/1460458217751013
3. Andrews, B., et al.: Teaching participatory design. ACM Int. Conf. Proc. Ser. 2, 203–204 (2014). https://doi.org/10.1145/2662155.2662202
4. Bate, P., Robert, G.: Toward more user-centric OD: lessons from the field of experience-based design and a case study. J. Appl. Behav. Sci. 43(1), 41–66 (2007). https://doi.org/10.1177/0021886306297014
5. Beaudry, J., Consigli, A., Clark, C., Robinson, K.J.: Getting ready for adult healthcare: designing a chatbot to coach adolescents with special health needs through the transitions of care. J. Pediatr. Nurs. 49, 85–91 (2019). https://doi.org/10.1016/j.pedn.2019.09.004, https://linkinghub.elsevier.com/retrieve/pii/S0882596318306006
6. Belfin, R.V., Shobana, A.J., Manilal, M., Mathew, A.A., Babu, B.: A graph based chatbot for cancer patients. In: 5th International Conference on Advanced Computing and Communication Systems, pp. 717–721 (2019)

7. Bibault, J.E., et al.: A chatbot versus physicians to provide information for patients with breast cancer: blind, randomized controlled noninferiority trial. J. Med. Internet Res. **21**(11), 1–7 (2019). https://doi.org/10.2196/15787

8. Brandtzaeg, P.B., Følstad, A.: Why people use chatbots. In: Proceedings of the 4th International Conference on Internet Science, pp. 377–392 (2017)

9. Chaix, B., et al.: When chatbots meet patients: one-year prospective study of conversations between patients with breast cancer and a chatbot. JMIR Cancer **5**(1), e12856 (2019). https://doi.org/10.2196/12856

10. Chen, Z., Lu, Y., Nieminen, M.P., Lucero, A.: Creating a chatbot for and with migrants: chatbot personality drives co-design activities. In: DIS 2020 - Proceedings of the 2020 ACM Designing Interactive Systems Conference, pp. 219–230 (2020). https://doi.org/10.1145/3357236.3395495

11. Danby, S., Taylor, C.: Increasing access to citizen services with conversational AI (2020). http://www.speech-interaction.org/CSCW2020/papers/6-LeeTaylor.pdf

12. Easton, K., et al.: A virtual agent to support individuals living with physical and mental comorbidities: co-design and acceptability testing. J. Med. Internet Res. **21**(5), e12996 (2019). https://doi.org/10.2196/12996, http://www.jmir.org/2019/5/e12996/

13. Fadhil, A., Schiavo, Gianluca Wang, Y., Yilma, B.A.: The effect of emojis when interacting with conversational interface assisted health coaching system. In: ACM International Conference Proceeding Series, pp. 378–383 (2018)

14. Gabrielli, S., Rizzi, S., Carbone, S., Donisi, V.: A chatbot-based coaching intervention for adolescents to promote life skills: pilot study. JMIR Hum. Fact. **7**(1), 1–7 (2020). https://doi.org/10.2196/16762

15. Greer, S., Ramo, D., Chang, Y.J., Fu, M., Moskowitz, J., Haritatos, J.: Use of the chatbot 'vivibot' to deliver positive psychology skills and promote well-being among young people after cancer treatment: randomized controlled feasibility trial. JMIR mHealth and uHealth **7**(10), 1–13 (2019). https://doi.org/10.2196/15018

16. Gröpper, S., van der Meer, E., Landes, T., Bucher, H., Stickel, A., Goerling, U.: Assessing cancer-related distress in cancer patients and caregivers receiving outpatient psycho-oncological counseling. Supp. Care Cancer **24**(5), 2351–2357 (2015). https://doi.org/10.1007/s00520-015-3042-9

17. Hwang, Y., Song, S., Shin, D., Lee, J.: Linguistic features to consider when applying persona of the real person to the text-based agent. In: 22nd International Conference on Human-Computer Interaction with Mobile Devices and Services, pp. 1–4 (2020)

18. Jain, M., Kumar, P., Kota, R., Patel, S.N.: Evaluating and informing the design of chatbots. In: DIS 2018 - Proceedings of the 2018 Designing Interactive Systems Conference, pp. 895–906 (2018)

19. Jassova, B.: The ultimate guide to conversational design (2019). https://landbot.io/blog/guide-to-conversational-design/. Accessed 3 Feb 2021

20. Jordan, M.E., et al.: The role of conversation in health care interventions: enabling sensemaking and learning. Implement. Sci. **4**, 15 (2009). https://doi.org/10.1186/1748-5908-4-15

21. Jovanovic, M., Baez, M., Casati, F.: Chatbots as conversational healthcare services. IEEE Internet Comput. **25**, 44–51 (2021). https://doi.org/10.1109/MIC.2020.3037151

22. Kataoka, Y., Takemura, T., Sasajima, M., Katoh, N.: Development and early feasibility of chatbots for educating patients with lung cancer and their caregivers in japan: mixed methods study. JMIR Cancer **7**(1), 1–7 (2021). https://doi.org/10.2196/26911

23. Khasnabish, S., Burns, Z., Couch, M., Mullin, M., Newmark, R., Dykes, P.C.: Best practices for data visualization: creating and evaluating a report for an evidence-based fall prevention program. J. Am. Med. Inform. Assoc. **27**(2), 308–314 (2020). https://doi.org/10.1093/jamia/ocz190

24. Kucherbaev, P., Psyllidis, A., Bozzon, A.: Chatbots as conversational recommender systems in urban contexts. In: Proceedings of the International Workshop on Recommender Systems for Citizens, pp. 1–2. ACM, New York, August 2017. https://doi.org/10.1145/3127325.3127331

25. Lucas, G.M., Gratch, J., King, A., Morency, L.P.: It's only a computer: virtual humans increase willingness to disclose. Comput. Hum. Behav. **37**, 94–100 (2014). https://doi.org/10.1016/j.chb.2014.04.043

26. McDuff, D., Czerwinski, M.: Designing emotionally sentient agents. Commun. ACM **61**(12), 74–83 (2018). https://doi.org/10.1145/3186591

27. Moran, K.: The four dimensions of tone of voice. (2016 [Nielsen Norman Group]), https://www.nngroup.com/articles/tone-of-voice-dimensions/. Accessed 09 Sep 2021

28. Moran, K.: The impact of tone of voice on users' brand perception (2016 [Nielsen Norman Group]), https://www.nngroup.com/articles/tone-voice-users/. Accessed 09 Sep 2021

29. Nadarzynski, T., Miles, O., Cowie, A., Ridge, D.: Acceptability of artificial intelligence (AI)-led chatbot services in healthcare: a mixed-methods study. Digit. Health **5**, 1–12 (2019). https://doi.org/10.1177/2055207619871808

30. Narimatsu, H., Sato, A.H.E., Suganuma, N.: Preliminary screening for hereditary breast and ovarian cancer using a chatbot augmented intelligence genetic counselor (preprint). JMIR Form. Res. **5**, 1–11 (2020). https://doi.org/10.2196/25184

31. Pears, M., et al.: Co-creation of chatbots as an educational resource- training the trainers workshop. In: INTED2021 Proceedings, vol. 1, pp. 7808–7815 (2021). https://doi.org/10.21125/inted.2021.1570

32. Piau, A., Crissey, R.B.D., Balardy, L., Nourhashemi, F.: A smartphone chatbot application to optimize monitoring of older patients with cancer. Int. J. Med. Inf. **128**, 18–23 (2019). https://doi.org/10.1016/j.ijmedinf.2019.05.013

33. Portela, M., Granell-Canut, C.: A new friend in our smartphone? observing interactions with chatbots in the search of emotional engagement. In: ACM International Conference Proceeding Series, p. F1311 (2017)

34. Potts, C., et al.: Chatbots to support mental wellbeing of people living in rural areas: can user groups contribute to co-design?, J. Technol. Behav. Sci. **6**, 652–665 (2021). https://doi.org/10.1007/s41347-021-00222-6, https://link.springer.com/10.1007/s41347-021-00222-6

35. Rapp, A., Curti, L., Boldi, A.: The human side of human-chatbot interaction: a systematic literature review of ten years of research on text-based chatbots. Int. J. Hum. Comput. Stud. **151**, 102630 (2021). https://doi.org/10.1016/j.ijhcs.2021.102630

36. Rosenbaum, E., Rosenbaum, I.: Coping with Cancer: Ten Steps Toward Emotional Well-Being Andrew, vol. 1 (2005). https://doi.org/10.7748/paed.1.7.6.s12

37. Rozga, S.: Practical Bot Development, 1st edn. Apress, Berkeley (2018). https://doi.org/10.1007/978-1-4842-3540-9

38. Siglen, E., et al.: Ask Rosa - the making of a digital genetic conversation tool, a chatbot, about hereditary breast and ovarian cancer. Patient Educ. Counsel. 0–1 (2021). https://doi.org/10.1016/j.pec.2021.09.027

39. Smestad, T., Volden, F.: Chatbot personalities matters: improving the user experience of chatbot interfaces, pp. 170–181, April 2019. https://doi.org/10.1007/978-3-030-17705-8_15

40. Medhi Thies, I., Menon, N., Magapu, S., Subramony, M., O'Neill, J.: How do you want your chatbot? an exploratory wizard-of-Oz study with young, urban Indians. In: Bernhaupt, R., Dalvi, G., Joshi, A., Balkrishan, D.K., O'Neill, J., Winckler, M. (eds.) INTERACT 2017. LNCS, vol. 10513, pp. 441–459. Springer, Cham (2017). https://doi.org/10.1007/978-3-319-67744-6_28

41. Timplalexi, E.: The human and the chatterbot: tracing the potential of transdimensional performance. Perform. Res. **21**(5), 59–64 (2016). https://doi.org/10.1080/13528165.2016.1223449

42. Triberti, S., Savioni, L., Sebri, V., Pravettoni, G.: ehealth for improving quality of life in breast cancer patients: a systematic review. Cancer Treat. Rev. **74**, 1–14 (2019). https://doi.org/10.1016/j.ctrv.2019.01.003

43. Webb, C.: How we created global anti-harassment chatbot, Maru (2020). https://www.linkedin.com/pulse/how-we-created-global-anti-harassment-chatbot-maru-dr-charlotte-webb/

44. Wiratunga, N., Cooper, K., Wijekoon, A., Palihawadana, C., Mendham, V., Reiter, E., Martin, K.: FitChat: conversational artificial intelligence interventions for encouraging physical activity in older adults (2020). http://arxiv.org/abs/2004.14067

45. Wong-Villacres, M., Evans, H., Schechter, D., DiSalvo, B., Kumar, N.: Consejero automatico, January 2019. https://doi.org/10.1145/3287098.3287149

46. Xu, X., Griva, K., Koh, M., Lum, E., Tan, W.S., Thng, S., Car, J.: Creating a smartphone app for caregivers of children with atopic dermatitis with caregivers, health care professionals, and digital health experts: participatory co-design. JMIR mHealth uHealth **8**(10), e16898 (2020). https://doi.org/10.2196/16898, http://mhealth.jmir.org/2020/10/e16898/

47. Zhang, J., Oh, Y.J., Lange, P., Yu, Z., Fukuoka, Y.: Artificial intelligence chatbot behavior change model for designing artificial intelligence chatbots to promote physical activity and a healthy diet: viewpoint. J. Med. Internet Res. **22**(9) (2020). https://doi.org/10.2196/22845

Individualized Learning Patterns Require Individualized Conversations – Data-Driven Insights from the Field on How Chatbots Instruct Students in Solving Exercises

Sebastian Hobert[1,2]([envelope]) [iD]

[1] University of Goettingen, Goettingen, Germany
shobert@uni-goettingen.de
[2] Campus Institute Data Science, Goettingen, Germany

Abstract. Chatbots can foster the learning success of students in educational settings. This has been shown in prior research studies, e.g., using laboratory studies in online learning settings. Actual evaluations of using educational chatbots in the field are nevertheless rarely reported. Thus, insights into the students' interactions with chatbots in long-term field settings are missing. In this research study, we aim at gaining insights into the students' interactions with an educational chatbot in a programming course. To this aim, we follow an explorative data-driven discourse analysis approach and show how students interacted with the chatbot during a field study lasting several months. We ground our analysis on a dataset from 54 students interacting with a chatbot while working on programming exercise tasks. We reveal how students interact with the chatbot and identify different types of usage patterns. The results imply that adaptive learning paths are one of the most important aspects of educational chatbot design for dealing with heterogeneous usage patterns.

Keywords: Educational chatbots · Digital tutors · Learning process · Field study · Evaluation

1 Introduction

Prior laboratory studies have shown that educational chatbots can improve learning in online-based education [1]. In educational settings, chatbots have the possibility to support learners individually in personalized conversations. Thus, they have the possibility to overcome resource constraints in teaching settings (e.g., a limited number of instructors or teaching assistants) [2]. Independently of the specific type of an educational chatbot (e.g., a chatbot as a lecturer or as a tutor), its representations or implementation (e.g., voice-based or text-based input and output), the overall aim of most educational chatbots is to foster the learners' learning outcome [3].

Many prior research studies in educational settings focus on design and evaluation studies that are not researched in the field but only in limited laboratory settings [4].

A. Følstad et al. (Eds.): CONVERSATIONS 2021, LNCS 13171, pp. 55–69, 2022.
https://doi.org/10.1007/978-3-030-94890-0_4

Due to this, we know only little about the actual learning processes of students and their interactions with chatbots in the field. In many other application domains like in business settings, this does not seem to be a problem as laboratory studies are perfectly useable to simulate a realistic usage setting. In educational settings, however, this seems to be problematic, especially when educational software is not only used during a short timeframe but during a whole lecture term of several months. In laboratory studies, such a long usage term of several months can usually not be simulated. To address this gap, we particularly focus on the long-term use of educational chatbots during a multi-month lecture term in this research study. To actually get insights into how students interact with chatbots in the long term, we conducted an explorative discourse analysis and followed a data-driven approach using field data. Using this approach, we focus on the first research direction identified by Følstad et al. [5], who demand "[…] to move from studies of chatbot users in general to studies of chatbot users and behaviours for particular demographics, domains, or contexts." [5] Following this direction, we aim at answering the following research question:

RQ: How do students interact with chatbots in long-term educational settings?

To address this research question, we rely on data from a field study in which we introduced an educational chatbot [6] into a programming course. We analyzed the discourses from approximately 50 novice programmers who worked in more than 1,000 sessions on solving programming tasks. While solving these tasks, the students were supported by the educational chatbot who discoursed with them and instructed them how to solve the task. Additionally, the chatbot is able to analyze the students' source code to provide personalized feedback automatically. By analyzing the approximately 30,000 chat interactions, we aim at contributing to the design of educational chatbots by outlining first insights into how students interact with educational chatbots.

The remainder of this paper is structured as follows: Subsequently, we briefly present related research on educational chatbots and outline the theoretical foundations of chatbot-based instructions in Sect. 2. This forms the basis for our research design in Sect. 3, in which we describe the field setting and the demographic background of the study participants, briefly present our chatbot used in the study, and summarize how we preprocessed the data and conducted the analysis. In Sect. 4, we present the results of our explorative data-driven research approach, focus on aggregated statistics on the students' interaction with the chatbot, and compare the interactions in easy and difficult exercises. Finally, we identify different types of interaction groups and outline that students interact differently with the chatbot. In Sect. 5, we discuss the results to derive implications and summarize our findings.

2   Theoretical Background

2.1   Related Research on Educational Chatbots

Chatbots have been used in educational settings for many years [7]. For instance, Tegos et al. [8] developed MentorChat, a chatbot that aims at supporting collaborative learning tasks in discussions. Graesser et al. [9] developed the AutoTutor software that focused on complex problems, and Winkler et al. [1] developed Sara, the lecturer that is able to interact with students in video-based settings [1]. It has also been used to support skills of learners – like verbal communication [10] or argumentation [11].

Like in other application domains, chatbots in educational settings can be defined as software-based agents that interact with learners using natural language conversation in dialogs [3, 12–15]. For instance, they use this form of human-computer interaction to mimic a natural language conversation between a learner and either a human teacher, instructor, tutor, or fellow student [3, 12–15].

In prior years, multiple literature reviews [3, 7, 16] have analyzed how chatbots have been researched in educational settings. Prior research indicates the potentials of utilizing chatbots for improving teaching and learning. It seems particularly useful as an additional tool for fostering learning support. For instance, it has been shown that chatbots are capable of (1) supporting video-based teaching in voice- or text-based conversations [1], (2) helping students to work on programming exercises [6], and (3) training factual knowledge using quiz bots [17]. These use cases in educational settings often differ from use cases in business settings (see [18] for exemplary use cases): In classical business use cases, like in customer support, users interact with chatbots typically with a particular goal or problem in mind. The aim of the conversations is usually to solve user needs as quickly as possible. In typical learning settings, chatbots are, however, usually not solely designed to improve the efficiency of the learning processes. Instead, increasing the effectiveness of skill improvement is often the main focus [3]. Thus, educational chatbots are usually used over a much more extended period of time. For instance, if teaching tasks are supported, the usage period may range up to a complete lecture term of several months in which the learners interact with the chatbot. Insights into educational, chatbot-enabled learning processes are still a research gap. To this aim, we focus on how a chatbot supports learners in a long-term educational setting in this explorative study.

2.2 Theoretical Foundations of Chatbot-Based Instruction

For designing educational chatbots, defining proper learning paths for enabling interactions are essential. Adaptive learning paths, as described by the Scaffolding concept [19, 20], enable chatbots to provide individual learning support. By adapting the conversations based on the students' individual needs, the chatbot is able to mimic the behavior of lecturers or tutors who also try to respond to each student individually. Adapting the conversations based on the learners' needs seems also be useful for creating meaningful discussions about learning content. The learners usually do not only want to get general learning support but also want to get individual help on their specific challenges. This seems also be useful as proposed by the ICAP framework [21]. The ICAP framework proposes that and increased learning engagement results in increased learning success. According to the framework, the highest engagement can be reached in interactive learning scenarios. As examples for such interactive learning, Chi and Wylie [21] propose conversations and discussions. Thus, educational chatbots should focus on offering students individualized learning paths to create rich and interactive conversations to foster learning success. In this study, we build upon the Scaffolding concept as well as the ICAP framework and introduce a chatbot in a field setting to observe the students' interaction with it in a long-term learning setting.

3   Research Design

In the following, we outline the research design of our field study. To this end, we briefly describe the field setting and the demographic background of the study participants before we present the chatbot implementation. Finally, we provide an overview of the data preprocessing and data analysis for answering our research question.

3.1   Field Setting

In this study, we report the findings from a field setting, in which we implemented a chatbot in an online programming environment for a full lecture period of approximately 14 weeks. During the lecture period, the students of a programming course at a larger German university had to work on programming exercise tasks on a weekly basis. Each week, the students should solve two to three exercises that were aligned to the course's schedule. The exercises were addressed to novice programmers and started with very simple tasks like programming a *Hello World* program in Java. During the lecture term, the difficulty of the tasks increased, and students needed to work on Iterators, user interface implementation, or implementations of more complex algorithms like the Euclidean algorithm for calculating the greatest common divisor of two numbers. The students should work on the provided exercise tasks as homework. To support the students while working on the exercise tasks, we implemented a chatbot in the course's web-based coding platform (see Subsect. 3.3).

3.2   Demographic Background of Study Participants

During the field study, 54 students of the programming course attended the course and agreed to participate in the study. Participation in the study was voluntary, and no incentives were provided. The vast majority of the students were enrolled in a Bachelor's program on information systems in their study entry phase. Most of the students were in their second to fourth semester, with only a few exceptions. Based on an anonymous self-evaluation at the beginning of the course, the sample can be classified with a novice level. With only a few exceptions, the students had only limited prior programming experience in Java. Nevertheless, basic computer science concepts were known to them as most of them passed a class on fundamentals in computer science before.

3.3   Chatbot Software Integrated into the Programming Course

During the field study, all 54 students participating in the study got access to the course's online programming environment. The online programming environment is based on the *Coding Tutor* system introduced in [6]. Within the online programming environment, the students got access to the course's programming task. For each programming task, a detailed task description and a web-based coding editor were provided. In addition to that, a chatbot was integrated into the programming interface as a popup overlay. As visualized in Fig. 1, the chatbot introduces itself at the beginning of each exercise task as a digital tutor before focusing on supporting the students.

Fig. 1. Exemplary screenshot of the chatbot at the beginning of an exercise task.

The digital tutor has the aim to support the students while working on the exercise tasks. To this end, the digital tutor offers the students multiple opportunities for supporting their learning processes: In the beginning, the chatbot introduces itself and explains the exercise task. The chatbot further offers the students individualized guidance on a step-by-step basis or on-demand help based on the students' individual requests. Suppose students would like to get individualized guidance. In this case, the chatbot is capable of explaining the theoretical background of the exercise task (e.g., the algorithm underlying the task) and guiding the students step-by-step (e.g., by outlining which methods are needed and which functionalities should be implemented).

An exemplary chat dialog showing the chatbot's capabilities in terms of individualized guidance and on-demand help is visualized in Fig. 2.

Additionally, students may always ask the chatbot to evaluate their code. In this case, the chatbot automatically analyzes the code using unit tests and provides individualized feedback. For instance, the chatbot reports the results of compiling and executing the source code and the unit tests. Based on this dynamic code analysis, the chatbot can provide individualized feedback to the students. Finally, the chatbot can proactively offer help to the students based on a background static code analysis. To this end, the chatbot automatically analyzes the students' written source code on a timely basis (i.e., several times per minute). If the static code analysis repeatedly reports coding errors, the chatbot proactively offers help and hints the students at the identified error.

An exemplary chat dialog showing the chatbot's capabilities in terms of individualized feedback based on dynamic code testing and proactive help based on static code analysis is visualized in Fig. 3.

To summarize, the chatbot offers (1) step-by-step guidance, (2) on-demand help based on students' questions, (3) individualized feedback based on dynamic code testing,

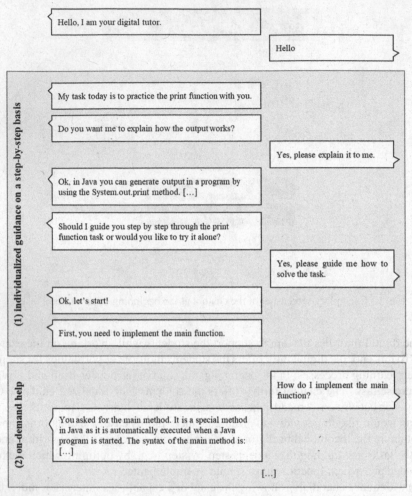

Fig. 2. Exemplary chat dialog showing (1) individualized guidance on a step-by-step basis and (2) on-demand help.

and (4) proactive help based on automated static code analysis. We summarize the first two types of interactions in the following as *instruction* and the last two as *feedback*.

To offer these conversation-based possibilities of learning support, the chatbot is theoretically grounded on the ICAP framework [21] and the scaffolding concept [19, 20] as outlined in the theoretical foundation in Sect. 2.2. To implement these concepts, the chatbot combines typical intent recognition techniques known from natural language processing with complex learning paths implemented using finite state machines that enable adaptive responses to the students' individual state of knowledge and their demands. Further information on the chatbot's architecture and the initial implementation is available as a separate conference paper, see [6] for further information.

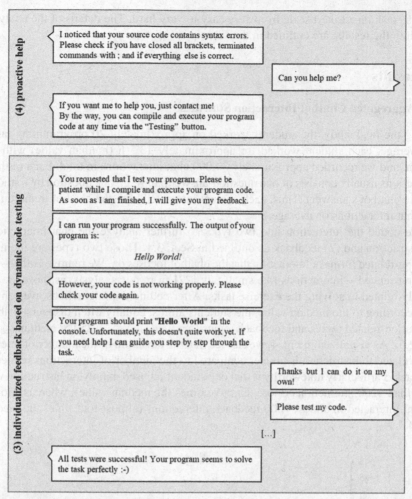

Fig. 3. Exemplary chat dialog showing (3) individualized feedback based on dynamic code testing and (4) proactive help based on automatic static code analysis.

3.4 Data Preprocessing and Analysis

During the field study, we collected pseudonymized usage data from the students' inter-action with the chatbot. The usage data only contains data from students who gave their informed consent. It is linked to the exercise tasks and includes a timestamp and the tex-tual conversations between the students and the chatbot. We labeled each interaction (a message from the user and a response from the chatbot) based on the intent classification and assigned it to two types of learning-related interactions: instruction and feedback (see Sect. 3.3).

We aggregated the usage logs by time and type of interactions to analyze the data. Additionally, we include the perceived difficulty of the exercise tasks in our analysis. The difficulty was measured by surveying the students and allowing them to rate each exercise task on a Likert scale from very easy to very hard. The details of the analysis, including the results, are outlined in the subsequent section.

4 Results

4.1 Aggregated Chatbot Interaction Statistics

During the field study, the students worked on approximately 20 programming tasks. On average, each student worked for approximately 13.5 h (median value) with the system, and we recorded approximately 30,000 chat interactions in total. Each of these interactions usually consists of one question-answer pair (e.g., one question by a student and the chatbot's answer). Thus, each student interacted with the chatbot in more than 550 chat interactions on average.

We coded the interaction into two types to further analyze the chat interactions: (1) instruction and (2) feedback as outlined in Sect. 3.4. Those two types are the main learning-related forms of interaction that the chatbot focuses on. We removed other – not learning-related – interactions like small talk [22] from our analysis, as those are not directly related to solving the exercise tasks. After coding the interactions, we can see that according to the median value, the students almost equally often discoursed about instruction-related topics and feedback topics ($median_{instruction} = 250{,}5$; $median_{feedback} = 252{,}5$). As visualized in Fig. 4, we can see that the deviation of the number of interactions related to instruction is greater compared to the number of interactions related to feedback. Particularly noteworthy is that one student focused mainly on instruction with more than 1200 interactions (more than five times the median value), whereas another student interacted in almost 1000 feedback interactions (almost four times the median value).

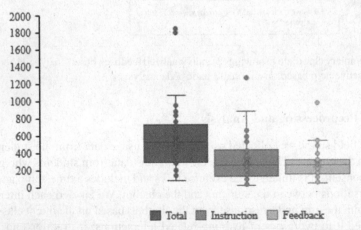

Fig. 4. Boxplots for comparing the distribution of instruction and feedback interactions.

For a more detailed analysis of the timing of the students' interactions with the chatbot, we mapped every single interaction to the relative timing in the processing of the task. To this end, we divided the time each student worked on each exercise into ten equally sized timeslots and counted how many interactions occurred (a value of 0 on the timeline means that a student just started to work on the exercise; a value of 100 means that a student finished her or his work on the exercise). The result visualized in Fig. 5 reveals that the students mainly interacted with the chatbot at the beginning of the exercises and at the end. In the beginning until approximately 10% of the task processing was completed, almost 15% of all interactions occurred. Most of them were related to instruction. The dialog analysis revealed that many students discoursed with the chatbot about the theoretical background and asked for more information on the algorithm required for solving the task. Afterward, the number of interactions dropped substantially and started increasing again after approximately 70% of the task processing was completed. This increase at the end of the task processing can be explained by a substantial increase in the interactions related to feedback. This does not seem surprising. After working on a solution for a given exercise task, the students asked the chatbot to test their solution and to provide feedback. Interestingly, this also resulted in an increase in the number of instruction-related messages. A close analysis of these dialogs shows that some students requested help to fix errors in their solutions. Thus, they asked the chatbot for guidance.

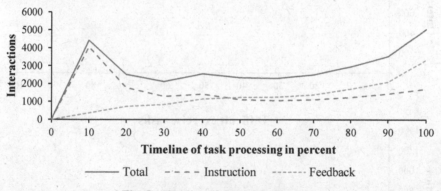

Fig. 5. Timeline of the chat interactions

Based on these observations, the interactions over time can be divided into three phases:

1. Instruction phase: The first phase in which students mainly focus on conversations related to instructions, i.e., students ask the chatbot for explanations of the theoretical background, the algorithm, or how to start the coding process.
2. Coding phase: In the second phase, the number of interactions decreases, and students mainly work on their solutions. This is the phase in which most of the source code is written.
3. Testing phase: In the last phase, the number of interactions related to feedback increases. The students aim at finalizing their source code and ask the chatbot for its assessment and feedback.

4.2 Comparing Interactions by Task Difficulty

To further investigate the students' interactions with the chatbot, we compared the number of interactions of easy exercise tasks to difficult exercise tasks. To determine which exercise tasks were perceived as easy or difficult, we asked each student to rate the exercises' difficulty. For the subsequent analysis, we selected the five easiest and the five most challenging exercise tasks as comparison groups.

The comparison visualized in Fig. 6 indicates that the interaction patterns differ substantially. The visualization of the interactions while working on easy exercise tasks shows that the total amount of interactions remains relatively constant during the whole time. In the beginning, the majority of interactions were related to instructions. Later, most interactions were related to feedback as the amount of instruction-based interactions declined.

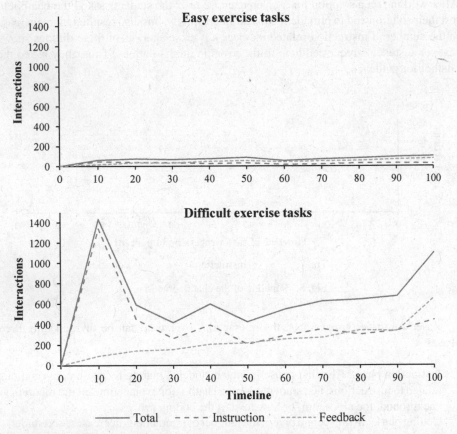

Fig. 6. Comparison of the timelines of chat interactions: easy exercises vs. difficult exercises

The interaction of the students while solving difficult tasks differs substantially from the easy ones. In the beginning, huge amounts of instruction-based interactions occur. This indicates that the students ask the chatbot for instructions on how to solve the task. Even if the number decreases after 10% of the task processing time, it remains higher than the maximum value for easy tasks at all times. Further, an almost monotone increase in the number of feedback-based interactions can be observed. It reaches its maximum at the end of the task processing time.

A comparison of Fig. 5 and Fig. 6 reveals that the aggregated timeline of all chat interactions (Fig. 5) is mostly dominated by the huge amount of interactions in difficult exercise tasks. This is reflected in the fact that both charts have an almost similar shape.

4.3 Identifying Different Types of User Groups

We have already shown that the amount of interactions depends largely on the difficulty of the exercise tasks. To further investigate the nature of the interactions, we now focus on the users. To this end, we aim at identifying different types of user groups.

As we have seen in Fig. 5, the students' interaction can be divided into three major parts: (1) instruction phase, (2) coding phase, and (3) testing phase. Due to this observation, we also split the timeline into three phases in the following, covering one-third of the timeline each. For each student, we analyzed the discourse log and labeled for each phase whether they performed above average in the phase. If this was the case, we coded this phase with $+1$, otherwise with -1. If a student interacted almost equally much in all phases, we coded this with 0. After labeling the phases for each student, we aggregated them and resulted in four distinct phases (see Table 1 and Fig. 7).

Table 1. Resulting groups after coding ($+1$: no. interaction above 1/3 of all interactions; -1 below 1/3 of all interactions; 0 approximately 1/3 of all interactions)

Group	No. students	Instruction phase	Coding phase	Testing phase
G1 Code on your own	13 (24%)	$+1$	-1	$+1$
G2 Feedback-driven	25 (46%)	-1	-1	$+1$
G3 Instruction-driven	10 (19%)	$+1$	-1	-1
G4 Balanced interaction	6 (11%)	0	0	0

All students could be assigned to these groups. We could not identify other combinations of $+1/0/-1$ in the three phases, even though they would be theoretically possible.

Group 1: Code on Your Own. The first group consists of 13 students (24%) and is characterized by many interactions in the instruction phase (approximately 200 interactions per student) as well as in the feedback phase (approximately 195 interactions). In the coding phase, the number of interactions is substantially lower (approximately 77 interactions). Thus, students in group 1 focus on interactions at the beginning and the end of the task processing time. In total, each student was involved in approximately 471 interactions.

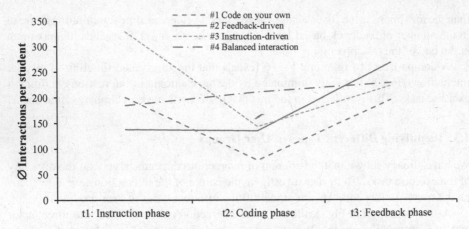

Fig. 7. Visualization of the amount of interaction per student in each identified group

Group 2: Feedback-Driven. In contrast to the first group, the 25 students in the second group mainly focus on interactions in the feedback phase (approximately 268 interactions). In the other two phases, the number is comparably low (approximately 134 resp. 137 interactions). Thus, the students in this group mainly interact with the chatbot to ask it to test their source code to receive feedback. The total number of messages in this phase is slightly larger compared to group 1 (approximately 539 interactions per student).

Group 3: Instruction-Driven. The third group can be defined as the opposite of group 2. The ten students in this group mainly interact with the chatbot to get instructions in each phase. This is represented in approximately 464 interactions related to instructions compared to only approximately 230 related to feedback. In contrast to group 2, we can see that the number of messages reaches a minimum in phase 2 and slightly increases in phase 3. In total, the students in this group interacted with the chatbot at most, with approximately 694 interactions per student.

Group 4: Balanced Interaction. The last group consists of only six students (11%). As visualized in Fig. 7, the amount of interactions is almost similar in all three phases. The number of interactions vary only slightly in the phases between approximately 184 and approximately 228.

5 Discussion and Implications

Evaluations from actual field data in educational settings rarely exist in current educational chatbot research. In this initial exploratory, data-driven study, we analyzed how approximately 50 students interacted with educational chatbots in approximately 30,000 interactions. The analysis of the field data allowed us to get first insights into how learners interact with educational chatbots in long-term educational settings. This allows us to address our research question:

RQ: How do students interact with chatbots in long-term educational settings?

The results of our explorative analysis of field data suggest that the students interacted in extensive discourses with the provided chatbot. We were particularly able to show that students interacted with the chatbot most often at the beginning and at the end of the processing time of solving given exercise tasks. Thereby, the interaction patterns differ depending on the perceived task difficulty: Easy tasks result in low, unvarying interactions. Difficult tasks result in a large number of interactions with a particular demand on instructions at the beginning and individualized feedback at the end of the task processing time.

We could further reveal that the learners do not interact homogenously. Instead, we could identify four different usage patterns that we labeled as (1) code on your own, (2) feedback-driven, (3) instruction-driven, and (4) balanced interaction.

These identified groups among the students reveal that there is no *one size fits all* approach for educational chatbots. Instead, educational chatbots need to be able to adapt to the students' desired interaction patterns. With these results, we were able to show that adaptive learning paths are essential when educational chatbots should adapt to the students' individual learning patterns. The Scaffolding concept [19, 20] seems to be a suitable approach for us for adapting the learning paths.

Further, the results suggest that the chatbot created an interactive learning setting, which seems desirable as recommended by the ICAP framework [21].

Overall educational chatbots might not be a *one size fits all* approach to instruct all students. Instead, educational chatbots might be one additional, promising educational technology that can be integrated into learning settings to foster learning success.

We argue that educational chatbots should not be used as the only tool or method to support learners. Using educational chatbots as a supplementary tool in in-class, blended, or online teaching settings seems most promising to us. In doing so, it would be possible to offer the students multiple different types of learning support (e.g., an in-class lecture for instructing the students at the university combined with an educational chatbot for answering on-demand questions at home). Nevertheless, as our initial study is explorative in nature, further field studies are needed to validate and extend the results. This seems particularly useful to get an in-depth understanding of chatbot users in the educational domain (see [5]). Additionally, it would be worth comparing in detail whether similar interaction patterns and user groups can be found when using other sophisticated learning support software systems in similar settings.

6 Conclusion

With our study, we contribute to the current educational chatbot research stream by providing data-driven insights into the interactions of students with chatbots in a long-term educational setting. Our results suggest that students request the individualization of learning paths as their way of interacting differs substantially. Focusing on the adaption of teaching and learning strategies seems to be a promising future research direction to us. Additionally, it would be interesting to get further insights into actual field data from other educational learning settings. As we only analyzed field data from one university course in this study, further case studies might help to validate or supplement our findings.

References

1. Winkler, R., Hobert, S., Salovaara, A., Söllner, M., Leimeister, J.M.: Sara, the Lecturer: improving learning in online education with a scaffolding-based conversational agent. In: Proceedings of the 2020 CHI Conference on Human Factors in Computing Systems. CHI 2020, pp. 1–14. Association for Computing Machinery, New York (2020). https://doi.org/10.1145/3313831.3376781
2. Maedche, A., et al.: AI-based digital assistants. Bus. Inf. Syst. Eng. **61**(4), 535–544 (2019). https://doi.org/10.1007/s12599-019-00600-8
3. Wollny, S., Schneider, J., Di Mitri, D., Weidlich, J., Rittberger, M., Drachsler, H.: Are we there yet? - A systematic literature review on chatbots in education. Front. Artif. Intell. **4** (2021). https://doi.org/10.3389/frai.2021.654924
4. Hobert, S.: How are you, chatbot? Evaluating chatbots in educational settings – results of a literature review. In: Pinkwart, N., Konert, J. (eds.) DELFI 2019, pp. 259–270. Gesellschaft für Informatik e.V, Bonn (2019). https://doi.org/10.18420/delfi2019_289
5. Følstad, A., et al.: Future directions for chatbot research: an interdisciplinary research agenda. Computing **103**(12), 2915–2942 (2021). https://doi.org/10.1007/s00607-021-01016-7
6. Hobert, S.: Say hello to 'coding tutor'! Design and evaluation of a chatbot-based learning system supporting students to learn to program. In: ICIS 2019 Proceedings, pp. 1–17 (2019)
7. Hobert, S., Meyer von Wolff, R.: Say hello to your new automated tutor – a structured literature review on pedagogical conversational agents. In: Proceedings of the 14th International Conference on Wirtschaftsinformatik, pp. 301–314. Siegen (2019)
8. Tegos, S., Demetriadis, S., Karakostas, A.: MentorChat: introducing a configurable conversational agent as a tool for adaptive online collaboration support. In: 2011 15th Panhellenic Conference on Informatics, pp. 13–17. IEEE (2011). https://doi.org/10.1109/PCI.2011.24
9. Graesser, A.C., Cai, Z., Morgan, B., Wang, L.: Assessment with computer agents that engage in conversational dialogues and trialogues with learners. Comput. Hum. Behav. **76**, 607–616 (2017). https://doi.org/10.1016/j.chb.2017.03.041
10. Catania, F., Spitale, M., Cosentino, G., Garzotto, F.: Conversational agents to promote children's verbal communication skills. In: Følstad, A., et al. (eds.) CONVERSATIONS 2020. LNCS, vol. 12604, pp. 158–172. Springer, Cham (2021). https://doi.org/10.1007/978-3-030-68288-0_11
11. Wambsganss, T., Soellner, M., Leimeister, J.M.: Design and evaluation of an adaptive dialog-based tutoring system for argumentation skills. In: ICIS 2020 Proceedings, Paper 2 (2020)
12. Brandtzaeg, P.B., Følstad, A.: Chatbots: changing user needs and motivations. Interactions **25**, 38–43 (2018). https://doi.org/10.1145/3236669
13. Følstad, A., Brandtzaeg, P.B.: Users' experiences with chatbots: findings from a questionnaire study. Qual. User Exp. **5**(1), 1–14 (2020). https://doi.org/10.1007/s41233-020-00033-2
14. Weizenbaum, J.: ELIZA - a computer program for the study of natural language communication between man and machine. Commun. ACM **9**, 36–45 (1966). https://doi.org/10.1145/365153.365168
15. Diederich, S., Brendel, A.B., Kolbe, L.M.: Designing anthropomorphic enterprise conversational agents. Bus. Inf. Syst. Eng. **62**(3), 193–209 (2020). https://doi.org/10.1007/s12599-020-00639-y
16. Winkler, R., Söllner, M.: Unleashing the potential of chatbots in education: a state-of-the-art analysis. In: Academy of Management Annual Meeting (AOM). Chicago (2018)
17. Ruan, S., et al.: QuizBot: a dialogue-based adaptive learning system for factual knowledge. In: Proceedings of the 2019 CHI Conference on Human Factors in Computing Systems, pp. 1–13. ACM, New York (2019). https://doi.org/10.1145/3290605.3300587

18. Meyer von Wolff, R., Hobert, S., Masuch, K., Schumann, M.: Chatbots at digital workplaces - a grounded-theory approach for surveying application areas and objectives. Pac. Asia J. Assoc. Inf. Syst. **12**, 64–102 (2020). https://doi.org/10.17705/1pais.12203

19. Kim, M.C., Hannafin, M.J.: Scaffolding problem solving in technology-enhanced learning environments (TELEs): bridging research and theory with practice. Comput. Educ. **56**, 403–417 (2011). https://doi.org/10.1016/j.compedu.2010.08.024

20. van de Pol, J., Volman, M., Beishuizen, J.: Scaffolding in teacher-student interaction: a decade of research. Educ. Psychol. Rev. **22**, 271–296 (2010). https://doi.org/10.1007/s10648-010-9127-6

21. Chi, M.T.H., Wylie, R.: The ICAP framework: linking cognitive engagement to active learning outcomes. Educ. Psychol. **49**, 219–243 (2014). https://doi.org/10.1080/00461520.2014.965823

22. Hobert, S., Berens, F.: Small talk conversations and the long-term use of chatbots in educational settings – experiences from a field study. In: Følstad, A., et al. (eds.) CONVERSATIONS 2019. LNCS, vol. 11970, pp. 260–272. Springer, Cham (2020). https://doi.org/10.1007/978-3-030-39540-7_18

Chatbots Supporting Collaboration
and Social Interaction

How Can a Chatbot Support Human Resource Management? Exploring the Operational Interplay

Tina Taule[1] (ID), Asbjørn Følstad[2(✉)] (ID), and Knut Inge Fostervold[1] (ID)

[1] Department of Psychology, University of Oslo, Oslo, Norway
tina.taule@gmail.com, k.i.fostervold@psykologi.uio.no
[2] SINTEF, Oslo, Norway
asbjorn.folstad@sintef.no

Abstract. Chatbots are increasingly taken up to support organizational functions and processes, particularly in support of the Human Resource Management (HRM) function. However, there is a lack of knowledge on the organizational implications of this support – in particular the operational interplay between the chatbot, the HRM function, and the organization at large. In this study, we contribute knowledge to the fields of chatbot research and digital HRM support through interviews with 13 HRM practitioners in organizations that had implemented chatbots to support their function. The findings show that a chatbot may support the HRM function through handling of repetitive inquiries and tailoring of HRM support in response to insights from analysis of chatbot use. At the same time, the chatbot impacts the HRM function in terms of new tasks and competence requirements. The findings also provide insight into characteristics of the organization and the chatbot which may impact uptake and effective use. Based on the findings, we suggest implications for theory and practice and point out future research needs.

Keywords: Chatbot · Human resource management · Work support

1 Introduction

In recent years there has been an emerging interest in chatbots as support of functions and processes internal to organizations, such as Human Resource Management (HRM) [23]. Specifically, chatbots are thought to support the HRM function in areas such as recruitment and selection, onboarding and training, automation of routine processes and answering employees' frequently asked questions [31].

Authors note an increased focus on employee experience and the use of consumer-oriented technologies, such as chatbots, to raise employee engagement and increase task efficiency in daily work [9, 10, 32]. To illustrate this trend, Gartner [17] predicted that in the near future, it will be common among white-collar workers to interact with conversational platforms on a daily basis, and organizations such as IBM have successfully applied chatbots for purposes internal to the organization [19, 21].

© Springer Nature Switzerland AG 2022
A. Følstad et al. (Eds.): CONVERSATIONS 2021, LNCS 13171, pp. 73–89, 2022.
https://doi.org/10.1007/978-3-030-94890-0_5

However, as the application of chatbots for organizational purposes is relatively new, there is a knowledge gap concerning the way in which the chatbot currently supports internal functions such as HRM [26]. Furthermore, there is a lack of research on chatbot implementation from an organizational perspective [29]. This knowledge gap is problematic, as a successful continued uptake of chatbots for organizational purposes depends on insight into how this technology may support and impact existing internal functions. Furthermore, there is a need to understand the resulting operational interplay between the technology and the functions it is intended to support, that is, their resulting distribution of tasks and responsibilities.

In response to this gap in current knowledge, we conducted a qualitative exploratory study, involving 13 HRM practitioners from 10 different organizations which all had implemented chatbots for HRM purposes. The study was conducted by semi-structured interviews allowing for needed exploration of the HRM perspective on chatbot implementation.

The study contributes to the existing state of the art in two main ways. First, by empirically exploring chatbot implementation and use from an organizational perspective, this study provides insight into a viable chatbot use area as well as factors that may prove to have significant impact on successful implementation and use. Second, taking a starting point in the assumption that chatbots are expected to support the HRM function in various ways, this study contributes insight into chatbots as a specific and relatively new HRM technology and empirically explores what characterizes the interplay between the HRM function and such chatbots. By empirically investigating the lived experiences of HRM personnel managing and working with the chatbot, this study sheds light on how HRM personnel experience the implementation of an internal chatbot, how this affects HRM work tasks and roles, as well as how this new interplay is perceived by HRM practitioners and the organization at large.

The remainder of the paper is structured as follows. First, we provide an overview of relevant background before detailing the research questions and methods. We then present study findings and discuss these relative to the current state of the art, addressing implications for theory and practice.

2   Background

2.1   Human Resource Management

HRM concerns organizational activities related to the management of people at work [30, 34]. This includes external activities such as recruitment and selection, and internal practices related to training and development, motivation, employee wellbeing, and design of work. The HRM department can also be a part of strategic and operational managerial activities such as change management and employee branding [28, 34].

One of the main concerns of the HRM function is to deliver value to key stakeholders, including employees, line managers, external customers and investors [30]. Due to the demands of both strategic contributions and cost-effectiveness, the HRM department is now seeking to reduce time spent on administrative tasks and strengthen the role as strategic business partner and change agent [34].

To support transition towards strategic HRM, routine HRM tasks are increasingly supported by digital solutions and automation [24, 34]. Digital HRM solutions are also held to potentially improve HRM service provision [4]. However, there may also be challenges in implementing digital HRM solutions; such solutions do not necessarily lead to a positive change for HRM [24] and HRM departments may experience difficulties in adopting new technologies [4]. Hence explorations of chatbots in support of the HRM function will need to consider both potential benefits and challenges.

2.2 Chatbots for Organizational Purposes

Chatbots have been described as the artificial intelligence (AI) application with the broadest set of potential uses for HRM [19].

There are several reasons why chatbots are seen as interesting to organizations. Chatbot may be convenient and efficient interfaces to information and services [6] and have also been marketed as "inexpensive to design, and quick to train" [19]. Due to the increasing volume of information, communication channels and applications, an essential advantage of chatbots for internal purposes, is the improvement of information management along with the automation of administrative and routine tasks [26, 32].

Furthermore, the conversational interface may be seen as aligned with employee expectations of user experience and contribute positively to collaboration in the workplace [17]. Self-service through chatbots internal to the organization is also suggested to contribute to higher employee engagement [11, 14, 23], and is seen in relation to organizational reputation and employee branding where investment in modern technology is key to attracting the right knowledge and sustain employee engagement [1, 23].

Although practitioners point to potential benefits of chatbots for organizational purposes, others note that the technology is still in an early stage and that uptake of chatbots for internal purposes is not yet widespread in organizational settings [1, 5, 26]. For example, some note that such chatbots need continuous training and human supervision, and output is limited to available content [1]. Furthermore, implementing a new technology is not only dependent on the system or tool itself; 'people factors' such as organizational culture, habits and attitudes are shown to have significant impact on the adoption of technologies [4]. Similarly, it has been argued that chatbots possess specific and special characteristics and that therefore it is important to gain understanding of their acceptance in the organizational context, as well as an understanding of the employee needs and expectations [5].

2.3 An Organizational Perspective on Chatbots?

Chatbots have been studied extensively from the perspective of user needs, behaviour and experiences [e.g. 15, 22], from the perspectives of design and implementation [e.g. 2, 18], and with regard to technology underpinnings such as dialogues systems and natural language processing [25]. However, while an important aspect of successful chatbot uptake is their organizational implementation and maintenance [20, 35], there is a surprising lack of research on the organizational aspects of chatbot.

Syvänen and Valentini [29] accentuated this point in their state-of-the-art analysis covering more than 60 articles on chatbot research. They found studies on implementational, marketing-oriented, and interactional aspects of chatbots to be dominating, and studies of organizational aspects of chatbot implementation to be remarkably absent.

Meyer von Wolff et al. [26] made a complementary observation in their literature review of chatbots in support of the digital workplace. Emerging research on work-oriented use of chatbots was found mainly to concern information acquisition, self-service, and the use of chatbots for education and training tasks. The authors pointed out as important future research challenges the need to understand the application areas viable for chatbots at the digital workplace, the need to understand prerequisites for such application areas, and factors supporting and inhibiting workplace use of chatbots.

Drawing on the field of digital HRM support, an organizational perspective on new technologies to support digital work may enable insight into the consequences of the technology. Research indicates that operational (cost savings and efficiencies) and relational (HRM service quality) consequences of digital HRM support is more steadily obtained [3, 13, 27], while several authors point to a lack of evidence concerning transformational consequences [4, 13]. Research addressing the organizational perspective of chatbots may benefit from addressing consequences at all three levels.

3   Research Questions

In order for chatbots to provide support and create value for the HRM function as well as the organization as a whole, it is important to study the interplay between the chatbot and the HRM personnel and gain empirical insights into central factors in this organizational change initiative. In response to the identified gap in the literature concerning organizational use of chatbots in general, and chatbots supporting the HRM function in particular, the following research questions were formulated:

1. How can a chatbot support the HRM function?
2. How does the implementation of a chatbot affect the HRM function?
3. How does organizational characteristics impact the implementation and use of the chatbot to support the HRM function?

Given the limited research available on chatbots as HRM technology, the research questions were set up so as to encourage an exploratory investigation.

4   Method

4.1   Research Design

While previous work has suggested potential benefits of chatbots to the HRM function, there is a lack of empirical knowledge on how chatbots actually support and affect this function, and the resulting interplay between the technology and the HRM practitioners. In consequence, the study applied a qualitative exploratory approach. The data-driven investigation afforded by this approach is valuable to investigate new areas of interest where there exists little prior knowledge.

Data collection was conducted through semi-structured interviews with HRM practitioners who held a role connected to an HRM chatbot. Semi-structured interviews are particularly suitable when the research focus concerns experiences connected to the phenomenon under study [33]. To gather the needed insights, data was collected from organizations that had already implemented a chatbot to support the HRM function.

4.2 Participants and Recruitment

Ten organizations that had implemented a chatbot for internal purposes were onboarded for the study through two collaborating chatbot providers. The organizations were all Norwegian, which is beneficial as Norway has relatively high levels of digitalization and findings here may also be relevant for other digitally advanced markets [12]. Nevertheless, the organizations represented a broad spectrum of enterprises across several market sectors and with varying size – from a few hundred to several thousand employees. The criteria for onboarding were that (1) the organization had already implemented or in the process of implementing a chatbot and (2) the chatbot was implemented for internal purposes and mainly belonged to the HRM function.

From the participating organizations, 13 participants were sampled through email with an invitation to participate in the project, based on their role in the organization and their role connected to the chatbot. The participants represented a broad range of experiences with the HRM chatbot, which was regarded as beneficial for data saturation considering the general exploratory approach of the study.

Ten of the participants worked directly with the chatbot at the time of the interview, three of them had worked with it previously. Seven of the participants reported that they had been involved with the chatbot project from the beginning, and some had held the role of project leader or driver of the chatbot initiative. The remaining six participants had not been involved in the early implementation phase and had only received chatbot responsibilities at a later point in time.

The participants represented organizations with different maturity in their chatbot implementation. For most, the chatbot had been implemented for one year or more – for a few, the chatbot had been implemented only months prior to the interview.

4.3 The HRM Chatbots

The chatbots in the participating organizations were retrieval-based, able to identify and respond to several hundred user intents on topics such as employment policies and regulations, aspects of the organization, and – in some – also facility management. By AI-based natural language processing, the chatbots predicted user intents from users' free text messages. Chatbot conversations could involve one or more user messages and chatbot answers could typically be refined through buttons with response alternatives.

In terms of chatbot implementation, the participating organizations had taken one of two different approaches. Although based on the same conversational platform, one approach was bespoke development of chatbot content, training, and integrations within the organization, the other approach was to get the chatbot provided as a service from a third-party vendor. The first approach will be referred to as *inhouse chatbot*, the second to *chatbot as a service* respectively. It is worth noting that these different types of chatbots account for parts of the variations observed in the participants' reports.

4.4 Interview Guide and Process

The interviews were conducted by the first author by way of video meetings. All interviews were recorded and transcribed prior to analysis. Participation in interviews followed only after informed consent, data were treated confidentially and anonymized following analysis, and the study was cleared by the relevant privacy regulatory body.

The interview guide consisted of four main topics with more detailed follow-up questions belonging to each of these.

- *Topic 1: The participant's role and experiences connected to the chatbot.* The purpose of this topic was to make the participant confident in the interview setting and share openly and generally about chatbot experiences.
- *Topic 2: The operational interplay between the HRM function and the chatbot.* These questions sought to explore the interplay between the HRM practitioner and the chatbot in greater detail. This included past and current experiences, as well as perceived possibilities and limitations.
- *Topic 3: How the implementation of an HRM chatbot affects the HRM function.* The purpose of this topic was to explore how the chatbot affects the HRM function. This included ways in which the chatbot has altered HRM work and how the chatbot is perceived by users in the organization, along with expectations regarding future chatbot impact.
- *Topic 4: Organizational conditions that can promote or inhibit successful implementation.* This topic addressed what the participants perceived to be relevant or impactful organizational aspects for a successful implementation of the chatbot.

4.5 Analysis

The qualitative data were made subject to a reflexive thematic analysis [7, 8]. In this approach to thematic analysis, the researcher's subjectivity is an important analytical resource, as is reflexive engagement with theory, data and interpretation. Coding is open and organic, and themes are developed iteratively throughout the process [8].

The analysis was conducted by using the analysis software Nvivo12 and was completed in a six-phase process detailed in Table 1.

5 Results

In the results section, we first provide an overview of findings concerning organizations' motivation for HRM chatbot implementation, before detailing findings related to the three research questions.

Table 1. Phases of the thematic analysis employed, including details and selected examples

Phase	Details	Examples
1. Familiarizing with the data	Transcription and initial review. Ideas for themes	An early theme idea concerned the allocation of tasks between HRM and information technology (IT) personnel
2. Generate initial codes	Initial coding. Revision of codes in several iterations	An initial code concerned experiences with the chatbot, and was split into several more detailed codes
3. Search for themes	Codes systematized in themes	Codes concerning tasks associated with chatbot implementation grouped in overarching theme
4. Review themes	Review and reworking theme conceptualizations	A theme concerning tailoring information support was reconceptualized as concerning chatbot support, rather than experience
5. Define and name themes	Labelling of themes to reflect data-driven conceptualization	Theme labels changed from concerning chatbot characteristics to concern impact of characteristics
6. Produce the report	Rich description of the themes and findings provided	Themes and findings provided in report and condensed in this paper

While the study is purely qualitative, it may be useful to the reader to get an indication of the prevalence of the different themes within the participant sample. To facilitate this, the following phrases are used when reporting the findings: a few (reported by 2–3), some (reported by 4–5), many (reported by 6–8), most (reported by 9–12).

5.1 Organization's Motivations for Taking up a Chatbot for the HRM Function

The organization's motivations for taking up an HRM chatbot were reported to concern both strategic and operational aspects.

Key strategic motivations concerned the internal users and their experiences when approaching HRM information services. Many of the participants noted that the user perspective was central when considering how the HRM function supports the organization and the employees, and that information regarding employment conditions and relationships should be easily accessible and available. Furthermore, many of the participants expressed that the implementation of a chatbot can contribute to HRM being perceived as technologically advanced, which ultimately may establish an experience of the HRM function as modern and user-oriented. Many of the participants also noted that by reducing the amount of routine and administrative tasks for HRM personnel, they may contribute more to developmental activities and other strategic initiatives.

Key operational motivations concerned administrative efficiency and automation to free up time for value-adding tasks for HRM personnel as well as employees and leaders. Many participants reported to see the chatbot as a tool to relieve the HRM function of high volumes of inquiries and increase self-service in the organization.

5.2   How the Chatbot Supports the HRM Function

Throughout the interviews, the participants reported on how the chatbot supports the HRM function in their daily tasks and routines, by relieving HRM workload and enabling HRM to provide better service to the organization.

Relieving the HRM Function. All participants reported relieving HRM workload to be a key benefit of the chatbot, and the most important way in which the chatbot support the HRM function. Such relief may manifest in reduced volume of inquiries and more time for HRM personnel to focus on more complex, human matters.

Most of the participants noted that the chatbot has a visible effect on the volume of common requests received by HRM personnel. The participants pointed out that all questions and queries answered by the chatbot represent a phone call, email or knock on the door that the HRM function do not have to engage with or get interrupted by.

> "[the chatbot] answers questions [...] that have a concrete answer. For example vacation, salary, so things that are regulated. That's a big area that he can answer. And then those routine questions, right. Overtime and flexible working time and home office, for example" (P10).

Some made a particular note that the chatbot allows the HRM function to formulate a good answer to a question once, instead of repeatedly answering the same question.

> "[...] I also feel that it saves a lot of time for us in HRM, because we get a lot of inquiries. That we instead of spending a lot of time on formulating an answer, we can just refer to the chatbot. Or you can find the answer there" (P9).

The participants also found the chatbot to be a potential support tool for them. Some reported that they frequently use the chatbot to quickly find needed information. A few also noted that the chatbot's assistance during the first period as an employee in HRM had been helpful for learning about the organization and finding needed information.

> "Yes, I use chatbot a lot myself. If I want some simple information that I've forgotten, whether it's a post address or organization number [...]. These standard things that you don't have written down anywhere" (P7).

Enabling the HRM Function to Provide Better Service. Although much emphasis was put on how the chatbot may relieve HRM work, it was also evident that the chatbot may support the HRM function by strengthening their service offering to employees.

Participants reported the chatbot to enable them to better tailor information to employees, as users' interactions with the chatbot provides rich insight into questions the employees have and how these are phrased. Some specifically noted that the chatbot logs offer insights into employees' actual needs for information and support.

"And we go in and analyze what people actually ask about. Because we thought that everybody asked very generally. But people ask very concretely. [...] Ask about different things than we thought that they ask about" (P6).

A few participants reported on how the chatbot can be used in a proactive manner. For example, based on insights from previous seasonal questions in the chatbot, HRM can prepare answers for the coming season in advance.

The chatbot may also enable the HRM function to have increased focus on value-adding services. Specifically, participants reported that the chatbot makes it possible to do more of the core HRM work, including employee follow-up and increased attention to those in need of more in-depth assistance.

"[...] we can deliver better quality on the services to those who really need our help. Because those who really just wondered about something simple, they can get help from the chatbot" (P10).

Such core HRM work was sometimes referred to as a reason why a chatbot can never fully replace HRM personnel. The participant's considered the professional guidance and support that may be provided by the HRM function to be too complex to be provided by chatbot technology alone.

5.3 How the Chatbot Affects the HRM Function

Throughout the interviews, the participants described various ways in which the chatbot affects the HRM function. This concerned development of competences and skills, novel tasks, and the operational interplay between the HRM personnel and the chatbot.

Implications for Needed HRM Competences. The participants reported that the chatbot requires HRM personnel to acquire knowledge and different technological competences to be able to implement and manage the chatbot.

Specifically, the participants noted a need to learn the basics of the chatbot technology. That is, to acquire sufficient understanding and knowledge of how the chatbot learns to understand the user's intentions, as well as how to train and test the chatbot. In addition, some participants had undertaken courses to become 'AI trainers' – to take on the role of maintaining the chatbot content and prediction capabilities.

"[...] one took all the courses that were needed to both be a content designer and also really train the chatbot, because HR decided that we would do everything ourselves" (P4).

The degree to which the chatbot required HRM personnel to develop new technological competences varied between the participants. Some of the participants who work with an *inhouse chatbot* reported the acquisition of new knowledge and skills through courses as an essential part of the chatbot project. Conversely, some of the participants who work with a *chatbot as a service* reported the need to have an initial understanding of how the chatbot technology works to be able to test the chatbot and update the replies. As such, the different ways of implementing a chatbot may pose different requirements with regards to the skills and competences needed.

Implications for HRM Work Tasks. Key tasks associated with implementing a chatbot involved preparations for the implementation, training and testing of the chatbot, along with continuous updating and improvements of the content and answers. For example, all participants reported that the chatbot implementation implied some level of involvement in building or training and testing the chatbot. Some of the participants who work with a *chatbot as a service* reported most of the needed intents already to be pre-trained by the vendor and described their involvement in the training of the chatbot as mainly limited to the implementation phase, as well as when the vendor creates new intents that need to be trained. Conversely, some of the participants who work with an *inhouse chatbot* reported training as a continuous task requiring substantial effort.

> *"[...] And not only are you supposed to train the chatbot, but it also needs to be maintained. [...] So that people don't get the wrong answer" (P1).*

Many of the participants noted that the chatbot needs to correspond with personnel handbooks or other forms of documents and web pages. Because of this, it is necessary to update chatbot answers whenever there are changes in organizational regulations, systems or handbook content.

> *"[...] it is a bit of extra work in terms of that I have to, if we are to update the personnel handbook, we also have to in parallel update his answer. [...] So that is something that I had to start doing. [...]" (P12).*

Another new task associated with the chatbot implementation is the promoting of chatbot use. Most of the participants reported that a central part of working with the chatbot concerns the organization-internal communication about the chatbot and its content. This was also expressed as an essential success factor. Continuous promotion regarding the chatbot and the types of inquiries that it can fulfil were noted as crucial to change employees' habits and to realize the full potential value of the chatbot.

> *"It is often nice and great if you implement it and then there is a 'oh, how fun to use', and then it's maybe especially HR's responsibility to make sure that people keep using him. [...]" (P13).*

The Operational Interplay Between the Chatbot and the HRM Function. Through the interviews, notions emerged regarding the participants' perceptions of a desired and functional distribution of tasks and roles between the HRM function and the chatbot.

Some of the participants noted that the chatbot typically answers easy, rule-based inquiries and, hence, serves as complementary support for employees to find information or complete specific routine tasks. Some described this as a service architecture with the chatbot as first line of support and where humans may provide support for more complex matters as second line.

"the chatbot becomes some kind of first line, and then HRM can become more of a second line [...] that answers more thoroughly regarding regulations and how we do things here then, maybe" (P8).

Building on this, some of the participants emphasized that the chatbot is intended as a supplement and not as a replacement of the HRM function. The still maturing chatbot technology and the human aspect of employee relations were noted as reasons for this. As such, the participants differentiated between answering routine questions, which the chatbot can do, and providing nuanced and tailored guidance to leaders and employees, for which human personnel is needed.

"There is always a need for someone who can give advice [...] the chatbot can present the alternatives, but we can give the advice, what is smart" (P10).

Some of the participants expressed this interplay in terms of future-oriented states, or what they wish to achieve with a full integration of the chatbot within the organization. The suggestive formulations may reflect an early stage of chatbot adoption, and the fact that such an interplay may take some time to establish.

"[...] I'm sure there is a lot that he can contribute with. And then I also think that you will never be able to replace the one-to-one dialogue with the employees, with a human. But I think that there are no limitations regarding different work tasks, it's just a matter of where you are in the development" (P7).

5.4   The HRM Chatbot in the Wider Organizational Context

The participants were also asked to report on their experiences regarding chatbot uptake, experiences of positive impact of the chatbot, along with perceived challenges.

Chatbot Uptake and Emerging Patterns of Use. Most of the participants reported a general positive reception when deploying the chatbot in the wider organization and experiencing how the internal users responded to the new tool. However, some participants noted a form of reluctance or resistance among some employees.

"[...] I experience it to be a bit divided. That many are satisfied and think that the chatbot is a resource, and some are a bit frustrated because they have higher expectations (to the chatbot)" (P9).

In terms of emerging patterns of chatbot use, the participants in particular reported on use for information on organizational policy and conditions of employment. This could include both general employee regulations as well as agreements and policies specific to the organization. The participants also reported on use for questions regarding holidays and vacations, different types of leave, work time, compensation, and company internal practices like insurances and pension – all considered typical high-volume HRM inquiries. Most of the participants also reported the chatbot to receive a high volume of questions regarding facility management (i.e., parking spaces, canteen, meeting rooms, etc.), other practical details connected to employment conditions (computers, access details, credit cards, etc.), IT, as well as where to find certain information.

> *"[...] topics connected to facility management, the facilities, premises, there are often a lot of questions from employees in a company there. How do I apply for a parking space? Questions about locker rooms [...] and access cards and canteen information, everything like that. [...]" (P2).*

Some noted that employees often ask concrete questions about personal details like salary, a reported case in the case management system, or how many vacation days they have left. These typically are questions that the chatbot currently cannot answer.

Experiences of Positive Impact of the HRM Chatbot. Most of the participants reported that the chatbot contributes to HRM and other personnel related information being perceived as more available and easily accessible, as the chatbot is available day and night. The participants pointed out that this had a positive impact on the employees' experiences with HRM in terms of lessening frustrations associated with HRM personnel being in meetings or out of office.

> *"[...] And what is so good about the chatbot, is that [...] it is available twenty-four hours, not all people are. We have different countries, right, that people ask from, right. So when we're off, somebody else goes to work. [...]" (P4).*

The chatbot was also seen as motivating fair and just treatment of employees. Specifically, many participants noted that the chatbot functionality promotes a consistent and identical answer to every employee. The participants considered this to facilitate a consistent practice and an experience of the HRM function as modern and professional.

> *"[...] All employees in the whole organization get the same answer. And that this is, in a way, perceived as a unified practice. [...] So that is important. That there are no different answers to questions [...]" (P8).*

Perceived Challenges During Chatbot Deployment. The participants also expressed challenges concerning the interaction between the chatbot and the internal users.

Most participants reported that different expectations of the chatbot and understandings of the chatbot technology could impact chatbot use in the organization. Such expectations concerned three different aspects. First, many noted employees to experience limitations in the chatbot scope, that is, to make inquiries the chatbot cannot answer. For example, that employees might ask questions concerning highly individual matters, suggesting their expectations may not fully be in line with the chatbot capabilities.

> *"The downside is that people expect him to be able to answer personal things. [...] This he won't be able to do. So we've received some feedback on that now after the launch, that 'but he couldn't answer for example how many vacation days I have'." (P11).*

Furthermore, many participants pointed to differences between employee groups, and how different groups may hold preferences or habits that impact the use of the chatbot. For example, the participants noted that they to a certain degree perceive older employees to prefer interacting directly with HRM personnel, and that this employee group may be less accustomed to chatting as a way of acquiring information.

"We have a pretty high average age. So I think there are very many employees who might not use chat functions as much as maybe the younger part does." (P1).

Finally, some participants expressed that the high frequency of changes in both systems and ways of working and communicating, can act as fatiguing factors that contribute to some employees being more hesitant about using the chatbot.

"It's tiring for employees that there are new computer systems arriving all the time. [...] people can get kind of digitalization fatigue" (P10).

6   Discussion

This study aimed to explore the operational interplay between the HRM function and a chatbot implemented for internal purposes. In the following we first discuss key findings relative to previous research, structured according to our three research questions, before detailing implications for theory and practice. Finally, we discuss limitations and avenues for future research.

6.1   The Operational Interplay Between the Chatbot and the HRM Function

How Can a Chatbot Support the HRM Function? (RQ1). Our findings suggest several ways in which the chatbot is perceived to currently support the HRM function, in particular concerning accessible support for repeated inquiries. This corresponds to assumptions from the literature on digital HRM support, where operational outcomes of such support is typically reported [3, 4]. However, the HRM chatbots were also found to provide relational outcomes, as the chatbot could enable the HRM function to provide better services for the organization. Additionally, factors such as the placement of the chatbot, the 24/7 availability of the chatbot, updated and right answers based on statistical insights, as well as equal treatment through standardized answers, were noted to contribute to improved communication and perception of HRM information and services. This corresponds to the general notion that digital HRM support should provide simplification of processes, provision of accurate data, and enhance the perceptions of the organization in order to positively impact HRM service quality (3, 13).

How Does the Implementation of a Chatbot Affect the HRM Function? (RQ2). The findings show how the chatbot requires the building of internal competences, skills, and knowledge regarding the chatbot technology. This echoes literature on adoption of AI technology, where it is noted that development and upskilling of employees are essential to work successfully with AI [9, 31].

The findings of the current study indicate that a potential interplay between the HRM function and the chatbot can be characterized by the chatbot managing routine employee inquiries, and HRM professionals keeping the chatbot relevant and valuable as well as counselling employees and leaders in non-routine and complex cases.

It is also interesting to note the need for HRM personnel to serve as internal marketers of the chatbot. In the literature, internal marketing in terms of system functionality, positive word of mouth and a system advocate that maintains enthusiasm for the new implementation is seen as critical for implementation success [4].

How Does Organizational Characteristics Impact the Implementation and Use of the Chatbot to Support the HRM Function? (RQ3). The organizational characteristics may impact how a chatbot supporting the HRM function is received. One example of this from the findings is the reported variation between employee groups in terms of enthusiasm for the chatbot. Another, the concern for fatigue when having too many digital change projects internally. Managing 'people factors' was considered essential for successful digital HRM support [4]. The findings also resonate with the chatbot literature, as user acceptance and managing user expectations are considered fundamental to successful chatbot use [16, 22]. Furthermore, Bondarouk et al. [4] proposed that length of employment can impact willingness to take up new technology. Similarly, different demographic groups have been found to perceive chatbot user experience differently [15].

6.2 Implications

Several implications may be drawn from the findings. We consider the following key.

Implications for Theory. The findings contribute to reducing the knowledge gap concerning chatbots in the enterprise context, specifically concerning the operational interplay between chatbots and the HRM function. Furthermore, chatbots have been reported to have various potential areas of use within the HRM function, and this study expands the literature by providing empirical insights regarding experienced chatbot support, challenges, and opportunities from the perspective of the HRM function. Lastly, the findings of this study also contributes insight into the importance of people factors in chatbot implementation and use.

Implications for Practice. The insights provided by this study may contribute to a better understanding of the factors that need consideration when an organization or HRM function seeks to adopt a chatbot. The findings may inform project planning and adoption of future chatbot implementation, as the study gives an overview of what it requires in terms of time, resources, as well as the scope of the chatbot content. This includes concrete tasks associated with the chatbot, where key takeaways concern the importance of internal marketing and sensitivity to user demographics. Other useful findings relate to how the chatbot is being used, and how many employees seek to use the chatbot in a way that is not yet realized (e.g. for concrete and personal inquiries).

6.3 Limitations and Future Work

A key limitation in the study is that it is conducted within one country, Norway, and mainly with organizations already having substantial experience with chatbots at the time of the study. The benefit of this study context is that there is a relatively high acceptance of new technology, and the participating organizations were mostly well-established users of HRM chatbots. However, findings in this study context may not be transferred directly to contexts that are highly different, for example in terms of technology uptake and use. Future research could therefore explore HRM chatbots in other contexts and types of organizations.

Furthermore, the study is based on interviews with HRM personnel only. Hence, it does not provide direct access to the perspectives of other users and stakeholders, something that limits the findings on the organizations' motivations for taking up a chatbot and on its wider organizational reception. Future research may benefit from including other users and stakeholders to gain a more comprehensive understanding of different factors affecting the implementation of the chatbot, and further explore how the chatbot can support the HRM function. Such studies could benefit from including data both on actual chatbot conversations, as well as data from users and stakeholders through interviews or questionnaire surveys.

Finally, this study only represents a single point in time for each of the participating organizations. Because of this, there is limited insight into any long-term developments of relevance for chatbot impact and use. Therefore, we foresee future research to include longitudinal studies investigating how the operational interplay between the chatbot and the HRM function develops over time.

Our study contributes an initial exploration of an important topic. We hope the findings encourage future work in this increasingly important area of chatbot research.

Acknowledgements. The work of the second author was supported by the Research Council of Norway, Grant No. 270940.

References

1. Accenture: Chatbots are here to stay - so what are you waiting for? Report (2018). www.acc enture.com/_acnmedia/pdf-77/accenture-research-conversational-ai-platforms.pdf
2. Araujo, T.: Living up to the chatbot hype: the influence of anthropomorphic design cues and communicative agency framing on conversational agent and company perceptions. Comput. Hum. Behav. **85**, 183–189 (2018)
3. Bondarouk, T., Harms, R., Lepak, D.: Does e-HRM lead to better HRM service? Int. J. Hum. Resour. Manag. **28**(9), 1332–1362 (2017)
4. Bondarouk, T., Parry, E., Furtmueller, E.: Electronic HRM: four decades of research on adoption and consequencs. Int. J. Hum. Resour. Manag. **28**(1), 98–131 (2017)
5. Brachten, F., Kissmer, T., Stieglitz, S.: The acceptance of chatbots in an enterprise context - a survey study. Int. J. Inf. Manag. **60**, 102375 (2021)
6. Brandtzaeg, P.B., Følstad, A.: Why people use chatbots. In: Kompatsiaris, I., et al. (eds.) INSCI 2017. LNCS, vol. 10673, pp. 377–392. Springer, Cham (2017). https://doi.org/10. 1007/978-3-319-70284-1_30

7. Braun, V., Clarke, V.: Thematic analysis. J. Positive Psychol. **12**(3), 297–298 (2017)
8. Braun, V., Clarke, V.: One size fits all? What counts as quality practice in (reflexive) thematic analysis? Qual. Res. Psychol. **18**(3), 328–352 (2020)
9. CIPD: People profession 2030: a collective view of future trends. Report (2020). www.cipd.co.uk/Images/people-profession-2030-trends-1_tcm18-86095.pdf
10. Deloitte: Introduction: Rewriting the rules for the digital age (2017). www.deloitte.com/us/en/insights/focus/human-capital-trends/2017/introduction.html
11. DiRomualdo, A., El-Khoury, D., Girimonte, F.: HR in the digital age: how digital technology will change HR's organization, structure, processes and roles. Strateg. HR Rev. **17**(5), 234–242 (2018)
12. European Commission: International Digital Economy and Society Index (DESI). Report. https://digital-strategy.ec.europa.eu/en/policies/desi
13. Florkowski, G.W.: HR technology goal realization: predictors and consequences. Pers. Rev. **50**(5), 1372–1396 (2020)
14. Forbes: How leveraging chatbots internally drives staff productivity (2019). www.forbes.com/sites/forbescommunicationscouncil/2019/06/20/how-leveraging-chatbots-internally-drives-staff-productivity/#62e4b27a5caa
15. Følstad, A., Brandtzaeg, P.B.: Users' experiences with chatbots: findings from a questionnaire study. Qual. User Exp. **5**(1), 1–14 (2020). https://doi.org/10.1007/s41233-020-00033-2
16. Følstad, A., Nordheim, C.B., Bjørkli, C.A.: What makes users trust a chatbot for customer service? An exploratory interview study. In: Bodrunova, S.S. (ed.) INSCI 2018. LNCS, vol. 11193, pp. 194–208. Springer, Cham (2018). https://doi.org/10.1007/978-3-030-01437-7_16
17. Gartner: Chatbots will appeal to modern workers (2019). www.gartner.com/smarterwithgartner/chatbots-will-appeal-to-modern-workers/
18. Go, E., Sundar, S.S.: Humanizing chatbots: the effects of visual, identity and conversational cues on humanness perceptions. Comput. Hum. Behav. **97**, 304–316 (2019)
19. IBM: The business case for AI in HR. Report (2018). www.ibm.com/downloads/cas/AGKXJX6M
20. Kvale, K., Freddi, E., Hodnebrog, S., Sell, O.A., Følstad, A.: Understanding the user experience of customer service chatbots: what can we learn from customer satisfaction surveys? In: Følstad, A., et al. (eds.) CONVERSATIONS 2020. LNCS, vol. 12604, pp. 205–218. Springer, Cham (2021). https://doi.org/10.1007/978-3-030-68288-0_14
21. Vera Liao, Q., Geyer, W., Muller, M., Khazaen, Y.: Conversational interfaces for information search. In: Wai Tat, Fu., van Oostendorp, H. (eds.) Understanding and Improving Information Search. HIS, pp. 267–287. Springer, Cham (2020). https://doi.org/10.1007/978-3-030-38825-6_13
22. Luger, E., Sellen, A.: "Like having a really bad PA": the gulf between user expectation and experience of conversational agents. In: Proceedings of CHI 2016, pp. 5286–5297. ACM, New York (2016)
23. Majumder, S., Mondal, A.: Are chatbots really useful for human resource management? Int. J. Speech Technol. **24**(4), 969–977 (2021). https://doi.org/10.1007/s10772-021-09834-y
24. Marler, J.H., Fisher, S.L.: An evidence-based review of e-HR and strategic human resource management. Hum. Resour. Manag. Rev. **23**, 18–36 (2013)
25. McTear, M.: Conversational AI. Dialogue systems, conversational agents, and chatbots. Morgan & Claypool (2020)
26. Meyer von Wolff, R., Hobert, S., Schumann, M.: How may I help you? – State of the art and open research questions for chatbots at the digital workplace. In: Proceedings HICCS 2019, pp. 95–104. ScholarSpace, Honolulu (2019)
27. Parry, E.: e-HRM: a catalyst for changing the HR function? In: Martínez-López, F.J. (ed.) Handbook of Strategic e-Business Management, pp. 589–604. Springer, Heidelberg (2014). https://doi.org/10.1007/978-3-642-39747-9_24

28. Storey, J., Ulrich, D., Wright, P.M.: Strategic Human Resource Management. Routledge, London (2019)
29. Syvänen, S., Velentini, C.: Conversational agents in online organization-stakeholder interactions: a state-of-the-art analysis and implications for future research. J. Commun. Manag. **24**(4), 339–362 (2020)
30. Ulrich, D., Dulebohn, J.: Are we there yet? What's next for HR? Hum. Resour. Manag. Rev. **25**, 188–204 (2015)
31. Vrontis, D., Christofi, M., Pereira, V., Tarba, S., Makrides, A., Trichina, E.: Artificial intelligence, robotics, advanced technologies and human resource management: a systematic review. Int. J. Hum. Resour. Manag. (2021). https://doi.org/10.1080/09585192.2020.1871398
32. White, M.: Digital workplaces: vision and reality. Bus. Inf. Rev. **29**(4), 205–214 (2012)
33. Willig, C.: Introducing Qualitative Research in Psychology, 3rd edn. Open University Press (2013)
34. Wilton, N.: An Introduction to Human Resource Management, 3rd edn. Sage Publications, Thousand Oaks (2016)
35. Zhang, J.J., Følstad, A., Bjørkli, C.A.: Organizational factors affecting successful implementation of chatbots for customer service. J. Internet Commer. (2021). https://doi.org/10.1080/15332861.2021.1966723

How to Find My Task? Chatbot to Assist Newcomers in Choosing Tasks in OSS Projects

Luiz Philipe Serrano Alves, Igor Scaliante Wiese, Ana Paula Chaves, and Igor Steinmacher[✉]

Universidade Tecnológica Federal do Paraná, Campo Mourão, Paraná, Brazil
luizphilipe@alunos.utfpr.edu.br, {igor,chavesana,igorfs}@utfpr.edu.br

Abstract. Open Source Software (OSS) is making a meteoric rise in the software industry since several big companies have entered this market. Unfortunately, newcomers enter these projects and usually lose interest in contributing because of several factors. This paper aims to reduce the problems users face when they walk their first steps into OSS projects: finding the appropriate task. This paper presents a chatbot that filters tasks to help newcomers choose a task that fits their skills. We performed a quantitative and a qualitative study comparing the chatbot with the current GitHub issue tracker interface, which uses labels to categorize and identify tasks. The results show that users perceived the chatbot as easier to use than the GitHub issue tracker. Additionally, users tend to interpret the use of chatbots as situational, helping mainly newcomers and inexperienced contributors.

Keywords: Chatbots · Open source software · Software engineering · Onboarding · Skills · Barriers · Newcomers

1 Introduction

Open Source Software (OSS) projects are open collaboration communities in which geographically distributed people develop software. To remain sustainable and grow, several of these communities rely on volunteers [13]. However, it is known that newcomers often face barriers during the joining process, which may lead them to give up on contributing [27]. Among these barriers, the difficulty to find a task to work on is a crucial one [3,26] since newcomers have a hard time attempting to match their interests and skill set to the community needs [34]. Still, the communities often expect new members to find their tasks instead of giving them specific work to do [33].

The literature [28] suggests that newcomers need specific guidance since finding the first task depends on the difficulty level, technology and modules affected. To help newcomers find tasks, social coding platforms, such as GitHub encourage the project maintainers to label the issues according to the difficulty

© Springer Nature Switzerland AG 2022
A. Følstad et al. (Eds.): CONVERSATIONS 2021, LNCS 13171, pp. 90–107, 2022.
https://doi.org/10.1007/978-3-030-94890-0_6

level or required skills. However, the labeling process may be complex and time-consuming [4]. To mitigate this problem, Santos *et al.* [25] proposed an approach that automatically labels the tasks by predicting the potentially required libraries for each task.

Still, newcomers are unfamiliar with the OSS tools and infrastructure, which bring many challenges when navigating the tasks on a traditional issue tracker interface [16]. Dominic *et al.* [9] suggests that a conversational interface may help engage the newcomers fully by recommending projects, artifacts, and experts as well as choosing an appropriate task. However, chatbots are not yet common in the OSS domain. A large number of GitHub projects adopt bots that assist contributors by performing repetitive tasks [35], such as quality assurance tasks (e.g., automating code reviews, assigning reviewers, reporting failures, etc. [35]) and artifacts recommendation [21]. Although these bots, in some sense, communicate with the community by, for example, posting comments or acting on mentions to them, they are not designed to hold interactive conversations with the community members.

In this paper, we walk toward using a conversational, interactive interface to support newcomers when finding the first task. We developed a chatbot that assists the users in navigating their skill set to select an appropriate task. We evaluated the acceptance of the before-mentioned chatbot by performing a user study that compares this tool to the traditional GitHub issue tracker. Our study focuses on answering the following research question:

RQ. *How does using a chatbot to find tasks compare to the use of the GitHub issue tracker?*

We conducted a survey-based within-subject study with 40 participants, including graduate students and industry practitioners that may or may not have previous experience with GitHub and OSS. Participants assessed each task-finder tool (chatbot vs. GitHub issue tracker) individually and comparatively, in the latter case, by informing which one they preferred. We compared the perceived usefulness and perceived ease of use of the tools according to the Technology Acceptance Model (TAM) [8]. Additionally, we analyzed the participants' qualitative feedback through a thematic analysis.

Our results show that participants perceive both the search feature and the chatbot as similarly useful, but the chatbot as easier to use. This result indicates that chatbots could be an effective way to help newcomers navigate through and find appropriate tasks. The qualitative analysis revealed positive aspects of the chatbot compared to the GitHub issue tracker and improvement opportunities. Our findings demonstrate that using a chatbot to find a task, as proposed by Dominic *et al.* [9], is feasible and relevant to support newcomers in OSS.

2   Related Work

Advances in natural language processing (NLP) and machine learning (ML) increased the adoption of chatbots in numerous applications. In the past decades, many companies have developed chatbots to the many existing messaging tools, such as Facebook Messenger, Skype, Telegram, and Slack. The website BotList[1] shows chatbots that are currently available in domains such as entertainment, education, games, leisure, culture, and sports.

The partnership between humans and chatbots makes it possible to create interactions around the activities performed by both [10]. Chatbots have shaped the interaction between companies and customers [5,19], teachers and learners [6, 37], patients and healthcare providers [12,17], among many other applications. These examples show that using a chatbot's interactive capabilities is useful for supporting users in their tasks.

In software engineering, chatbots are often called only "bots", regardless of their ability to hold an interactive conversation. Many of the bots for the software engineering domain are "non-conversational," in the sense that their focus is task automation [29,35]. Even though they often post messages and comments they are not able to respond to the users in a conversational style [36].

Chatbots have been used in OSS projects, especially on GitHub[2], but they appear more timidly than the task-automation bots. The literature presents a couple of examples of chatbots in OSS. For example, Abdellatif and Shihab [2] developed a chatbot called MSRBot that supports users finding answers to questions about specificities of software repositories. They argue that the conversational nature of chatbots potentially lowers barriers that newcomers face when first contributing to a project.

Dominic *et al.* [9] raises a discussion about the ways that newcomers may benefit from interacting with chatbots during the onboarding process. The authors envision the creation of a chatbot to help newcomers find projects and tasks to contribute and provide guidance throughout their first contributions by playing the role of a mentor. Since these claims have not yet been further investigated in the literature, we have hypothesized that a chatbot would increase users' ease of use and perceived usefulness. Therefore, we opted to use an already validated instrument that covers these two constructs, the Technology Acceptance Model [8] (more details in Sect. 3.1).

3   Method

To conduct this research, we first set up the necessary tools and materials for the study; then, we collected the data through a within-subject study and analyzed the outcomes using mixed methods. The research steps are summarized in Fig. 1 and detailed below.

3.1   Materials

Task Classifier: finding an appropriate task requires ways to filter the available tasks according to the user's expectations. Labeling issues is a way to make it easier for users to find tasks according to their interests. In this study, we used the

---

[1] https://botlist.co/.
[2] Social Coding Platform, available at https://github.com.

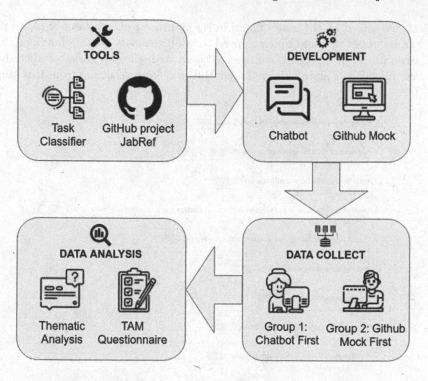

Fig. 1. A summary of the method followed in this study.

task classifier created by Santos *et al.* [25] that predicts labels to GitHub issues. We have chosen this task classifier because of its assertiveness when predicting and relevance for newcomers. We used this task classifier to generate the labels used in the GitHub mock and filter the tasks in the chatbot interface.

GitHub Project JabRef: to evaluate whether a chatbot help developers find tasks, it is necessary to choose a project which contains a history of open and closed issues. We chose the JabRef project [18], which is an open-source bibliography reference manager developed by a diverse community, including contributors that are not familiar with computer science. Also, the project is mature (created in 2003) and active on GitHub (migrated in 2014) with a large number of commits (15.7k+), 42 releases, 337 contributors, 2.7k closed issues, and 4.1k closed pull requests. JabRef is frequently investigated in other scientific studies [11,22] and it interacts conveniently with the task classifier used in this study [25] since the classifier was trained with issues extracted from this project.

GitHub Mock: since we are not authorized to add labels to JabRef issue tracker on GitHub, we developed two tools that consume the output produced by the task classifier. The first tool is a mock of JabRef's issue tracker page. We used the mock to control the task labels that a participant sees on the issue tracker page to match with the task labels used in the chatbot environment. To build the mock, we first forked the JabRef project to a new repository. In this now project, we copied all the issues found in the Santos *et al.*'s dataset of issues [25] (the same dataset of issues that was used to train the classifier). Before including the issues in the new project, we labeled them with the categories predicted by the task classifier. Figure 2 show the GitHub mock-up resulting from this step.

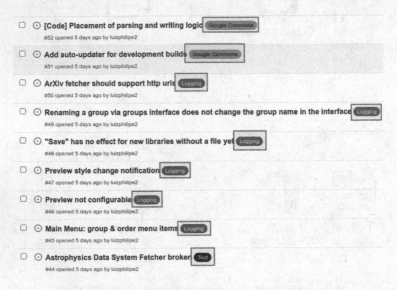

Fig. 2. Labels put on the GitHub cloned project.

Chatbot: besides the GitHub mock, we also developed the task-finder chatbot (in Brazilian Portuguese) using the Watson Assistant platform[3]. We designed the conversational flow based on the hierarchical categorization proposed in Santos *et al.* [25] (Fig. 3), which is based on JabRef's source code and was specifically generated for that project. The chatbot's conversation, as shown in Fig. 4, is based on clickable predefined answers (buttons instead of free text) and aims to deliver a link to a task as soon as possible. The chatbot starts the conversation by introducing itself and asking whetherif the user has collaborated on an OSS project before. This question works to acclimate the respondent to the clickable answers. After that, the chatbot asks about the contributor's preference regarding the following possible options: *development, systems integration,* and *user interface.* Depending on the chosen option, the chatbot may follow up with options to filter the subcategories. Categories and sub-categories are organized in three layers (*User Interface, Development* and *System Integration*), as presented in the Fig. 3. The categories and subcategories are specific to this project and were generated automatically by the task classifier. The options were purposely generated to fit the suggested layers and end up one in each layer level.

---

[3] https://cloud.ibm.com/catalog/services/watson-assistant.

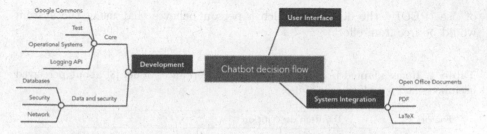

Fig. 3. Mind map of sub-categories that the tasks were categorized.

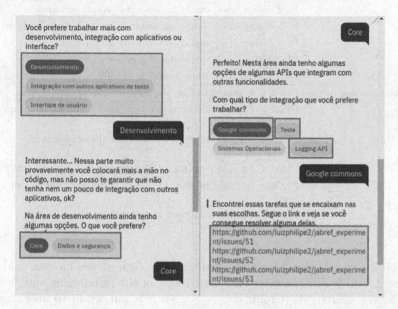

Fig. 4. Chatbot interaction, sub-categories as defined on Table 3 and predefined answers. The last level of the interaction is the same labels as put on Fig. 2. The tasks link will conduce to GitHub.

Questionnaire: To answer the question *How does the use of a chatbot to find tasks compare to the use of the GitHub issue tracker?*, we conducted a questionnaire study using Google Forms, divided into three sections. The first two sections contain the instructions to interact with each tool (chatbot or GitHub issue tracker), along with questions about their experience. The experience of the participants was measured using a questionnaire based on version 1 of the TAM instrument [8] followed by open-ended questions aiming to capture general feedback about the pros and insights on how to improve each tool. We present the items in Table 1. The TAM items were measured using a 5-points Likert scale. We evaluated two factors: perceived usefulness (PU—the degree a person believes that the tool would enhance their job performance); and perceived ease of use (PEOU—the degree to which a person believes that using the system would be free from effort).

Table 1. Items adapted from the Technology Acceptance Model [8] about perceived usefulness and perceived ease of use.

Factor	ID. Item description
Perceived usefulness	PU1. Using [tool] would enable me to accomplish tasks more quickly
	PU2. Using [tool] would improve my job performance
	PU3. Using [tool] in my job would increase my productivity
	PU4. Using [tool] would enhance my effectiveness on the job
	PU5. Using [tool] would make it easier to do my job
	PU6. I would find [tool] useful in my job
Perceived ease of use	PEOU1. Learning to operate [tool] would be easy for me
	PEOU2. I would find it easy to get [tool] to do what I want it to do
	PEOU3. My interaction with [tool] would be clear and understandable
	PEOU4. I would find [tool] to be flexible to interact with
	PEOU5. It would be easy for me to become skillful at using [tool]
	PEOU6. I would find [tool] easy to use

Table 2 presents the descriptive statistics for each of the factors, and each treatment, which demonstrates the consistency of the instrument and that the scales found are reliable (Cronbach's $\alpha \geq 0.8$). It is important to note that the participants answered the same questions just after interacting with each tool. In the third part of the questionnaire, we included one question to ask the preferred tool (GitHub issue tracker, Chatbot, or Any) followed by demographics questions (presented in Fig. 5).

Table 2. Descriptive statistics for the Likert Items

Factor	Tool	Mean	Median	SD	Cronbach's α
Perceived usefulness (PU)	Chatbot	4.19	4	0.94	0.88
	GitHub search	4.18	4	0.95	0.83
Perceived ease of use (PEOU)	Chatbot	4.55	5	0.78	0.92
	GitHub search	4.18	4	0.97	0.93

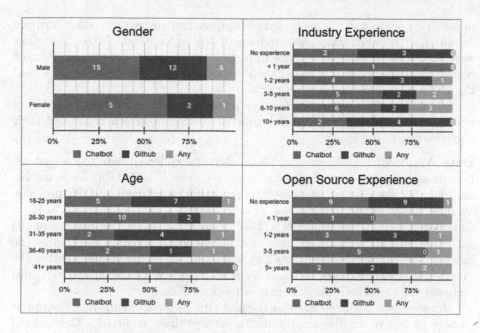

Fig. 5. Demographics of respondents.

3.2 Procedures

Participants: We used a convenience sampling approach and openly invited prospective participants from the university where the research has been conducted and from the authors' contacts, kindly asking them to spread the word in their companies. Participants received the invitation link by email and voluntarily responded to it. We received 40 responses to the study, including undergraduate and graduate students as well as software developers. As depicted in Fig. 5, 75% of the respondents are men, 50% are between 26–30 years old, and the majority of them have more than 3 years of industry experience and less than 2 years of OSS experience.

Study Task: When the participants clicked on the invitation link, they were redirected to the Google Forms page with the study description. Participants were invited to simulate the scenario of choosing an issue from the JabRef project that they would like to work on. Since we performed a within-subject study, each participant had to complete this scenario twice, using each of the two provided tools: once using the mock of the GitHub issue tracker (control condition) and once using the chatbot (experimental condition). Before each scenario, the participants were introduced to the task they had to perform, followed by the sentence *"Now you are requested to interact with the [TOOL] available at the link below until you find an issue you consider suitable for you"*—replacing [TOOL] with "chatbot" and "GitHub Search." After completing each scenario, participants answered the TAM questionnaire for the ease of use and usefulness of the tool they had just used, along with the two open-ended questions about their impressions of the tool. This portion of the questionnaire was the same for both conditions. To avoid biases, we randomized the order in which the conditions were presented to the participants through a simple redirecting script. Almost half of the participants (19) used the chatbot first, and the remaining 21 used the GitHub issue tracker interface first.

After concluding both scenarios, the participants answered the comparative and demographics questions and submitted the forms, which concluded their participation in the study.

Data Analysis: The last step was to analyze the collected data to understand how using a chatbot to find a task compares to using the GitHub issue tracker and whether the chatbot is useful for supporting newcomers on OSS projects. We first analyzed the participants' answers to the TAM questionnaire using a Cumulative Link Mixed Model (CLMM) for ordinal data [7]. We fitted a model with the rates for each Likert item as the dependent variable, the tool as the independent variable (GitHub mock vs. chatbot), and a factor representing the measured construct (perceived usefulness and perceived ease of use). We also included the individual Likert item as a random effect.

Moreover, we evaluated whether the participants' profiles influence their preferences for one or another condition. To achieve that, we fitted a Generalized Linear Model [14] with binomial class, where the dependent variable is the participant's preferred tool (chatbot vs. GitHub mock), and the independent variables are the participant's age, gender, years of industry experience, and years of OSS experience. The results of the quantitative analysis can be found in Sect. 4.1.

We also analyzed the open-ended questions through a thematic analysis method [31]. We inspected the answers to identify themes and assigned codes that summarize the key points. By constantly comparing the codes [30], we grouped them into categories to give a high-level representation of the codes. This coding process was conducted by one researcher and constantly discussed with two experienced researchers until reaching a consensus on the codes and categories. These findings are presented in Sect. 4.2.

4   Results

In this section, we present the results of our study. Firstly, we focus on the quantitative analysis, which compares the use of a chatbot to find a task to the use of the traditional GitHub issue tracker. After that, we present our findings related to the qualitative analysis, pointing out the pros and cons of each tool according to the participant's feedback.

4.1   Quantitative Analysis

Figures 6 and 7 depict the results for the TAM questions regarding the perceived usefulness (PU) and perceived ease of use (PEOU), respectively. Participants rated both tools positively for their ease of use and usefulness. PU2 and PU3 received the highest number of negative scores. These questions focused on job performance and productivity, which were not sufficiently explored in the study since participants were not required to solve the selected task.

Although participants were mostly positive about both tools, Fig. 7 suggests that there is a trend toward the chatbot receiving higher scores than the GitHub mock for the perceived ease of use factor. The results of the CLMM analysis confirmed this inference, as the estimated contrast $(chatbot - GitHub_{mock})$ is

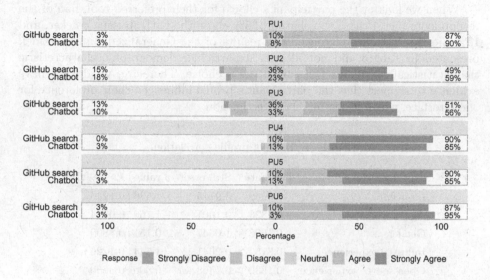

Fig. 6. Perceived usefulness: chatbot vs. GitHub issue search tool

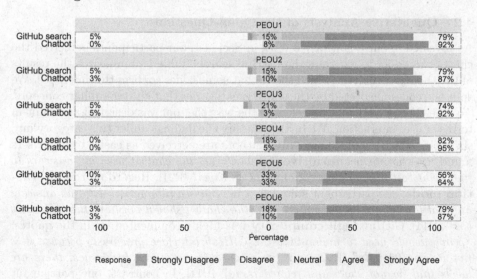

Fig. 7. Perceived ease of use: chatbot vs. GitHub issue search tool

0.42 ($SE = 0.13$, $p\text{-}value < 0.001$, $\alpha = 0.05$), which means that one-unit increase in the GitHub mock score would result in $exp(0.42) = 1.52$-unit increase in the chatbot score (odds ratio of higher scores equals to approximately 52%). The contrast per factor showed that the perceived ease of use influenced this difference (estimate $= 0.92$, SE $= 0.19$, p-value $< .0001$), while we found no difference in the perceived usefulness (estimate < -0.001, SE $= 0.18$ p-value $= 0.99$). Therefore, we concluded that although participants perceived both tools as similarly useful, they perceived the chatbot as easier to use.

When we look at the participant's choice for their preferred tool, half of the respondents (50%) chose the chatbot, 35% chose the GitHub issue tracker, and 15% did not have a preference. The results of the Generalized Linear Model, presented in Table 3, did not identify a particular demographic characteristic that statistically explains the participant's choice. Therefore, we do not have evidence to support that the participant's profile influenced their preference for one interface, which needs further investigation.

Table 3. Table of profile correlation.

	Estimate	Std. error	z-value	Pr $(> |z|)$
Intercept	6.0068	3.9115	1.536	0.1246
Age	−0.2828	0.1601	−1.766	0.0774
Gender	0.1608	1.0647	0.151	0.8800
Industry experience	0.3152	0.2041	1.544	0.1226
Open source experience	−0.1330	0.1468	−0.906	0.3650

4.2 Qualitative Analysis of the Open-Questions

As revealed in our quantitative work in Sect. 4.1, our participants perceived the chatbot as easier to use than the GitHub search. Table 4 summarizes the results of the thematic analysis, which shows that some codes confirm this inference. We split the codes uncovered by the analysis categories that cluster similar concepts.

The category UI DESIGN refers to the way the tool was designed and built-in terms of user interaction. We further classify the findings under this category into six topics which clearly shows why chatbots are perceived as easier to use. Users found the chatbot has **intuitiveness** because *"the chatbot uses my answers to find what best fits my expectations and abilities"* [P21]. Regarding the **interaction mode**, one participant stated that he *"missed interaction with my answers and not the defined by the options box, the chatbot should not have the text entry box"* [P11]. GitHub **high complexity** was highly commented, as in the quotes: *"people would need to understand the GitHub interface previously because it is not newbie friendly"* [P02] and *"it is complex the search for issues, there are labels that do not show any related issue"* [P11]. In contrast, one participant dropped a comment on the chatbot's **user friendliness**: *"as a newcomer to the programming environment, the chatbot was more user-friendly"* [P02]. We also

Table 4. Thematic analysis from user's open answers about negative and positive aspects about both tools

Categories		Chatbot		GitHub	
		Negative	Positive	Negative	Positive
Communicability	Context recovery	7			
	Lack of information on how to interact	7		4	
	Better options to filter		1		
	Search efficiency		6		1
UI design	Intuitiveness		2		
	Interaction mode	1			
	High complexity			10	
	User friendliness		1		
	Tool limitation			5	
	Ease to use		10		4
Maxim of quantity	Information overload			4	
	Too few recommendations	6			
	Lack of information preview	4			
	More information about the task				7
Profile dependency	Personal choice	2	1		1
	Situational use		1		
Side results	Lack of prioritization	2		1	
	Categorization dependency	2		11	

found some comments regarding **tool limitations**. Some participants mentioned the advanced search options (on GitHub) (e.g., *"there is no way to search using the asterisk as a wildcard"* [P27] and *"I can not store my searches even logged in, I wanted to save predefined filters"*). Participants reported the **ease of use** as a positive aspect for both tools. For example, [P32] reported that the chatbot was *"easy to use, it is prepared to give results directly following the user's profile, probably inexperienced users can not do an open search"*. Regarding the GitHub issue tracker, a participant mentioned that *"the tasks are already on GitHub, so it is easier to use GitHub to filter than a redirecting chatbot"* [P23].

The Grice's MAXIM OF QUANTITY defines the informativeness of a contribution and states that a message should be as informative as required [15]. Four codes are grouped under this category, but we highlight the first one because it shows a negative aspect of GitHub that may have influenced our quantitative result. Some participants found that GitHub's **information overload** leads to a time-consuming experience. For example, one participant complained: *"I had to analyze all the tags to find one that fits my profile"* [P18].

In contrast to what we found so far, our study revealed other aspects of the interaction that may not have influenced the quantitative results. Participants reported that the chatbot had **too few recommendations** and they wanted more (e.g., *"it limits the task options. Using the chatbot, I cannot explore all open issues or choose to detail an issue that already has a discussion"* [P25]. Participants reported **lack of information preview** as a negative aspect of the chatbot, as in the following quote: *"the chatbot does not provide a task preview, so the developer needs to click suggested links to verify"* [P31]. GitHub, on the other hand, offered **more information about the task**: *"in the GitHub search, I have a broader view for a search. Some tasks complement each other, and with the search, it is possible to visualize this. In the chatbot, I had to follow the GitHub link"* [P06].

COMMUNICABILITY, the ability of a tool to communicate, is subdivided into four codes. Users from the chatbot did not like that they could not **recover the context** of the conversation. For example, one participant said that *"the chatbot should have an option to go back to previous questions in the middle of a conversation without the need to finalize the whole selection flow"* [P15]. Another participant commented that *"changing this path is not easy as going back to the previous question"* [P20]. Besides, there are negative aspects of both chatbot and GitHub interfaces about the **lack of information on how to interact** with the tool. The following quotes demonstrate this need:

"At first I thought I would need to use the keyboard to interact with the chatbot and it gave me no answer at all, I had to ask how to interact to know that I needed to click on options" [P19].

"I would like a basic introduction, few words or images, where the basics of how to use the search tool are shown" [P02].

One participant mentioned that the hierarchical structure of the chatbot conversation provided **more options to filter** and classify the tasks helped him: *"I had the impression that the fact of the chatbot had levels (network, databases) has helped me to identify the tasks according to my interests"* [P11]. Regarding **search efficiency**, [P04] mentioned that *"using the chatbot, I could abstract tasks that would not have caught my attention and choose only among the ones I really would like to do"*. In contrast, another participant reported *"I believe that the search from GitHub is way faster and easier to find my task"*.

We found some topics that depend on the user's **personal choice** and **situational use**, so we categorized them as PROFILE DEPENDENCY. We evidenced that participants who had a negative experience with chatbots before the study leaned toward a traditional interface, as reported by one participant: *"I particularly do not like to use chatbots because my experiences were the worst"* [P36]. Other participants just prefer to search on their own (e.g., *"I prefer search engines to chatbots. Normally until it gives me what I need, I have already found a simple search query."* [P40]), and there were those who just think chatbots are more practical. Regarding the **situational use**, a participant stated that the chatbot would only be useful for a newcomer: *"As I am a newcomer to Open Source Software, the chatbot would be great, but I do not believe I would use this for a long time because the search engine visualization gives me a sense of responsibility and ownership"* [P30]. Another participant explained that choosing between the tools would *"depend on the intention of the moment if it is to explore the tasks or find the task easily"* [P25]. These statements complement what we have found on the quantitative analysis since newcomers would benefit more from a tool easier to use.

SIDE RESULTS correspond to the answers that are not directly related to the research goal but can also help improve its outcome. When talking about the chatbot, participants reported that there is a **lack of prioritization** when displaying the tasks: *"I missed other categories or subcategories like priority and difficulty"* [P11]. While this is related to the lack of information about tasks (under "Maxim of quantity"), it is a problem related to how the development team labeled the tasks. We point out that this is a more general problem related to the project's information architecture rather than the chatbot design. Participants also mentioned issues with the **categorization dependency**. They reported that *"if the categorization is wrong, the search using labels would be ruined"* [P20], and *"the contributor may give up if the task is not categorized correctly."*. This concern is important and should be taken into consideration. However, it goes beyond the scope of the study, which only used the task classifier as a tool to set up the environment.

5   Discussion

This section provides additional insights on our results and how they impact practice and improve the existing state-of-the-art.

As our quantitative results showed, the chatbot interface was perceived as easier to use. When analyzing the reasons for choosing the preferred tool, the thematic analysis revealed a pattern for those who chose chatbot along the lines of being *"simpler, easier, more intuitive."* This outcome is clearly evidenced in Table 4, in which USER FRIENDLINESS, INTUITIVENESS, and EASE OF USE are heavily reported as chatbot's positive aspects. Going in-depth, we learned that the design of the search engine may negatively affect the perception of ease of use of people who are not used to the tools. As some participants mentioned, *"[GitHub engine] has too much information to process and decide"* [P8] and *"it is complex to understand the issue list"* [P14]. We learned that the simplicity of the chatbot using predefined answers (buttons) makes it intuitive and easy to use, as compared to the UI offered by GitHub.

The results show the benefits of a chatbot for newcomers, supporting the insights from Dominic *et al.* [9] by showing that chatbots support these newcomers in the process of choosing an appropriate task [26]. This was evidenced by several participants who mentioned that *"As a newcomer, I preferred the chatbot because it is simpler"* [P26]. The thematic analysis also revealed that the complexity of the GitHub search engine gives the user more control over the search, but this same characteristic is overwhelming for someone who is not familiar with the issue tracker interface, as reported by [P31]: *"for a newcomer, the chatbot helps a lot...while GitHub tends to facilitate the work of more experienced developers."* As an implication, we suggest that the effort should lay on designing the chatbot to increasingly unveil complexity so that the users can move slowly from the chatbot to the issue tracker interface.

Regarding the usefulness, our quantitative results indicate that both the chatbot and GitHub search engine are not perceived differently. Both of the approaches supported our participants in their tasks. However, the thematic analysis revealed some chatbot negative aspects related to the efficiency in finding appropriate results. This is noticeable in Table 4, when we look at the mentions to TOO FEW RECOMMENDATIONS and LACK OF INFORMATION PREVIEW as negative aspects of the chatbot versus the MORE INFORMATION ABOUT THE TASK as a positive aspect of the GitHub search. At the same time that this is a potential improvement to the chatbot, previous discussions regarding conversational search [20] have already pointed out that an effective result from a conversational search cannot be as rich as the augmented results from a traditional web search. Furthermore, this may be related to personal preferences or the diversity of information processing styles [23], which deserves further investigation.

The recent research on chatbots for software engineering has mainly focused on exploring the intent discovery [2] and the precision of the information returned [1, 24, 32] rather than looking at the interaction aspects. This study complements the existing literature, shedding light on the importance of understanding not only the precision of the information provided by the chatbots, but also focusing on how the users perceive their usefulness and ease to use.

5.1 Limitations

Participants may be subject to learning effects since they have evaluated two tools to perform the same task. To mitigate that, we designed our experiment to follow a within-subject approach. In this case, the participants assessed the tools in random orders and answered the questionnaires in different orders, thus reducing potential biases by learning effect. Moreover, this enabled us to analyze the tools separately to understand if there is any chance of learning bias that may have caused any impact on the data collected.

Although we used strategies to avoid learning bias, we are still vulnerable to the selection bias since we did not actively search OSS contributors or potential contributors or selected only newcomers. In fact, we selected people randomly in a non-probabilistic way. There was no specific characteristic that we were looking for when selecting participants; the only crucial thing was the software development background.

We have not deployed the chatbot on a server, and we did not track all the paths users used to decide their tasks. We may have missed some important information in this process. Also, the chatbot was outside of GitHub, which does not simulate the real environment that we expect to use, which is the corner of the GitHub official platform. This might have led users to face difficulties that would not be a problem if the chatbot had been deployed inside GitHub.

The GitHub labeling system is not capable of reproducing the hierarchical structure that we created for the chatbot. This may have influenced the participants' experience. However, this is an issue with the GitHub search feature, which we could not change. Thus, we interpret this as a chatbot differential.

We cannot claim that our work is generalizable. We built our experiment considering specific variables: project, label classifier, and GitHub environment. To seek generalizability, other studies need to be conducted with different projects in different domains. Moreover, all participants of this study are Brazilian, which may have introduced a cultural bias. We encourage replications of this study with participants from other countries to assess how it may affect the perception of the chatbot.

6 Conclusion

Our paper proposed a new way to interact with OSS projects. Since there are no studies evaluating chatbots in software engineering, we used the technology acceptance model to understand whether users would find it easy to use and useful. Our results showed that a chatbot could help newcomers to find their first task to work on. This is the first step towards solving this problem already discussed by the literature.

As the chatbot was perceived as easier to use, we claim that this interface would be more appropriate for the newcomers, who may find it harder to onboard with little experience with the GitHub issue tracker interface. Although we could not evidence an association between the participants' choice and their profile, we understand that having a chatbot that helps newcomers filter their interests and deliver a small number of options is a good starting point, which we also evidenced in the qualitative analysis. In short, to answer our research question, we conclude that a chatbot is as useful as the GitHub issue tracker to find a task. Still, the chatbot is easier to use, which primarily benefits the newcomers.

As a future avenue, we will use the results of the qualitative analysis to improve the chatbot design, which may lead to a new round of studies to address the problems we found and mitigate the potential biases that we missed in this research. Another potential future direction is to analyze the preference of people with different learning styles and cognitive facets and explore other aspects of the user's profiles that could influence their preference for one or another interface.

References

1. Abdellatif, A., Badran, K., Costa, D., Shihab, E.: A comparison of natural language understanding platforms for chatbots in software engineering. IEEE Trans. Softw. Eng. (2021)
2. Abdellatif, A., Badran, K., Shihab, E.: MSRBot: using bots to answer questions from software repositories. Empir. Softw. Eng. **25**(3), 1834–1863 (2020). https://doi.org/10.1007/s10664-019-09788-5
3. Balali, S., et al.: Recommending tasks to newcomers in OSS projects: how do mentors handle it? In: OpenSym 2020, pp. 1–14 (2020)
4. Barcomb, A., Stol, K., Fitzgerald, B., Riehle, D.: Managing episodic volunteers in free/libre/open source software communities. IEEE Trans. Softw. Eng. 1 (2020)
5. Brandtzaeg, P., Følstad, A.: Chatbots: changing user needs and motivations. Interactions **25**, 38–43 (2018)
6. Catania, F., Spitale, M., Cosentino, G., Garzotto, F.: Conversational agents to promote children's verbal communication skills. In: Følstad, A., et al. (eds.) CONVERSATIONS 2020. LNCS, vol. 12604, pp. 158–172. Springer, Cham (2021). https://doi.org/10.1007/978-3-030-68288-0_11

7. Christensen, R.H.B.: Ordinal–regression models for ordinal data (2019). https:// CRAN.R-project.org/package=ordinal
8. Davis, F.D.: Perceived usefulness, perceived ease of use, and user acceptance of information technology. MIS Q. **13**(3), 319–340 (1989)
9. Dominic, J., Houser, J., Steinmacher, I., Ritter, C., Rodeghero, P.: Conversational bot for newcomers onboarding to open source projects. In: BotSE 2020, pp. 46–50 (2020)
10. Faraooq, U., Grudin, J.: Human-computer integration. Interactions **23**(6), 27–32 (2016)
11. Feyer, S., Siebert, S., Gipp, B., Aizawa, A., Beel, J.: Integration of the scientific recommender system Mr. DLib into the reference manager JabRef. In: Jose, J.M., et al. (eds.) ECIR 2017. LNCS, vol. 10193, pp. 770–774. Springer, Cham (2017). https://doi.org/10.1007/978-3-319-56608-5_80
12. Fitzpatrick, K., Darcy, A., Vierhile, M.: Delivering cognitive behavior therapy to young adults with symptoms of depression and anxiety using a fully automated conversational agent (Woebot): a randomized controlled trial. JMIR Ment. Health **4**, e19 (2017)
13. Forte, A., Lampe, C.: Defining, understanding, and supporting open collaboration lessons from the literature. Am. Behav. Sci. **57**, 535–547 (2013)
14. Friedman, J., Hastie, T., Tibshirani, R.: Regularization paths for generalized linear models via coordinate descent. J. Stat. Softw. **33**(1), 1–22 (2010)
15. Grice, H.P.: Logic and conversation. In: Cole, P., Morgan, J.L. (eds.) Syntax and Semantics: Volume 3: Speech Acts, pp. 41–58. Academic Press, New York (1975)
16. Guizani, M., Steinmacher, I., Emard, J., Fallatah, A., Burnett, M., Sarma, A.: How to debug inclusivity bugs? An empirical investigation of finding-to-fixing with information architecture. Technical report, EECS, Oregon State University (2020)
17. Höhn, S., Bongard-Blanchy, K.: Heuristic evaluation of COVID-19 chatbots. In: Følstad, A., et al. (eds.) CONVERSATIONS 2020. LNCS, vol. 12604, pp. 131–144. Springer, Cham (2021). https://doi.org/10.1007/978-3-030-68288-0_9
18. JabRef: JabRef project (2019). https://jabref.org/
19. Janssen, A., Rodríguez Cardona, D., Breitner, M.H.: More than FAQ! Chatbot taxonomy for business-to-business customer services. In: Følstad, A., et al. (eds.) CONVERSATIONS 2020. LNCS, vol. 12604, pp. 175–189. Springer, Cham (2021). https://doi.org/10.1007/978-3-030-68288-0_12
20. Joho, H., Cavedon, L., Arguello, J., Shokouhi, M., Radlinski, F.: First international workshop on conversational approaches to information retrieval. SIGIR Forum **51**(3), 114–121 (2018)
21. Pazzani, M.J., Billsus, D.: Content-based recommendation systems. In: Brusilovsky, P., Kobsa, A., Nejdl, W. (eds.) The Adaptive Web. LNCS, vol. 4321, pp. 325–341. Springer, Heidelberg (2007). https://doi.org/10.1007/978-3-540-72079-9_10
22. Olsson, T., Ericsson, M., Wingkvist, A.: The relationship of code churn and architectural violations in the open source software JabRef. In: Workshop on Software Architecture Erosion and Architectural Consistency, pp. 152–158. ACM (2017)
23. Padala, S.H., et al.: How gender-biased tools shape newcomer experiences in OSS projects. IEEE Trans. Softw. Eng. (2020)
24. Romero, R., Parra, E., Haiduc, S.: Experiences building an answer bot for Gitter. In: BotSE 2020, pp. 66–70 (2020)
25. Santos, F., Wiese, I., Trinkenreich, B., Steinmacher, I., Sarma, A., Gerosa, M.A.: Can i solve it? Identifying APIs required to complete OSS tasks. IEEE Trans. Softw. Eng. 1 (2020)

26. Steinmacher, I., Conte, T., Gerosa, M.A.: Understanding and supporting the choice of an appropriate task to start with in open source software communities. In: 48th Hawaii International Conference on System Sciences, pp. 5299–5308. IEEE (2015)
27. Steinmacher, I., Conte, T.U., Redmiles, D.F., Gerosa, M.A.: Social barriers faced by newcomers placing their first contribution in open source software projects. In: ACM Conference on Computer-Supported Cooperative Work and Social Computing (CSCW 2015), pp. 1–13 (2015)
28. Steinmacher, I., Treude, C., Gerosa, M.A.: Let me in: guidelines for the successful onboarding of newcomers to open source projects. IEEE Softw. 1 (2018)
29. Storey, M.A., Zagalsky, A.: Disrupting developer productivity one bot at a time. In: Foundations of Software Engineering (FSE), pp. 928–931 (2016)
30. Strauss, A.L., Corbin, J.M.: Basics of Qualitative Research: Techniques and Procedures for Developing Grounded Theory. Sage Publications, Thousand Oaks (1998)
31. Terry, G., Hayfield, N., Clarke, V., Braun, V.: Thematic analysis. In: SAGE Handbook of Qualitative Research in Psychology, vol. 2, pp. 17–37 (2017)
32. do Nascimento Vale, L., de Almeida Maia, M.: Towards a question answering assistant for software development using a transformer-based language model. In: BotSE 2021 (2021)
33. von Krogh, G., Spaeth, S., Lakhani, K.: Community, joining, and specialization in open source software innovation: a case study. Res. Policy **32**(7), 1217–1241 (2003)
34. Wang, J., Sarma, A.: Which bug should i fix: helping new developers onboard a new project. In: 4th International Workshop on Cooperative and Human Aspects of Software Engineering, CHASE 2011, pp. 76–79 (2011)
35. Wessel, M., et al.: The power of bots: characterizing and understanding bots in OSS projects. In: ACM on Human Computer Interaction. CSCW, vol. 2, p. 182 (2018)
36. Wessel, M., Wiese, I., Steinmacher, I., Gerosa, M.A.: Don't disturb me: challenges of interacting with software bots on open source software projects. In: ACM Conference on Computer Supported Cooperative Work and Social Computing (2021)
37. Meyer von Wolff, R., Nörtemann, J., Hobert, S., Schumann, M.: Chatbots for the information acquisition at universities – a student's view on the application area. In: Følstad, A., et al. (eds.) CONVERSATIONS 2019. LNCS, vol. 11970, pp. 231–244. Springer, Cham (2020). https://doi.org/10.1007/978-3-030-39540-7_16

Incorporating Social Practices
in Dialogue Systems

Eren Yildiz$^{(\boxtimes)}$ iD, Suna Bensch iD, and Frank Dignum iD

Umeå University, Umeå, Sweden
{eyildiz,suna,dignum}@cs.umu.se

Abstract. Current dialogue management systems do not take social concepts such as norms, conventions, roles etc. into account when managing dialogues. Neither do they keep track of the personal (mental) state such as goals, needs, etc. While the data-driven approaches work quite well in some cases, they are usually domain/user dependent and not transparent. On the other hand, the rule-based methods can only work on the predefined scenarios and are not flexible in that sense. In addition, these approaches are limited to modeling only the dialogue system and do not include the human participant as part of the overall dialogue. This makes the current dialogue systems not well suited for complex and natural dialogues. In this paper, we present a dialogue management system framework that incorporates the notion of social practices as a first step to extend the type of dialogues that can be supported. The use of social practices is meant to give structure to the dialogue without restricting it to a fixed protocol. We demonstrate the use of the proposed system on a scenario between the doctor and patient roles where the doctor is a medical student and the patient is simulated by the dialogue management system.

Keywords: Dialogue systems · Social AI · Conversational AI · Social practices · Chatbots

1 Introduction

Dialogue management is a component in a dialogue system that controls the flow of conversations between the participants or actors. It decides on the next step (i.e., system response) taking into account the user utterance, user intention, current state, dialogue history, context, and purpose of the dialogue [3]. In general dialogue management systems perform a syntactic, semantic and intention analysis to determine what an utterance means and what purpose it has. The context and purpose of a dialogue are the specific settings in which a dialogue occurs, for example, sales or information gathering. They can limit the search space to those utterances, intentions, etc. that are relevant in that particular setting.

Existing approaches for dialogue management are rule based [32], machine learning based [20] or hybrid ones that combine both rule and learning

© Springer Nature Switzerland AG 2022
A. Følstad et al. (Eds.): CONVERSATIONS 2021, LNCS 13171, pp. 108–123, 2022.
https://doi.org/10.1007/978-3-030-94890-0_7

based approaches [1,16]. The machine learning and information retrieval based approaches have the disadvantage of requiring huge amounts of data sets to work [22], which is not available for domains such as doctor-patient interactions. The rule based systems are too restricting in terms of utterance-response selection. Moreover, it is difficult for the dialogue systems to manage when the utterances become more realistic and natural [30]. This is of utmost importance in many domains such as communication training, teamwork, and service provision.

In order to start supporting more natural dialogues, we should include aspects such as social conventions and knowledge (i.e., social practices). Social practices [7] belong to the foundation of natural and efficient interaction between humans and we introduce a dialogue management framework that incorporates social practices for more natural and efficient dialogue systems.

Social practices which are defined as accepted ways of doing things enclose the components of the social context [7]. Social practices not only influence but to a large degree create expectations on the character of a dialogue, in particular *what*, *when*, and *how* we say things.

Incorporating social practices allows us to build dialogue management systems that

- encode all dialogue participants' perceptions and expectations rather than only modeling the system's (i.e., Theory of Mind),
- are transparent and make it easier to find unwanted discriminatory social practices [9],
- make it possible to incorporate reasoning capabilities,
- accommodate non-identical educational or cultural backgrounds of users (e.g., utterances are influenced by the experiences and social environment),
- model the interdependence of separate aspects of social practices, which, for example, can dictate when and how to say things during a dialogue,
- explain dialogue phenomena such as turn-taking, misunderstanding or non-understandings as deviations from social practices.

We argue that the problem of generic responses and the requirement of pre-training the system can be solved to some extent by utilizing social practices. Data-driven systems are weak against new interactions since they are only trained to match the same patterns they have faced in the data. On the contrary, our system is able to deal with unexpected interactions (i.e., the ones that the DMS has not seen before), since social practices do not expect a fixed type of interaction but give handles to the dialogue system to search for an alternative one that is flexible yet still related to the practice based on the capabilities and the knowledge of the roles, available resources, personal traits of the actors, norms based on different cultures, etc. The system uses social practices to create states (i.e., slots) and rules that are loosely coupled. In general, a social practice will state that a conversation will start with a greeting, but does not prescribe exactly how the greeting is done. It also will indicate in a doctor-patient anamnesis dialogue that first the symptoms of the patient are discussed and only after that possible causes and finally the remedies are discussed. This is different than the current rule based systems where the intent extraction fills the slots that are isolated whereas in our case, the dialogue management system uses the components of social practices to have slots that are connected.

We show the validity of our ideas by implementing the proposed dialogue management system in a project with the purpose of training the communication skills of medical students with patients. The dialogue system simulates different virtual patients with whom the medical students engage in conversation. The dialogue system incorporates social practices of common doctor-patient interactions and focuses on creating challenging dialogues including a variety of patient behaviors (still fitting the practices).

The paper is organized as follows. In Sect. 2 we give an overview of other existing approaches and identify that most of the existing dialogue systems overlook to incorporate social practices. In Sect. 3 we explain in more detail social practices and in Sect. 4 we discuss how to incorporate social practices into dialogue management. We draw some conclusions about our approach in Sect. 5.

2   Related Work

First versions of the dialogue management systems were based on hand-crafted rules such as ELIZA which simulates a psychotherapist [29], PARRY which acts like a paranoid patient, and ALICE which uses pattern-matching algorithms to generate a response. The rule-based systems utilized variations of Markov decision processes [12,31] to track the states of dialogue and generate responses more accurately, which were then succeeded by the recent neural network models that are often called neural belief tracking systems [20,21,23]. Although they perform well in some contexts [8], due to the black-box nature of neural models, the intentions of users are not interpretable and become vague behind the deep neural layers. Generic responses such as "I don't know", or "Okay" are still common in these systems and remain a challenge [25,27,28]. Furthermore, data-driven approaches require a large set of data [4] to work, and even then, responses of these chatbots are too general despite the recent work on speaker consistency and meaningful responses [13–15].

In recent studies, it has become apparent that social intelligence is needed to have engaging dialogues [6]. There were various attempts to construct social intelligence for robots. For example, in order to make users feel comfortable and trust the robot, social talk (i.e., small talk) can be used [2] by utilizing specific dialogue acts and sequences [10]. In another related work, researchers synthesized speech cues to dialogues such as; filled pauses, word repetitions, silences, explicit acknowledgments [19], and with different social cues such as; greetings, self-disclosure elicitation, self-disclosure, suggestions, general statement, simple yes/no answers, acknowledgments, praises, and terminations [11] with the aim of improving the naturalness of the dialogues for more social conversations. In addition, researchers also use the terminology trust and rapport alongside social dialogues. For example, one of the previous works found that social dialogues can help with recovering from agents' conversational mistakes if it is designed carefully [18]. In another work, researchers investigated the effects of the culture of social dialogue's capability of mitigating trust loss when the agents make errors [17]. Their results showed that culture has crucial role on repairing trust and social dialogue can mitigate the negative effects of conversational errors depending on the culture.

The previous works on social dialogues (i.e., socially aware dialogues) accumulated mainly around *enhancing* the dialogues by either adding some rules or cues to them. These approaches are not based on any sociological theory which makes them very specific and context-dependent solutions. In order to have social dialogues, we first need to understand how conversations really work. For example, in [5], conversations are defined as socially joint activities (i.e., joint projects) where joint action is performed by one actor and taken up by the others. Social practices which are defined as accepted ways of doing things that are routinized over time [24] encapsulate this definition and extend it to include various other social concepts such as norms and conventions.

3   Extending the Dialogue Management Systems

Social practices consist of both physical and mental routinized activities which are performed between participating actors in a specific context [24]. They are the patterns we apply in our daily lives [7].

For example, when we go to the hospital when we get sick is a social practice. Firstly, we check ourselves on whether we really feel bad enough to need to go to the hospital. If the pain does not go away, we leave the house and either call a taxi or drive by ourselves if the pain is manageable. Then we tell our problem to the hospital receptionist and wait for our turn. Finally, we enter the doctor's office and explain to her our problem. Although different actions can be taken (e.g., calling a taxi or driving by ourselves), overall the pattern of the social practice would be the same. The power of the social practice is, it does not only give the necessary information to perform a sequence but also grants the flexibility that is necessary to handle unexpected and unknown events when they occur. For instance, for the same social practice, a person without a driving license would consider taking different paths because he cannot drive.

We use the formalized version of a social practice [7] for dialogue systems which explains each component of social practice in detail. These components are as follows:

- **Context** is composed of *roles, actors, resources, affordances, places, time*
  - *Roles* define the type of actor that is necessary to deliberate about expectations
  - *Actors* are the participating humans and agents who fulfill the roles in the interaction that is specific to the social practice they are being part of
  - *Resources* are the objects used in the interaction
  - *Affordances* are the features that allow certain resources to be used interchangeably in a specific context
  - *Places* are the locations where the social practice happens or are related to it

- *Time* is the component that provides temporal information about the social practice
- **Meaning** is composed of *purpose, promoted values*, and *counts-as*
  - *Purpose* is the component that indicates the state wanted to be achieved with the social practice
  - *Promoted values* is the component that highlights the values which can be promoted or demoted by certain actions of the actors.
  - *Counts-as* are the relations that connects certain speech acts to other acts by the actions of actors.
- **Expectations** is composed of *plan patterns, norms, strategies, start condition*, and *end condition*
  - *Plan patterns* are the action patterns that are expected to occur in the practice with a particular order
  - *Norms* are the deontic rules of obligations, prohibitions, and permissions
  - *Strategies* are the triggers that start certain action sequences for interaction without having an explicit thought behind
  - *Start condition* is the condition of the states where the scenario is ready to start
  - *End condition* or duration is the component that indicates in which conditions the social practice ends. It can be either temporal (e.g., 10 min, 2 h, etc.) or static (e.g., the fire alarm went off) values
- **Activities** is composed of *possible actions*, and *competences*
  - *Possible Actions* are both verbal and non-verbal actions that often occur during the social practice
  - *Competences* are the skills that the actors are expected to have in order to perform certain actions

In the following sections, we describe what each of these components encapsulate in an interaction and explain how the dialogue management system we propose utilizes it.

3.1   Context

Context provides the necessary information about the materials of the social practice. It has *roles, actors, resources, affordances, places*, and *time*.

Roles come with predefined sets of expected actions. The role of the user defines the general goal of the role, its norms, and other behaviours that we expect to see in that role. E.g., we expect the doctor (i.e., one of the roles of the social practice) to know about medical practices. Our proposed dialogue management system uses this information to parse the utterances from the dialogue based on the roles as some of the actions are expected to occur (e.g., CHECK ("eye") from the doctor role, SIT (place = "chair") from the patient role). Moreover, the roles information also allows the dialogue management system to track the flow of dialogue as there are expected set of action sequences from each role. E.g., the dialogue system expects the doctor to calm the patient down after the patient starts worrying about something.

Actors is used to track the specifics of the actor in the dialogue system. E.g., if an actor is a human, the dialogue management system stores information about this actor such as; sex, age, personal goals, beliefs, etc. This information is used to track expectations in a scenario where an actor may perform an action that does not come from its role. E.g., a patient may be uncooperative and therefore may not follow the directives of the doctor. If the actor data is hidden to the dialogue management system (e.g., when parsing from a new scenario), instead of breaking apart, the proposed dialogue management system allows agents to take different (i.e., unseen) routes in a scenario. This is one of the benefits of using social practices in dialogue management systems as it does not strictly follow a set of rules but uses handles that are provided by social practices to keep continue doing its tasks. This means that the actors are not forced to follow the rules of their roles but may perform different actions which are based on their beliefs and personal goals.

Resources are the objects used in the interaction like a chair to sit or a medical tool to check the patient's eye. Every social practice has a unique set of resources that are relevant to that particular social practice. Every actor in the interaction has different types of access to resources at certain times. E.g., medical tools are only accessible to the doctor, and only after the patient has presented his problem. The dialogue management system uses this component to have expectations of which resources may be used with the combination of what actions in which phases and creates the repository of available objects for each agent.

Affordances component is used, for example, when the doctor uses an "oph-thalmoscope", the dialogue management system can parse the resource as a "medical tool" because it affords to be a medical tool. The affordances compo-nent of a social practice especially helps to build diverse dialogues and make them parsable since the system does not look for a specific resource but an affordance of a resource.

Places component is used by the dialogue management system to know whether the actors are in the expected places during the interaction at certain times. E.g., it is expected to see the patient sit on the chair (i.e., one of the places) during the first phase (i.e., opening phase) and then switch to the exam-ination chair (i.e., one of the places) during the physical examination phase. This component also provides information about which resources are expected to be used at which places.

Time component is used by the dialogue management system to handle the expectations of the time-specific interactions (e.g., the doctor expects to check the patient's eye not more than 5 min) and the expected duration of the phases are expected to happen at certain times (e.g., it is expected move on to problem presentation phase after 2 min maximum which is enough for the opening phase to be completed).

3.2 Meaning

Meaning is about how we perceive the social practice, i.e., how the social practice functions as intermediation between the participants. It describes the role of the practice. E.g., doctors wearing white coats and sitting behind a desk give them a place of authority, which makes it easier to accept their judgement and advice. It has *purpose*, *promoted values*, and *counts-as* components.

Purpose is used by the dialogue management system to look into the states of the actors to check whether the social practice has already finished and the goals are accomplished. E.g., for the doctor's visit (i.e., social practice) to end as expected; (i) the patient has to know the name of his problem, (ii) the reason why it has happened, and (iii) what is the treatment for it. Knowing the purposes of the social practice, the dialogue management system can check at every step whether the purpose is still achievable or is already achieved. E.g., if the patient has a serious problem that cannot be treated at the current hospital due to lack of medical expertise, then the purpose of knowing the treatment will never be achieved, thus the possible actions of the actors will change accordingly in a way that the system will no longer expect to see the actions related to previously achievable phases. The dialogue management system that utilizes social practices can create different plans which aim to reach the new purpose and expect to see the actions which align with it. Moreover, the purpose of a social practice does not necessarily have to be the same as the goals of the actors. For example, while it is expected to see a patient goes to the hospital to get treatment, it is also possible that the patient might have a different goal like wanting to get a prescription for antibiotics. This means that the purposes of actors may differ from the purposes of the social practice, and the dialogue management system can use this information to create new plans and thus expect different action sequences throughout the dialogue.

Promoted Values component exists in the dialogue management system to handle the unexpected interactions. For instance, patients are expected to wait for their turn in the waiting room. Any patient who does not follow this rule (e.g., cutting in line) would face its consequences like getting a warning. Here, the dialogue management system keeps track of the values such as *courtesy* in the aforementioned example which is *demoted* due to the patient's action. The dialogue management system we propose keeps track of not only the values themselves but also *when* and *how* they are promoted or demoted. This makes it possible for the dialogue management system to create a different set of expectations which enables continuous monitoring of the dialogue. Promoted values in this case help the dialogue management system to handle the unexpected interactions by adapting the system to the new plan accordingly.

Counts-As component makes it possible for the dialogue management system to refer one interaction to others that are based on the same intention and meaning. E.g., the patient nodding counts as acknowledging the doctor's speech whereas the doctor nodding counts as showing that the patient is being listened to. These links allow our proposed dialogue management system to be flexible when parsing and monitoring the dialogue as the system treats different interactions equally which perform the same task in the same context.

3.3   Expectations

Expectations hold the necessary information about the sequential behaviours and their conditions of social practice. The relevant components are *plan patterns*, *norms*, *strategies*, *start condition*, and *duration*.

Plan Patterns component helps with managing the phases and the expected actions for each interaction. For example, in a typical doctor's visit the phases are; opening, problem presentation, history taking, physical examination, diagnosis, treatment and recommendations, and closing [26]. In this social practice, each phase yields different plans and thus interaction sets. The dialogue management system uses this information to prioritize the relevant interactions over others while parsing and monitoring the dialogue. For instance, in the doctor's visit social practice, the dialogue management system expects to see introductory interactions at the greeting phase and valedictory interactions at the closing phase. Plan patterns also serve as back-chain planning in a way that it sets up the expectancy of the dialogue management system for the most favourable outcome (i.e., purpose or desired state) before the plan is initiated.

Norms should be performed by its actor in its relevant phase and role. Otherwise, it will be a violation and would result in either punishment or reconsideration of the interaction. Punishment happens when the actor unreasonably does not perform the expected action, and thus gets an unfavourable outcome as a result. On the other hand, if the actor has a good reason for not executing the norm, then it triggers the reconsideration of the interaction. E.g., it is expected that the patient follows the doctor's directives. If the patient violates this norm, for example, the patient does not listen to the doctor telling him to stop touching the medical tools, then the punishment for this particular norm would be the doctor calling the security to deal with the patient's vulgar behaviour. On the other hand, if the patient has a good reason to violate this norm such as being deaf, instead of punishing the patient for it, the doctor will reconsider her action to accommodate the patient's disability such as approaching the patient with a physical language (i.e., gestures and facial expressions). This also means that there are certain actions that are either permitted or forbidden to be executed by the actors of the practice at the specific times of each plan. E.g., the norm "Doctor notifies the patient before having physical contact with him" is permitted to be executed by the doctor only at the physical examination phase. If the doctor is to perform this norm in the *opening phase*, for example, it is necessary to interpret the action differently (e.g., the patient may need the doctor's assistance to sit on a chair). The permitting and the forbidding features of the norms create handles for the dialogue management system so that it does not fall apart when an unexpected event happens. It uses all of this information to set up the expected interactions set of the actors.

Strategies component is used in the dialogue management system to set rules for basic interactions that always occur when they are triggered. For instance, when a person calls someone and says *hello*, the other person would reply with *hello* immediately without thinking. Strategies serve as basic dialogue building blocks and combined with other action sequences like norms, they complete the dialogue. There are different strategies planned for each phase and they are only triggered when certain conditions are met. This means that not every single strategy needs to happen in the dialogue but they are always triggered when their conditions are met. Unlike norms, strategies do not have any violation rules since they are always executed when triggered.

Start Condition component describes a condition or a set of conditions that are necessary for the dialogue to start. It uses resources, actors, roles and other components that are available.

End Condition component signals dialogue management system that the scenario is expected to be finished.

3.4   Activities

Activities give us the repository of available actors' actions. It has *possible actions*, and *competences*.

Possible Actions is the repository of actions for the actors. Basically, this repository is checked when a plan has to be made to execute (parts of) the social practice and it is used to generate expected actions from other participants.

Competences component in the dialogue management system provides crucial information about the roles' and actors' skills which consist of abilities (e.g., the doctor can use the medical tools) and knowledge (e.g., the doctor knows eye disorders).

4   Exemplifying the Usage

In this section, we briefly describe the example scenario first and then explain the settings for the dialogue management system before the scenario starts and how it is used in the example scenario.

4.1   An Example Scenario with Alternative Dialogues

The following scenario takes place between a patient who seeks treatment for his eye problem and a doctor who is responsible of treating the patient's problem and informing him about the problem. The social practice of "doctor's visit" starts from the point that the patient enters the doctor's office and continues until the patient leaves. Due to the page limits, we only share a part of the dialogue in Fig. 1, its alternative version in Fig. 2, and its states in Fig. 3. We discuss how the dialogue management system handles the flow of the dialogue for that part specifically in the following subsections.

(1) **Patient**: Ah, my eye burns very bad doctor.

(2) **Doctor**: That sounds painful. Let me see.

(3) **Doctor**: When did it start?

(4) **Patient**: Last night. I could not sleep from the pain.

(5) **Doctor**: Hm hmm.

(6) **Patient**: I mean, I was able to still sleep but it wasn't comfortable.

(7) **Doctor**: Why is that so?

(8) **Patient**: Because it kept getting watery.

(9) **Patient**: Has it ever happened to you, doctor?

(10) **Doctor**: Don't worry.

(11) **Doctor**: It isn't uncommon to see that in the spring season.

Fig. 1. A part of the dialogue between the patient Alex and the doctor Helena from the doctor's visit social practice where the patient is **cooperative** and **calm**

In the first dialogue presented in Fig. 1, the patient Alex is a calm person and follows the doctor's directives. The patient reveals some of his symptoms during the dialogue and the doctor acknowledges them by sympathizing with the patient's pain (i.e., that sounds painful) or back-channelling (i.e., by saying hm hmm). The dialogue in Fig. 1 starts with the problem presentation phase (lines 1–2) and quickly moves to history taking phase (lines 2–11) shown in Fig. 1 where the doctor asks questions about the patient's problem. The doctor Helena tries to create a comfortable environment for the patient by letting him talk and taking the passive role in the interaction by mostly listening to what the patient has to say about his problem. This encourages the patient to share more about his eye problem and results in revealing more symptoms of it. At the end of the dialogue, the patient asks the doctor whether she has experienced the same eye disorder before (line 9). The doctor acknowledges the patient's statement but does not answer the question that is directed to her (lines 10–11). Instead, she shares general information about the eye disorder to make the patient feel that the problem is not to be worried about. If the doctor were to answer this question (line 9), it might give a wrong impression to the patient, or the patient may think that it is okay to have certain things because his doctor has it too. The medical social practice here highlights that the doctor's action of keeping her personal life to herself promotes the value *professionalism* in Fig. 3 and therefore the dialogue continues to reach the most favourable outcome as expected.

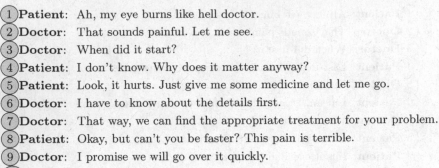

1 Patient: Ah, my eye burns like hell doctor.

2 Doctor: That sounds painful. Let me see.

3 Doctor: When did it start?

4 Patient: I don't know. Why does it matter anyway?

5 Patient: Look, it hurts. Just give me some medicine and let me go.

6 Doctor: I have to know about the details first.

7 Doctor: That way, we can find the appropriate treatment for your problem.

8 Patient: Okay, but can't you be faster? This pain is terrible.

9 Doctor: I promise we will go over it quickly.

10 Doctor: Now tell me please, when did it start?

11 Patient: Last night.

Fig. 2. A part of the dialogue between the patient Jack and the doctor Helena from the doctor's visit social practice where the patient is **uncooperative** and **impatient**

In the second dialogue shared in Fig. 2, the patient Jack is an uneasy person and does not want to bother with the whole process of the treatment. He aims to get a prescription for a medicine that will ease the pain of his eye. The doctor starts speaking the same as in the first dialogue but changes the way she talks after recognizing the patient's unorthodox goal and his uncooperative behavior (lines 4–5) shown in Fig. 2. In order to cope with the situation, the doctor explains that she needs to more about the patient's problem first before prescribing a medicine for his treatment if it is necessary (lines 6–7). The patient understands that the doctor has to follow certain procedures first to grant his desire and asks for quicker treatment (line 8). The doctor acknowledges the patient's request, finds it reasonable, and informs the patient that she will be faster (lines 9–10). At the end of the dialogue, we see that the patient starts answering the doctor's questions again (line 11).

4.2   Setting up the System for the Scenario

In this section, we explain how the dialogue management system is configured before the scenario starts. In Fig. 3 we show how all the aspects of the social practice are filled in. Note that the aspects in the dialogue management system are not configured for the example scenarios only, but overall for the social practice of *doctor's visit*. This shows that the proposed system is not only capable of managing a single scenario but many other possible ones as well. Note that the social practice does not contain information about the actual actors of a scenario. That information is kept by the dialogue management system in an actor base and merged with the social practice information whenever it is known that a particular actor plays one of the roles of the practice.

The active roles of the social practice which are the *doctor* and the *patient* are selected. The actors for each role, Alex for the patient and Helena for the

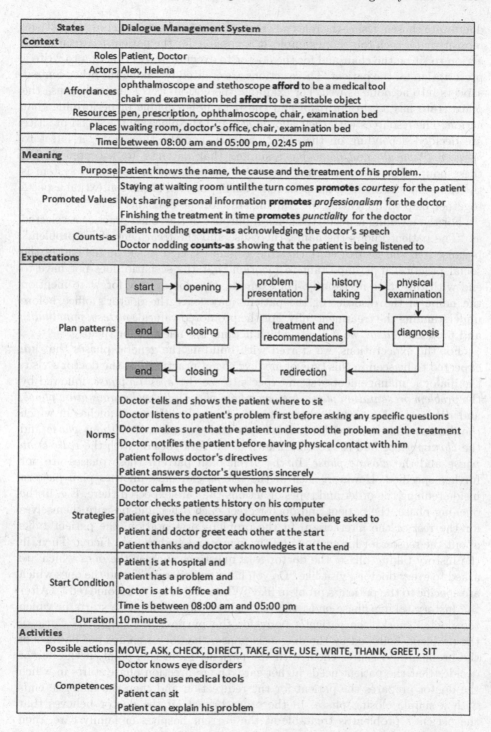

States	Dialogue Management System
Context	
Roles	Patient, Doctor
Actors	Alex, Helena
Affordances	ophthalmoscope and stethoscope **afford** to be a medical tool chair and examination bed **afford** to be a sittable object
Resources	pen, prescription, ophthalmoscope, chair, examination bed
Places	waiting room, doctor's office, chair, examination bed
Time	between 08:00 am and 05:00 pm, 02:45 pm
Meaning	
Purpose	Patient knows the name, the cause and the treatment of his problem.
Promoted Values	Staying at waiting room until the turn comes **promotes** *courtesy* for the patient Not sharing personal information **promotes** *professionalism* for the doctor Finishing the treatment in time **promotes** *punctiality* for the doctor
Counts-as	Patient nodding **counts-as** acknowledging the doctor's speech Doctor nodding **counts-as** showing that the patient is being listened to
Expectations	
Plan patterns	*[flowchart: start → opening → problem presentation → history taking → physical examination; physical examination → diagnosis → treatment and recommendations → closing → end; diagnosis → redirection → closing → end]*
Norms	Doctor tells and shows the patient where to sit Doctor listens to patient's problem first before asking any specific questions Doctor makes sure that the patient understood the problem and the treatment Doctor notifies the patient before having physical contact with him Patient follows doctor's directives Patient answers doctor's questions sincerely
Strategies	Doctor calms the patient when he worries Doctor checks patients history on his computer Patient gives the necessary documents when being asked to Patient and doctor greet each other at the start Patient thanks and doctor acknowledges it at the end
Start Condition	Patient is at hospital and Patient has a problem and Doctor is at his office and Time is between 08:00 am and 05:00 pm
Duration	10 minutes
Activities	
Possible actions	MOVE, ASK, CHECK, DIRECT, TAKE, GIVE, USE, WRITE, THANK, GREET, SIT
Competences	Doctor knows eye disorders Doctor can use medical tools Patient can sit Patient can explain his problem

Fig. 3. The aspects of a dialogue management system that incorporates social practices

doctor are chosen. Using the roles we create the first subset of the possible actions repository for each role. For example, it is possible for the patient to execute *SIT* action to sit on the chair and for the doctor to execute *WRITE* action to write a prescription for the patient. These actions are created by taking the other context aspects into account as well. For example, the action *WAIT* exists because the place state has a *waiting room* and the patient is capable of performing that action. The resources with their affordances and the places of the social practice are decided depending on the social practice. For the time state, it is set to *between 08:00 am and 05:00 pm* assuming that patients are accepted during these hours. The other time state used by the dialogue management system is the time that the scenario happens (e.g., 02:45 pm). All of the contextual aspects together help with creating the starting state of the dialogue.

For the meaning aspects, the general purpose of the social practice is selected as "The patient knows the name, the cause and the treatment of his problem" because it is the *desired state* that the system expects to see at the end of the social practice. It is important to mention that the scenario does not have to end with this state necessarily. For example, the doctor may forget to mention the name of the disorder or the patient may leave the doctor's office before understanding the treatment fully. For the promoted values *courtesy*, *punctuality* and *professionalism*, we indicate which actions are relevant for them.

For the expectations, we started with building the general phases that are expected to be seen in this type of medical social practice. For the doctor's visit, the dialogue management system expects to see the *opening phase*, followed by the *problem presentation phase, history taking phase, physical examination phase*, and *diagnosis phase* which then might fork into 2 different branches in which the first one continues with the *treatment and the recommendations phase* and the *closing phase* and the second branch of the fork goes on with the *redirection phase* and the *closing phase*. In the given plan pattern these phases are not further specified. However, each of the blocks can have another plan pattern inside refining the order and types of actions that are expected there. E.g. in the opening phase, the patient and doctor greet each other and prepare themselves for the rest of the interaction. In the problem presentation, the patient talks about the reason for his coming and the symptoms he has been facing. Then, in the history taking phase, the doctor asks questions such as the ones which are asked to every doctor's visit like "Do you have any allergies?" and the ones which are specific to the patient's problem like "When did your eye become red?". After the history taking phase ends, the physical examination phase starts in which the doctor checks the patient's body for the purpose of finding the cause of the problem. Followed by the diagnosis phase, the doctor shares her findings of the problem and shares them with the patient. From this point, if the doctor decides that the patient needs higher care, the redirection phase starts in which the doctor prepares the patient for the redirection and then the dialogue ends with a simple closing phase. In the other branch, if the doctor believes that the patient's problem is treatable at the current hospital or family care, then the doctor explains the treatment to the patient. The patient also may ask for possible changes in the treatment due to his lifestyle (e.g., the patient is a night worker and cannot take drugs in the morning as he sleeps during that time). After both the patient and the doctor agree on the treatment, the social practice ends with the closing phase. In each phase, actors are expected to conform to certain norms and strategies which are specific to that phase. For example, the norm "doctor tells and shows the patient where to sit" only happens in the *opening phase* explicitly. The expected norms and strategies also determine which actions are expected to be used with the combination of which context states. E.g., the resource *ophthalmoscope* can be used in the *CHECK* action by Helena who is the doctor during the physical examination phase.

For the activities, we listed the possible capabilities and knowledge as competences which are the requirements for the roles to be able to perform a certain action. For example, the capability of using the medical tools belongs to the doctor role. As for the knowledge part of the competences, it is a requirement for the doctor to know the eye disorders to fulfill the role. Therefore, the requirements which are expected from the roles are written in this state.

It is important to mention that the aspects which the proposed dialogue system uses for management are interconnected. Therefore, when we design the dialogue management system using social practices, we take all of its components into account at the same time.

5   Discussion and Conclusion

In this paper, we introduced a dialogue management system that incorporates social practices and uses their components to manage the dialogue states. Each component captures a different aspect of the dialogue yet they are interconnected under the same practice which allows the dialogue management system to deal with unexpected interactions. Our proposed dialogue management system has the advantage over traditional rule-based systems by not strictly expecting one interaction, but having the repository of possible interactions that are transparent both in the selection and the utilization processes meaning that the system knows why and how they are used. Moreover, our system also puts the model of the other persons into the deliberation process. In contrast to other studies where the focus is solely on enhancing the dialogue by adding various rules, our system is based on a sociological theory (i.e., Social Practice Theory) and aims to add a deliberation process that deals with human behavior. This means that it is possible to use our system alongside others to achieve social dialogues. For example, for the slot-filling approach where each slot (i.e., state) represents a certain value in the dialogue such as location or room number, our system can add social slots such as norms, conventions, rituals, etc. to track the social behavior of the actors. As the chatbots are used in a domain that is known to its developers, some of these social slots can be configured before the dialogue begins. Furthermore, more social slots can be created dynamically (i.e., during the dialogue) based on, for example, the definition of norms. For data-driven approaches, our system can be used to annotate the data using the components of social practices. We believe that the presented framework will be useful for the implementation of not only the medical chatbots but all socially aware chatbots as the components of the social practices such as norms, competences, etc. can be transferred to other cases.

References

1. Andrew, G., Gao, J.: Scalable training of L1-regularized log-linear models. In: Proceedings of the 24th International Conference on Machine Learning, pp. 33–40 (2007)
2. Bickmore, T., Cassell, J.: How about this weather? Social dialogue with embodied conversational agents. In: Proceedings of the AAAI Fall Symposium on Socially Intelligent Agents (2000)
3. Chen, H., Liu, X., Yin, D., Tang, J.: A survey on dialogue systems: recent advances and new frontiers. ACM SIGKDD Explor. Newsl. **19**(2), 25–35 (2017)
4. Chizhik, A., Zherebtsova, Y.: Challenges of building an intelligent chatbot. In: IMS, pp. 277–287 (2020)
5. Clark, H.H.: Using Language. Cambridge University Press, Cambridge (1996)
6. Dautenhahn, K.: Socially intelligent robots: dimensions of human-robot interaction. Philos. Trans. Royal Soc. B Biol. Sci. **362**(1480), 679–704 (2007)
7. Dignum, F.: Interactions as social practices: towards a formalization. arXiv preprint arXiv:1809.08751 (2018)
8. Goel, R., Paul, S., Hakkani-Tür, D.: Hyst: A hybrid approach for flexible and accurate dialogue state tracking. arXiv preprint arXiv:1907.00883 (2019)
9. Hellström, T., Dignum, V., Bensch, S.: Bias in machine learning - what is it good for? In: Proceedings of the First International Workshop on New Foundations for Human-Centered AI (NeHuAI) co-located with 24th European Conference on Artificial Intelligence (ECAI 2020). CEUR Workshop Proceedings, vol. 2659, pp. 3–10 (2020)
10. Klüwer, T.: "I Like Your Shirt" - dialogue acts for enabling social talk in conversational agents. In: Vilhjálmsson, H.H., Kopp, S., Marsella, S., Thórisson, K.R. (eds.) IVA 2011. LNCS (LNAI), vol. 6895, pp. 14–27. Springer, Heidelberg (2011). https://doi.org/10.1007/978-3-642-23974-8_2
11. Lee, H., Lee, S.Y., Choi, J., Sung, J.E., Lim, H., Lim, Y.: Analyzing the rules of social dialogue and building a social dialogue model in human-robot interaction
12. Levin, E., Pieraccini, R., Eckert, W.: Using Markov decision process for learning dialogue strategies. In: Proceedings of the 1998 IEEE International Conference on Acoustics, Speech and Signal Processing, ICASSP 1998 (Cat. No. 98CH36181), vol. 1, pp. 201–204. IEEE (1998)
13. Li, J., Galley, M., Brockett, C., Gao, J., Dolan, B.: A diversity-promoting objective function for neural conversation models. arXiv preprint arXiv:1510.03055 (2015)
14. Li, J., Galley, M., Brockett, C., Spithourakis, G.P., Gao, J., Dolan, B.: A persona-based neural conversation model. arXiv preprint arXiv:1603.06155 (2016)
15. Li, J., Monroe, W., Ritter, A., Galley, M., Gao, J., Jurafsky, D.: Deep reinforcement learning for dialogue generation. arXiv preprint arXiv:1606.01541 (2016)
16. Lison, P.: A hybrid approach to dialogue management based on probabilistic rules. Comput. Speech Lang. **34**(1), 232–255 (2015)
17. Lucas, G.M., et al.: Culture, errors, and rapport-building dialogue in social agents. In: Proceedings of the 18th International Conference on Intelligent Virtual Agents, pp. 51–58 (2018)

18. Lucas, G.M., et al.: Getting to know each other: the role of social dialogue in recovery from errors in social robots. In: Proceedings of the 2018 ACM/IEEE International Conference on Human-Robot Interaction, pp. 344–351 (2018)

19. Marge, M., Miranda, J., Black, A.W., Rudnicky, A.: Towards improving the naturalness of social conversations with dialogue systems. In: Proceedings of the SIGDIAL 2010 Conference, pp. 91–94 (2010)

20. Mrkšić, N., Séaghdha, D.O., Wen, T.H., Thomson, B., Young, S.: Neural belief tracker: data-driven dialogue state tracking. arXiv preprint arXiv:1606.03777 (2016)

21. Mrkšić, N., Vulić, I.: Fully statistical neural belief tracking. arXiv preprint arXiv:1805.11350 (2018)

22. Prakash, A., Brockett, C., Agrawal, P.: Emulating human conversations using convolutional neural network-based IR. arXiv preprint arXiv:1606.07056 (2016)

23. Ramadan, O., Budzianowski, P., Gašić, M.: Large-scale multi-domain belief tracking with knowledge sharing. arXiv preprint arXiv:1807.06517 (2018)

24. Reckwitz, A.: Toward a theory of social practices: a development in culturalist theorizing. Eur. J. Soc. Theory 5(2), 243–263 (2002)

25. Serban, I., Sordoni, A., Bengio, Y., Courville, A., Pineau, J.: Building end-to-end dialogue systems using generative hierarchical neural network models. In: Proceedings of the AAAI Conference on Artificial Intelligence, vol. 30 (2016)

26. Sidnell, J., Stivers, T.: The Handbook of Conversation Analysis, vol. 121. Wiley, New York (2012)

27. Sordoni, A., et al.: A neural network approach to context-sensitive generation of conversational responses. arXiv preprint arXiv:1506.06714 (2015)

28. Vinyals, O., Le, Q.: A neural conversational model. arXiv preprint arXiv:1506.05869 (2015)

29. Weizenbaum, J.: Eliza-a computer program for the study of natural language communication between man and machine. Commun. ACM 9(1), 36–45 (1966)

30. Williams, J.D.: Web-style ranking and SLU combination for dialog state tracking. In: Proceedings of the 15th Annual Meeting of the Special Interest Group on Discourse and Dialogue (SIGDIAL), pp. 282–291 (2014)

31. Williams, J.D., Young, S.: Partially observable Markov decision processes for spoken dialog systems. Comput. Speech Lang. 21(2), 393–422 (2007)

32. Young, S., Gašić, M., Thomson, B., Williams, J.D.: POMDP-based statistical spoken dialog systems: a review. Proc. IEEE 101(5), 1160–1179 (2013)

Socially Aware Interactions: From Dialogue Trees to Natural Language Dialogue Systems

Inês Lobo[1]([⊠]), Diogo Rato[1], Rui Prada[1], and Frank Dignum[2]

[1] INESC-ID and Instituto Superior Técnico, University of Lisbon, Lisbon, Portugal
{ines.lobo,diogo.rato,rui.prada}@tecnico.ulisboa.pt
[2] Umeå University, Umeå, Sweden
dignum@cs.umu.se

Abstract. In this paper, we present a prototype of a human-agent dialogue system, in which the scenarios are easy-to-author, as in tree-based dialogue tools. These, however, only allow for scripted and restricted dialogues. For this reason, we focused on developing a flexible and robust deliberation mechanism as well, based on the Cognitive Social Frames model and the theory of social practices, so that the conversational agent could provide acceptable responses according to different social contexts. Having access to sequences of frames containing small dialogue trees, the agent activates the most salient frame to reply appropriately to the user's input. As a proof of concept, we designed a medical diagnosis scenario between a doctor and a patient in which the agent could play both roles given different settings of the scenario. In this prototype, the user had to choose from a limited set of alternatives, based on the current context, in order to respond to the agent; however, in the future, we intend to allow users to write freely, expecting to be able to map their utterances to the appropriate context.

Keywords: Conversational agent · Context-aware dialogue · Social context · Dialogue authoring · Dialogue training · Medical diagnosis

1 Introduction

There is a growing demand for realistic social behaviour of agent systems in a variety of computational fields [7]. In this document, we will focus on dialogue systems. These systems should be aware of their social context in order to cooperate effectively with humans and other AI systems, meaning that social aspects of the context should be considered to manage interactions between these systems and other entities. This will allow for an efficient and focused dialogue aimed towards a specific goal that is endorsed by all participants of a given interaction.

In tree-based dialogue tools, the social context is taken into consideration solely through the authors of the dialogue, meaning that the conversation lacks flexibility. For instance, the Dialogue Trainer software[1] is a system that allows

---

[1] https://www.dialoguetrainer.com/en.

A. Følstad et al. (Eds.): CONVERSATIONS 2021, LNCS 13171, pp. 124–140, 2022.
https://doi.org/10.1007/978-3-030-94890-0_8

for authoring very simple yet directed dialogues, with limited choices available, to train medical students throughout the process of an anamnesis. In this tool, the responses of the conversational agent are scripted by an author in a large dialogue tree, so the agent does not need to adapt to changes in the context, displaying a restrictive and unrealistic behaviour [17]. Natural language dialogue systems, on the other hand, are flexible and capable of managing user errors, but their authoring mechanisms are typically not intuitive or general enough, preventing authors from easily configuring dialogue data for different settings. With this in mind, we would like to address the following research question:

Is it feasible to create a flexible and robust dialogue system that adapts to changes in the social context, while maintaining the authoring property of tree-based dialogue tools?

Our main goal will be to find a middle ground between the identified dialogue systems or tools, in order to model and develop a system that meets the requirements of flexibility, robustness and authoring. Then, we will be required to use the social context to manage a dialogue between a user and an artificial agent, based on defined social practices and identities, norms, conventions and values. This will enable us to build flexible and robust dialogue management systems that take the human as a starting point and that are necessary to create a human-based user interface. Moreover, we will have to ensure that the authoring property of the system is maintained, since it is essential for the quick set up of the domain knowledge and resources required to support the agent.

Considering the prior statements, we designed and implemented a dialogue system's software prototype based on the Cognitive Social Frames model [12], as well as the theory of social practices [13]. The key contribution of our work was how we decided to organize the data in the system to enable authorable socially-aware dialogues. We attempted to make it intuitive, controllable and general, so that dialogue scenarios could be easy-to-author and, simultaneously, be given as input to a conversational agent that deliberates and exhibits an appropriate behaviour according to different social contexts. These could vary based on location, time, conversation state, type of relation, and many other factors. For example, it could be as simple as saying "good morning" or "good afternoon" depending on the time of the day, or, in an anamnesis setting, being more formal to an unfamiliar doctor as opposed to being more friendly to a doctor the agent already knows and trusts. Additionally, we selected Twine[2], a widely known authoring tool, to configure the dialogue scenarios of the system. Finally, we defined a medical diagnosis scenario to demonstrate how the system operated.

2   Background

The human-agent interaction field, where agents should operate as partners to humans, as well as serious games and social simulations, all require more believable social behaviour of agent systems [7].

---

[2] https://twinery.org/.

Dignum et al. [7] proposed five key ingredients to generate realistic social behaviour in agents: social motives, identity, skills, values and social reality. In essence, social agents should have personal goals and preferences, while abiding by the norms and values of the social group to which they belong. Moreover, they should have their own knowledge and beliefs about the world, as well as the ability to recognize and understand other agents. Given these components, the main idea is to design believable social agents that have sociality at the centre of their reasoning, rather than simply adding "a few social modules" to their architectures.

We will start this section by outlining the social context and its dimensions. Following that, we will introduce social theories based on social identities and practices, which support the development of agents that adapt to the social context. Additionally, we will go over a few models and architectures inspired by these theories, culminating in a section on the Cognitive Social Frames model.

2.1 Social Context

Dey reviewed former attempts of defining context within the field of computer science, finding that previous definitions were extremely challenging to apply in the context-aware computing area [5]. As a result, Dey proposed a generally accepted definition of context, aiming to help software developers easily outline the context for a specific application scenario:

> "Context is any information that can be used to characterise the situation of an entity. An entity is a person, place, or object that is considered relevant to the interaction between a user and an application, including the user and applications themselves."

Zimmermann et al. found the prior definition to be too general, deciding to enclose this same concept "by a formal and an operational part" [20]. In regards to its formal extension, they identified five fundamental categories to classify the context information:

– **Individuality**: Includes the characteristics of the entity to which the context is associated.
– **Activity**: Entails the entity's current and future goals, tasks and actions. Tasks are goal-oriented and can comprise operation sequences with concrete goals.
– **Location**: Describes an entity's physical or virtual location, and other spatial details, such as speed and orientation.
– **Time**: Describes an entity's time information, like the user's time zone, the current time, any virtual time, time intervals, and so on.
– **Relations**: Depicts the relations of an entity with other entities. Depending on the relation, each entity plays a particular role.

In terms of the context's operational extension, Zimmermann et al. highlighted its dynamic properties, caused by context transitions (e.g., changes in the relevance or accessibility of context attributes), or by sharing contexts between multiple entities (e.g., establishment of new relations or knowledge exchange). Context is then defined using a structured approach, with the goal of "bridging the user-developer gap" - giving users an intuitive understanding of this concept and facilitating developers' implementation of a context model for context-aware systems.

Based on this understanding of context, Zimmermann et al. highlighted a few context-aware applications in [21]. These included a museum guide system that provided personalised audio information to users regarding the exhibitions, based on their location, head rotation, interest, among other factors, as well as an advertising board system that changed its content based on the noise level, time of day, or whether or not people were paying attention. These contextualized and personalized systems adapted not only to the current environmental state, but also to the user's needs and preferences, being able to support and relate to the humans who surrounded or used them. Nevertheless, we can assume that the described context categories are suitable to describe the agent of a system as well.

There is also an ongoing concern about establishing trustworthy relationships between agents and users in these types of systems. Zhao et al. [18,19], for example, developed a rapport management model, tying conversational strategies, associated with verbal and non-verbal cues, to specific goals that, when achieved, resulted in rapport. This model was eventually incorporated into a socially-aware virtual assistant.

2.2 Social Identity Theory and Social Practice Theory

Social Identity Theory (SIT), formulated by Tajfel and Turner [14], relies on "the group in the individual" [15]. It proposes that people exhibit all sorts of "group behaviour", such as cooperation, within their in-group and prejudice against out-groups. Individuals identify with groups or social categories for self-reference, following the prototypical behaviour of the group to which they belong [9]. As a result, the group's social status and prestige will influence the self-esteem of its members. Therefore, as an attempt to increase the reputation of their in-group, they will engage in a "process of social comparison with relevant out-groups".

Self-Categorization Theory also shares the concept of social identity, however it proposes that personal and social identities represent distinct levels of self-categorization, depending, respectively, on whether a person is in the presence of only their in-group or if more social categories are available [15]. Then, when a shared social identity becomes more salient, people start perceiving themselves as representatives of a shared social category membership rather than distinct individuals with their own personality [16].

These two theories have inspired various models for designing and developing social agents, such as the Dynamic Identity Model for Agents [8] or the Cognitive Social Frames framework [12], explained in depth in Sect. 2.3. In addition, Dignum et al. developed an abstract architecture for social reasoning [6], using not only the Social Identity Theory, but also the Social Practice Theory.

Practice Theory is a type of cultural theory, in which social order is rooted in collective cognitive structures - a "shared knowledge" - allowing to ascribe meaning to the environment in a socially shared manner [13]. Its "smallest unit of social analysis" is the practice, a "routinized type of behaviour" constituted by various interlinked and mutually dependent elements: physical and mental activities, resources and their use, and background knowledge required to understand the world's objects and agents.

Holtz [10] applied this theory in an agent-based model aimed at generating social practices to understand resource consumption behaviours. In this approach, social practices were viewed as independent social structures useful to provide valuable insights into a range of social behaviours, however they can also be used as "input and filter on the individual's deliberation process" [6], as in Dignum et al.'s previously mentioned architecture.

2.3 Cognitive Social Frames

Cognitive Social Frames (CSFs) is defined by Rato et al. [12] as "a framework that enables the adjustment of the agent's cognition" depending on the social context. The agent's cognition is enclosed into abstract blocks known as Cognitive Resources, which can hold knowledge and processes used to guide the agent's behaviour.

According to the model, the agent has to follow specific steps. The agent starts by observing the environment with its sensors, resulting in a set of perceptions that are sent to the agent's Sensory Memory. Then, the agent filters the previous perceptions given the salient CSF, transforming them into social perceptions and constructing the Social Context, which is transferred to the agent's Working Memory. Following this, the agent updates the previous salient CSF, selecting the CSF with the highest salience - computed as a balance between fitness to the social context and personal preferences of the agent - from the set of CSFs in the agent's Long-Term Memory. So, the salient CSF in the Working Memory is updated, meaning that the set of deployed Cognitive Resources, associated with the salient CSF, is also modified. Finally, the updated collection of deployed Cognitive Resources is executed, and the agent will now reason, decide or interact with the environment in accordance with the social context.

3   Related Work

Dialogue training tools are widely used in a variety of fields, existing a particular interest in tools to train medical students, as we will see along the following paragraphs. In this section, we will start by discussing the benefits and drawbacks of using tree-based dialogue training tools. Then, we will describe natural language dialogue systems that seek to address the problems associated with scripted dialogues. Lastly, we will highlight ongoing concerns about these systems.

3.1   Scripted Dialogues

Communicate! [11] is a serious game for developing social skills, in particular for training health-care professionals - players - in their interactions with patients - agents - with the goal of improving the communication between them. These entities will be required to speak in a scripted dialogue, such as a tree-like structure, and players will be given options for each utterance. Furthermore, when a scenario ends, feedback is given. Agents' emotions e.g., facial expressions, provide immediate feedback as well. In addition, scenarios can be authored, meaning that utterances, feedback, emotional reactions, scores and other parameters can be configured in an editor. With that said, the Dialogue Trainer Software, mentioned earlier, shares the same attributes of the prior game, being a commercial tool for communication training.

Nevertheless, as identified by Weideveld, there are a number of problems in using the previous tools to teach adequate communication skills [17]. From the user's standpoint, since the dialogue is not self-made, players will be unable to properly apprehend relevant communication abilities such as clarity, understanding and appropriateness. Furthermore, in the agent's perspective, given that their responses are scripted, the dialogue ends up being predetermined, implying that the agent does not need to adapt to changes in the context, or, better yet, the "adaptive" behaviour of the agent is controlled by the editor of the scenario, which results in a lack of authenticity and flexibility. Finally, from the viewpoint of the editor, while the dialogue content is easy to author, managing a big dialogue tree may be challenging and repetition is prone to happen - the same utterances may have to be specified more than once in distinct conversation paths.

3.2   Context-Aware Conversational Agents

Inspired by the Communicate! tool, the Social Agents for Learning in Virtual Environments (SALVE) [1] game was developed. SALVE is a dialogue-based serious game in which players can experiment various scenarios and act in different roles, while communicating with an agent, whose avatar is shown in a graphical interface. The agent expresses emotions and reactions in response to the user's inputs, detecting also repetition during the conversation. In addition, the game allows to evaluate the player's abilities, scoring their empathy, social interpersonal behaviour, and communication skills, among others.

In SALVE, the agent interprets the players' utterances using AIML and a rule-based approach, together with the concept of Social Practices, as a way of restricting the scope of the dialogue [17]. Then, the game scenarios will follow predefined social practices (e.g., the practice associated to an anamnesis scenario, as seen in Table 1 [2]), and the agent will be able to appropriately respond to the user, due to its pattern matching mechanisms.

In relation to the previous scenario, a dialogue system including a virtual patient was recently developed by Campillos-Llanos et al. [4], using a "knowledge-based and rule-frame-based approach". A medical instructor could

Table 1. Example of a social practice in an anamnesis scenario [2]

Abstract social practice	Doctor patient dialogue
Physical context	
Resources	Current time, Medical instruments
Places	Hospital, Office
Actors	User, Agent
Social context	
Social interpretation	Consulting room, Consulting time
Roles	Doctor, Patient
Norms	Patient is cooperative (gives truthful and complete answers), Doctor is polite
Activities	Welcome, Resentation, Data gathering, Symptom description, Speech acts
Plan patterns	Welcome, Presentation, Data gathering, Symptom description, Therapy
Meaning	Support the patient, Create trust, Eliciting patient's problems and concerns, Empathic response
Competences	Listening effectively, Being empathic, Use effective explanatory skills, Adapt conversation

edit the patient's medical record in a simple interface, allowing the system to run multiple medical cases by modifying the agent's health state (e.g., symptoms, lifestyle). The user of this system, commonly a medical student, could type text to the agent, which would consequently be processed by a natural language understanding module. The dialogue manager would then receive a semantic frame containing information about the dialogue state and context information of the user's input, querying this to find the appropriate answer. According to this answer, the agent selected relevant information from the patient's record, replying to the user using a template-based generator.

These systems are clearly an improvement compared to scripted dialogues: not only do they allow users to enter their own input with the keyboard, but they are also more flexible and capable of handling errors in the conversation. Authoring new or existing scenarios, on the other hand, becomes more difficult, especially if no authoring tool is available, as in SALVE. Regarding the second system, while it is possible to author different health states for the agent, the system is still limited to the domain of a medical diagnosis. As a result, no new scenarios can be created; instead, only the content of an existing one can be altered. Given these examples, what is lacking is an efficient method of structuring dialogue data so that it can be easily configured and controlled by its authors in a variety of settings, while also being accepted as input by the deliberation process of a socially-aware agent. Then, we will need to search for a compromise between scripted and rigid dialogue tools - where authoring is usually simple, enabling for different scenarios to be configured - and natural language dialogue systems - where flexibility and error handling are present, however intuitive authoring methods that can be used across different domains are absent.

4   Dialogue System

We considered flexibility, robustness, and authoring to be the most important requirements for modelling and implementing this prototype of a dialogue system. Tree-based dialogue tools restrict the flow of the conversation by preventing it from taking various alternative paths. A flexible dialogue system, on the other hand, will adapt to changes in the conversation's context, allowing it to be less rigid and, consequently, more natural to the user. This adaptation mechanism should be robust, meaning that the system should be able to generalize to different contexts without collapsing. Robustness also includes the system's ability to handle user errors or unexpected actions. Moreover, it should be possible to create new dialogue scenarios or edit existing ones in a simple and controllable manner, given that the easier it is to author, the more people will be able to use the system, not being required to have any particular technical skill to do so.

An additional requisite we considered was for users to be able to easily play different roles in a conversation, allowing them to experience the same scenarios from multiple perspectives.

We applied the Cognitive Social Frames model, combined with Social Practices, in order to achieve these goals. Regarding the Social Context components, we followed Zimmerman's definition of context and its five fundamental categories. The following sections detail the agent's deliberation cycle, as well as our implementation and authoring process. In addition, we specified an anamnesis scenario to demonstrate an application example of the developed tool.

4.1   Deliberation Cycle

The agent's architecture is depicted in Fig. 1 and it was greatly inspired by the Cognitive Social Frames model. The key elements of the agent's deliberation cycle are the social practices, the frames, the cognitive resources, the context and the knowledge base.

Both the agent and the user have access to a "shared knowledge", in the form of social practices, conventions and values, aiming to limit the scope of their interaction. In a dialogue, social practices include collections of interlinked frames, whose connections convey expectations on how the conversation should follow, just like the "plan patterns" in Table 1. Then, for a particular scenario, we assume that one or more social practices are available. Concerning the frames, they are composed by a set of cognitive resources, which represent dialogue pieces - small dialogue trees with one or more utterances - created given the norms, motivations and beliefs of the dialogue's entities.

Regarding the context, as mentioned before, we considered Zimmerman's five dimensions of context. Then, in a human-agent dialogue, we propose that the context presents itself like this:

- **Time:** time of the day (e.g., morning, night)
- **Location:** physical location (e.g., university, hospital)

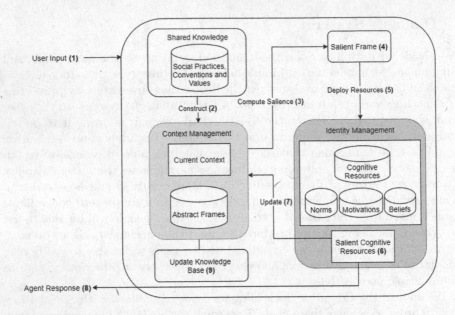

Fig. 1. Agent's architecture in the dialogue system

- **Activity:** state of the conversation (e.g., greeting, farewell), as well as goals, which, in this case, are associated with specific information that the entities of the conversation want to acquire (e.g., name, age, particular symptoms if in a medical scenario)
- **Relation:** social roles (e.g., doctor/patient, teacher/student), and type of relation (e.g., formal, friendly)
- **Individuality:** emotional state (e.g., being happy, being angry) - physical features were not yet considered given that we are only using written dialogue

These components of the context will work as a "filter", which means that, by mapping a given input to a context, the agent will be able to filter the most relevant frames that are appropriate for that same context, providing an acceptable response. As for the knowledge base, it simply represents the information (e.g., name, age, symptoms) that the agent manages to obtain throughout the conversation.

As shown in Fig. 1, the user starts by sending their input to the agent (**1**). After receiving it, the agent is able to translate this input into the relevant dimensions of the context (**2**), updating it accordingly - Context Management. Having access to sets of interconnected frames and considering the updated context, the agent computes the salience of each frame (**3**). The most salient frame (**4**) is then selected and its cognitive resources are deployed (**5**). The agent proceeds to identify the salient cognitive resource (**6**) from the collection of deployed resources, so that an appropriate response can be given - Identity Management. Finally, given this resource, the agent responds to the user (**8**). In addition, the context will be updated again (**7**) based on the salient frame. The knowledge base may be modified throughout this cycle as well (9), depending on whether relevant information is provided by the user or agent in their dialogue.

4.2 Application

The dialogue system application, implemented in Python, comprises the dialogue interface and deliberation cycle of the agent. In the dialogue interface, we list the sentences - associated with the cognitive resources - that the user can select at a specific step of the conversation, given the current context. In its deliberation process (Algorithm 1), the agent will receive the user's input and deliver an appropriate response, meeting the system's flexibility requirement.

The agent begins by updating the current context and the knowledge base, repeating this update close to the end of the algorithm as well. If the agent detects that the current dialogue tree has not been visited all the way through, it will continue on the current tree, following its course. Otherwise, it will calculate the salience of the frames in order to determine the resources that the agent could use as a response. The salience of a frame is calculated by the following formula:

$$Salience_{frame} = Frequency_{frame} + KnowledgeBaseMatch_{frame} \qquad (1)$$

The frame frequency corresponds to the number of times the frame appears after the current frame, which is the one associated with the current context. The resulting set of salient frames will have to be filtered to select the ones whose resources can be used by the agent, according to its role. If no frames are found, the agent will stay in the current frame. Therefore, the agent may be able to move through the practices, by altering the frame, or simply follow the lead of the user, by remaining in the same frame. In addition, if more than one frame is salient, the agent will randomly select the most salient frame, the same applying to the resources' selection. In the end, the agent returns the sentence associated with the most salient resource.

Following this cycle, the agent's response appears in the dialogue interface, and the user's possible inputs are updated based on the agent's response, using a reasoning process similar to the agent. There is no need to randomize the frames and cognitive resources in this case, since the user should have all the possible options, given the current context, available.

Besides being flexible, the dialogue system also demonstrates robustness, by being able to handle different contexts and dialogue scenarios without breaking, due to its general and simple deliberation mechanism. We also took into consideration the possibility of user error, which is quite common in dialogue systems. Thus, the system should include an error management mechanism that can perform error detection and recovery, i.e., the ability to recognize and respond to mistakes.

At the moment, we only implemented the "timeout error": if the users take an unusually long time to answer, the agent should acknowledge that it is waiting for their response. Having access to a timeout frame that is not linked to other frames, the agent can activate the respective frame at any time during

Algorithm 1. Agent's Deliberation Cycle

1: **function** AgentDeliberation(*UserInput*)	**(1)**
2: *CurrentSocialContext* = *UserInput.Tags*	**(2)**
3: *KnowledgeBase*.Add(*UserInput.Knowledge*)	**(9)**
4: *PossibleResources* = *UserInput.NextResources*	
5: **if** Length(*PossibleResources*) = 0 **then**	
6: *CurrentFrame* = FindFrame(*CurrentSocialContext*)	
7: *SalientFrames* = ComputeSalientFrames(*CurrentFrame*)	**(3)**
8: *PossibleFrames* = CheckFramesRole(*SalientFrames, AgentRole*)	
9: **if** Length(*PossibleFrames*) = 0 **then**	
10: *PossibleFrames*.Add(*CurrentFrame*)	
11: **end if**	
12: *SalientFrame* = Random(*PossibleFrames*)	**(4)**
13: *CurrentSocialContext* = *SalientFrame.Tags*	**(7)**
14: *PossibleResources* = CheckResourcesRole(*SalientFrame.Resources,*	
AgentRole)	**(5)**
15: **end if**	
16: *SalientResource* = Random(*PossibleResources*)	**(6)**
17: *KnowledgeBase*.Add(*SalientResource.Knowledge*)	**(9)**
18: **return** *SalientResource.Sentence*	**(8)**
19: **end function**	

The right-aligned comments correspond to the numbered steps in the agent's architecture (Fig. 1)

the conversation. This enables the agent to manage errors in the conversation in a robust and flexible manner. Then, when it is the user's turn in the conversation, the agent begins counting the time until the user responds. If the user does not say anything within the timeout value defined in the timeout frame (error detection), the agent will enter this frame and select one of its cognitive resources' utterances to say, checking if the user is still present (error recovery). The user's options will be updated based on the agent's utterance. Finally, once the user replies, the agent will repeat what it said before entering the timeout frame, restarting the conversation from where it was left (error recovery).

This same mechanism of having one general, unconnected frame, that deals with a single unexpected event, could be applied to other errors in the user's discourse, such as repetitions, contradictions, providing insufficient or excessive information in their utterances or switching to topics unrelated to the current context [3].

4.3   Authoring

The data that the agent requires to manage a dialogue with a user is organized in the system's architecture in such a manner that configuring it in an authoring tool is fairly straightforward, thereby satisfying the authoring requirement mentioned earlier. For this purpose, we selected Twine as an authoring tool, given that it is an easy-to-edit storytelling platform that enables us to represent all of the architecture's elements. A Twine add-on allowed us to export the data from the editor to a JSON file, which was then imported and read by the system's application, in order to store the frames, cognitive resources, and social roles.

Twine allows editors to create graphs divided into passages. A passage may include a title and tags, which are useful to categorize it, as well as a content and links to other passages. In Twine, we structured the passages as follows:

- **Social Practices and Frames:** a frame is defined as a passage tagged with context tags (e.g., greeting, morning, formal, hospital) and tags of knowledge acquired during the conversation. As previously stated, connected frames represent the plan patterns of a social practice, which means that frames tagged with the same context tags might appear in different social practices.
- **Cognitive Resources:** a cognitive resource is linked to a frame by its tags (e.g., if a frame is labelled with "greeting, formal", all cognitive resources tagged with these two tags belong to that frame). The title of a cognitive resource passage represents the associated utterance. These passages can be labelled with a role tag based on whether their utterances work for both social actors (no role tag necessary) or just one of them. Cognitive resources can be connected or not to other cognitive resources, being part of small dialogue trees with one or more elements. We can also specify knowledge base updates in these passages.
- **Roles:** the social roles of the user and the agent can be easily switched in a predefined passage tagged with "roles".

Further details on how to edit the dialogue data can be seen in the dialogue system's GitHub page[3]. It is worth noting that we modelled the social practices, frames and cognitive resources ourselves in Twine, tags included, aiming to verify if the dialogue system worked for a specific example (as seen in Sect. 4.4).

4.4 Anamnesis Scenario

We created a short anamnesis scenario in Twine, inspired by the social practice in Table 1, defining the roles of the user and the agent (doctor or patient), the timeout variable (30 s), the frames ("greeting friendly or formal", "introduction", "gather info", "ask symptoms", "diagnosis", "ask fever or cough", ...), their connections (practices), and their associated dialogue trees (cognitive resources). Then, we ran the dialogue system using this scenario as input.

In Fig. 2, the user plays the "patient" role, while the agent plays the "doctor" role. In this case, it is possible to observe the agent changing the frame according to the received user input. For example, when the user reports having a fever (U1), the agent will progress from frame "Fever" to frame "Cough" (A3), following the conclusion of the "Fever" dialogue tree path. As seen in the practices represented in Twine, there are two frames linked after "Fever": "Diagnosis" and "Cough". These have the same frequency, implying that the choice of the salient frame should be, presumably, random. However, the agent added

---

[3] https://github.com/GAIPS/socially-aware-interactions

to its knowledge base the information that the user had a fever, so, given that the frame "Cough" has a "fever" knowledge tag, its knowledge base match and, consequently, its salience, will be higher.

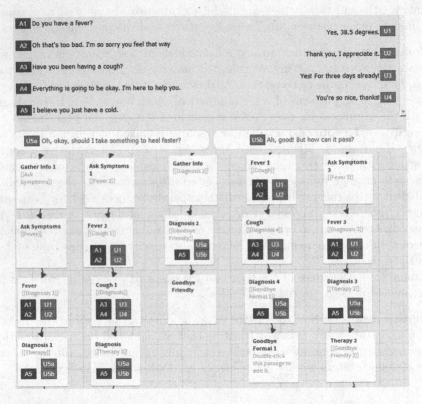

Fig. 2. Chat interface and twine - anamnesis scenario: agent (red labels) is doctor and user (green labels) is patient (Color figure online)

In Fig. 3, the roles of the dialogue entities switch. In this situation, we can see the agent following the user's lead, continuing on the same frame as the user input frame. Moreover, we can verify that the user options always adapt to the context. For instance, once the dialogue tree associated with the frame "Gather Info" finishes (A4), the options given for the user input are associated with the frames following this frame, such as "Ask Symptoms" (U5a, U5b) or "Diagnosis" (U5c, U5d). Regarding the timeout error (highlighted in blue), there is a moment in which the user is not saying anything, so the agent activates the "Timeout" frame, stating "Is everything okay? You are not replying...". When the user finally replies, the agent proceeds to repeat the previous utterance, making the conversation return to its previous state, in this case, the frame "Gather Info".

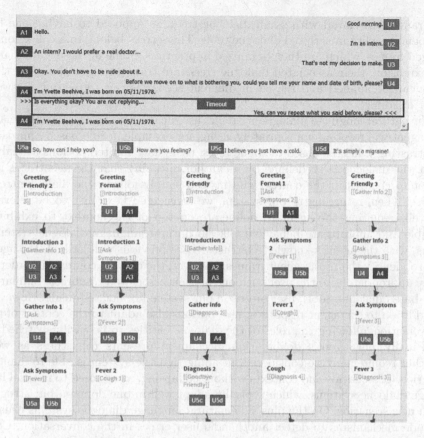

Fig. 3. Chat interface and twine - anamnesis scenario: agent (red labels) is patient and user (green labels) is doctor (Color figure online)

5   Discussion

The proposed dialogue system is a hybrid of scripted dialogue tools [11] and natural language dialogue systems [1,4,17], with certain similarities and differences, aiming to address the key concerns of these approaches, while considering their strengths.

In tree-based dialogue tools, authoring dialogue scenarios is very intuitive. A minor issue, however, is that authors must configure a single dialogue tree, which may be overwhelming in large scenarios. On the other hand, natural language dialogue systems lack good authoring mechanisms and thus do not allow scenarios to be easily edited or created for new domains. As a result, authoring was one of the system requirements we addressed, meaning we had to ensure that the dialogue data was structured in an intuitive and easy-to-manage manner, in contrast with the natural language dialogue systems we presented. We illustrated this using Twine, a well-known story-telling tool, in which an author can create and modify dialogue scenarios by altering the context tags and utterances associated with small dialogue trees, as opposed to having one big dialogue tree like in scripted dialogue tools. These trees belong to a collection of tagged frames, which are then organized in practices. Some of these frames and, by extension, their associated dialogue trees, are transversal, in the sense that they can be applied and reused in different scenarios (e.g., greeting, farewell, error handling).

In natural language dialogue systems, users can write their own input, and the agent will respond appropriately, using, for example, a rule-based approach. Contrastingly, in tree-based dialogue tools, users have limited options available. Also, the dialogue is predefined by its author, meaning that the agent does not adapt to changes in the context and instead simply follows the dialogue tree's course. Then, returning to our system, we considered flexibility to be relevant as well, requiring the agent to deliberate on top of the context to exhibit a flexible and appropriate behaviour, like in natural language dialogue systems. Thus, with the agent's knowledge structured as previously described, the agent has to identify the most salient frames, based on the current context, in order to reply appropriately to the user with one of their associated resources. Similar to tree-based dialogue tools, user inputs in our system are not self-made. However, in addition to the agent responses, user options also adapt to the context of the conversation, allowing the roles of the dialogue entities to be easily switched.

Finally, our agent's deliberation mechanism presents robustness as well, another requirement we considered, meaning that the system is able to manage a variety of scenarios and contexts without collapsing, as opposed to natural language dialogue systems, which typically adapt well in one domain, but struggle with new scenarios. On the plus side, natural language dialogue systems usually include mechanisms to detect and handle user errors in the conversation. Considering this, we are also in the early stages of dealing with user errors, but so far we have only handled the "timeout error". Our approach is based on having general frames that deal with unexpected events and that can be activated at any time during the conversation.

In essence, the existing contrast between tree-based dialogue tools and natural language dialogue systems has led us on the search for a compromise between the two. In our system, this middle ground relies on the fact that we have small easy-to-author dialogue trees grouped in tagged frames that can, in turn, be activated according to the context of the conversation, using a general and static deliberation mechanism that functions in a simple, flexible, and robust manner. The presented work, therefore, adds to the development of context-aware conversational agents by proposing a novel approach to organizing the agent's knowledge that meets the requirements of authoring, flexibility, and robustness.

One of our system's main limitations is the fact that it was not tested with users, not only those interacting with the agent, but also the ones configuring the agent's knowledge, being this an essential step for the future. Furthermore, user inputs should be self-made to ensure that they acquire the necessary communication skills for a specific scenario. Consequently, by allowing users to enter their own input, more errors will occur, such as contradictions, repetitions, unrelated information, among others, which will have to be identified and managed by an improved error handling mechanism. Moreover, the structure of the conversation, in terms of its speaking turns, requires more flexibility and should allow dialogues to present not only a simple turn-taking behaviour, but also interruptions and no specified turns to speak.

6   Conclusion

Our work began with the following research question: "Is it feasible to create a flexible and robust dialogue system that adapts to changes in the social context, while maintaining the authoring property of tree-based dialogue tools?". Based on the Cognitive Social Frames model and the theories of Social Practices and Social Identities, we then developed a prototype of a dialogue system that contributes to the creation of context-aware conversational agents. We deemed authoring, robustness, and flexibility to be the most relevant system requirements, having small dialogue trees arranged into interconnected frames, which can be activated by the agent to give an appropriate response according to the current context. With the mentioned requirements met, new scenarios, such as the anamnesis scenario we provided as a demonstration, can be easily configured and played, allowing users to go through a variety of conversation paths. Therefore, this method of structuring the conversational agent's knowledge allows dialogues to be intuitive to configure, while also enabling the agent to adapt to context changes. As future steps, we would like to include users in the system evaluation, translate user inputs to context tags, handle additional dialogue errors, support conversations with unspecified speaking turns, and, finally, create richer scenarios using crowd-sourced data.

Acknowledgement(s). The presented work was funded by the European Commission as part of the Humane-AI-net project, under grant agreement number 952026. It was supported by national funds through Fundação para a Ciência e a Tecnologia (FCT) with reference UIDB/50021/2020. Diogo Rato acknowledges his FCT grant (SFRH BD/131024/2017).

References

1. Augello, A., Gentile, M., Dignum, F.: Social agents for learning in virtual environments. In: Bottino, R., Jeuring, J., Veltkamp, R.C. (eds.) GALA 2016. LNCS, vol. 10056, pp. 133–143. Springer, Cham (2016). https://doi.org/10.1007/978-3-319-50182-6_12
2. Augello, A., Gentile, M., Weideveld, L., Dignum, F.: Dialogues as social practices for serious games. In: Proceedings of the Twenty-second European Conference on Artificial Intelligence, pp. 1732–1733 (2016)
3. de Bayser, M.G., et al.: A hybrid architecture for multi-party conversational systems. arXiv preprint arXiv:1705.01214 (2017)
4. Campillos-Llanos, L., Thomas, C., Bilinski, É., Neuraz, A., Rosset, S., Zweigenbaum, P.: Lessons learned from the usability evaluation of a simulated patient dialogue system. J. Med. Syst. 45(7), 1–20 (2021)

5. Dey, A.K.: Understanding and using context. Person. Ubiquit. Comput. **5**(1), 4–7 (2001)
6. Dignum, F., Dignum, V., Prada, R., Jonker, C.M.: A conceptual architecture for social deliberation in multi-agent organizations. Multiagent Grid Syst. **11**(3), 147–166 (2015)
7. Dignum, F., Prada, R., Hofstede, G.J.: From autistic to social agents. In: Proceedings of the 2014 International Conference on Autonomous Agents and Multi-Agent Systems, pp. 1161–1164 (2014)
8. Dimas, J., Prada, R.: Dynamic identity model for agents. In: Alam, S.J., Parunak, H.V.D. (eds.) MABS 2013. LNCS (LNAI), vol. 8235, pp. 37–52. Springer, Heidelberg (2014). https://doi.org/10.1007/978-3-642-54783-6_3
9. Hennessy, J., West, M.A.: Intergroup behavior in organizations: a field test of social identity theory. Small Group Res. **30**(3), 361–382 (1999)
10. Holtz, G.: Generating social practices. J. Artif. Soc. Soc. Simul. **17**(1), 17 (2014)
11. Jeuring, J., et al.: Communicate!-a serious game for communication skills-. In: Design for Teaching and Learning in a Networked World, pp. 513–517. Springer, Cham (2015).https://doi.org/10.1007/978-3-319-24258-3
12. Rato, D., Prada, R.: Towards social identity in socio-cognitive agents. Sustainability **13**(20), 11390 (2021)
13. Reckwitz, A.: Toward a theory of social practices: a development in culturalist theorizing. Euro. J. Soc. Theory **5**(2), 243–263 (2002)
14. Tajfel, H., Turner, J.C.: An integrative theory of intergroup conflict. In: Hogg, M.A., Abrams, D. (eds.), Intergroup Relations: Essential Readings, pp. 94–109. Psychology Press (1979)
15. Trepte, S.: Social identity theory. In: Bryant, J., Vorderer, P. (eds.) Psychology of Entertainment, pp. 255–271. Routledge, London (2006)
16. Turner, J.C., Oakes, P.J., Haslam, S.A., McGarty, C.: Self and collective: cognition and social context. Person. Soc. Psychol. Bull. **20**(5), 454–463 (1994)
17. Weideveld, L.: Social agents for learning in virtual environments. Master's thesis, University of Utrecht (2017)
18. Zhao, R., Papangelis, A., Cassell, J.: Towards a dyadic computational model of rapport management for human-virtual agent interaction. In: Bickmore, T., Marsella, S., Sidner, C. (eds.) IVA 2014. LNCS (LNAI), vol. 8637, pp. 514–527. Springer, Cham (2014). https://doi.org/10.1007/978-3-319-09767-1_62
19. Zhao, R., Sinha, T., Black, A.W., Cassell, J.: Automatic recognition of conversational strategies in the service of a socially-aware dialog system. In: Proceedings of the 17th Annual Meeting of the Special Interest Group on Discourse and Dialogue, pp. 381–392 (2016)
20. Zimmermann, A., Lorenz, A., Oppermann, R.: An operational definition of context. In: Kokinov, B., Richardson, D.C., Roth-Berghofer, T.R., Vieu, L. (eds.) CONTEXT 2007. LNCS (LNAI), vol. 4635, pp. 558–571. Springer, Heidelberg (2007). https://doi.org/10.1007/978-3-540-74255-5_42
21. Zimmermann, A., Lorenz, A., Specht, M.: Applications of a context-management system. In: Dey, A., Kokinov, B., Leake, D., Turner, R. (eds.) CONTEXT 2005. LNCS (LNAI), vol. 3554, pp. 556–569. Springer, Heidelberg (2005). https://doi.org/10.1007/11508373_42

Chatbot UX and Design

The Impact of Chatbot Linguistic Register on User Perceptions: A Replication Study

Ana Paula Chaves[1][(✉)] and Marco Aurelio Gerosa[2]

[1] Federal University of Technology - Parana, Campo Mourão, PR, Brazil
anachaves@utfpr.edu.br
[2] Northern Arizona University, Flagstaff, AZ, USA
marco.gerosa@nau.edu

Abstract. Chatbots often perform social roles associated with human interlocutors; hence, designing chatbot language to conform with the stereotypes of its social category is critical to the success of this technology. In a previous study, Chaves et al. performed a corpus analysis to evaluate how language variation in an interactional situation, namely the linguistic *register*, influences the user's perceptions of a chatbot. In this paper, we present a replication study with a different corpus to understand the effect of corpus selection in the original study's findings. Our results confirm the findings in the previous study and demonstrate the reproducibility of the research methodology; we also reveal new insights about language design for tourist assistant chatbots.

Keywords: Chatbot · Register · User perceptions

1 Introduction

Many companies have adopted chatbots to offer 24/7 customer support [20] and to reduce the need for human support for several domains. Accordingly, chatbots often assume social roles traditionally associated with a human service provider, for example, a tutor [46], a healthcare provider [34], or a tourist assistant [42]. Human interlocutors usually have a mental model of the interaction with a representative of these roles. Grounded in the media equation theory [18,40], which states that people respond to communication media and technologies as they do to other people, it is reasonable to assume that chatbot users project expectations in their interactions with chatbots.

One way to enhance a chatbot's impersonation of a social role is to carefully plan their use of language [23,33]. When a chatbot uses unexpected levels of (in)formality or incoherent language style, the interaction may result in frustration or awkwardness [33]. Previous research has analyzed user preferences regarding chatbot language use [1,17,43,45]; however, these studies focus on varying levels of formality or style, which is often disassociated from the

© Springer Nature Switzerland AG 2022
A. Følstad et al. (Eds.): CONVERSATIONS 2021, LNCS 13171, pp. 143–159, 2022.
https://doi.org/10.1007/978-3-030-94890-0_9

particular interactional situation. Similar consideration can be made for some commercially available chatbots. For example, Golem[1], a chatbot designed to guide tourists through Prague (Czech Republic), utters sentences extracted from an online travel magazine[2] without any adaptation to the new interactional situation.

In sociolinguistics, the concept that defines how humans adapt their language use depending on the interactional situation is called "register" [4,8]. Register consists of the relationship between the occurrences of *core linguistic features* in a conversation given the *context*. For example, the core linguistic features a person uses when writing an email to their supervisor are different from those used when texting a friend due to variation in the situational parameters (e.g., a supervisor vs. a friend; email vs. chat messaging tool). The *linguistic features* are the grammatical characteristics in the conversation (e.g., nouns, personal pronouns, or passive voices). The *context* is determined by a set of *situational parameters* that characterize the interactional situation (e.g., the participants and the relationship between them, channel, production circumstances, topic, and purpose) [8]. Despite being considered as one of the most important predictors of linguistic variation in human-human communication [5], register has not yet been widely explored as a theoretical basis for chatbot language design.

Previous studies [11,12] explored language variation in the context of tourism-related interactions. The results confirmed that the core linguistic features vary as the situational parameters vary, resulting in different language patterns. A more recent study identifies whether register influences the user's perceptions of their interaction with chatbots [13], based on a corpus analysis approach. The findings show an association between linguistic features and user perceptions of appropriateness, credibility, and overall user experience, which point to the need to consider register for the design of chatbots.

The study presented by Chaves et al. [13] is grounded on corpus analysis. Although corpus analysis is a powerful approach to detect register characteristics [15], it may also bring a limitation: the nature of the corpus may influence how extreme the study's participants perceived the register differences. For example, if the register of the selected corpus is too far away from the expected language patterns, then the likelihood that participants perceive it as uncanny may increase. Therefore, the question remains whether the conclusion presented in that study is supported if a different corpus is selected.

In this paper, we present a methodological replication study of [13], as we applied the same methods as the original study but used a different corpus of conversations in the tourism domain. Our goal is to investigate the effect of corpus selection on the previous outcomes and demonstrate whether the relations between linguistic features and user perceptions still stand for the new setting. According to [16], replication is a valuable scientific resource as it allows methodological enhancement and improves confidence in the scientific findings.

---

[1] Available at http://m.me/praguevisitor. Last accessed: November, 2021.
[2] https://www.praguevisitor.eu.

2   Background

Chatbots are disembodied conversational interfaces that interact with users in natural language via a text-based messaging interface [14,25]. Human-chatbot interactions are built upon the use of language. Therefore, scholars have put effort into improving chatbot conversational skills on several fronts. Research on natural language generation has heavily focused on ensuring that chatbots produce coherent and grammatically correct responses and on improving functional performance and accuracy (see e.g. [31,38]). Other studies have focused on comparing how humans adapt their language when interacting with chatbots, for example, by matching with the chatbot vocabulary [30] or with the language style [26]. However, the literature has overlooked how the chatbot should sound.

In the chatbot field, language often complies with the individual characteristics of one intended persona [24,27], which fits the definition of style [8]. Recent studies have focused on evaluating the effect of language style on the user's perceptions [17,37,43,44], many of them comparing different levels of formality. However, the formality of a chatbot should depend on how much the human interlocutors associate formality to the social category that the chatbot represents. The association between one's language use and the interactional situation goes beyond the scope of language style, inviting designers to account for *register*.

As introduced in Sect. 1, the linguistic register consists of the functional association between the occurrences of linguistic features and a given context. Register has not been widely investigated in the context of chatbots, with only a few studies pointing to its relevance [2,22,35]. As an effort to introduce the linguistic register as a theoretical basis for chatbot's language design, Chaves et al. [13] performed a study to evaluate how human interlocutors perceive register differences in a chatbot's discourse. The authors concluded that register could work as a tool to define what language pattern is appropriate for a given context, encapsulating the varying language styles that a persona-based chatbot might have. We are not aware of other studies that evaluate the influence of register on user experience with chatbots or the effect of corpus selection on the outcomes of register analysis. Thus, this paper presents a replication study to understand the influence of corpus selection on the study performed by Chaves et al. [13].

3   User Perceptions of Register: the Original Study

This section summarizes the method applied in [13], which we replicate in this study. In Sects. 4 through 7 we detail these steps for the replication study.

Chaves et al. [13] explored the extent to which behavioral aspects of user experience (namely perceived appropriateness, credibility, and user experience) relate to the register a chatbot uses. The authors invited participants to compare excerpts of conversations expressed in two different registers. To isolate the effect of register, the content of the conversation needed to be equivalent, which means using parallel data–natural language texts with the same semantic content, but expressed in different forms [41]. Since this kind of data is rarely available, the study's approach includes the production of parallel corpora. Actual conversations were carefully manipulated to mimic the register characteristics of a different corpus. The research methodology followed the steps outlined below (see [13] for details):

Step 1–Data collection: the baseline corpus, named FLG, consists of text-based interactions between three human tourist assistants and tourists from Flagstaff, Arizona, USA. The corpus comprises 144 interactions with about 540 question-answer pairs. A second corpus is used for comparison purposes. In that study, the authors extracted this corpus from a larger one named $DailyDialog$ [36].

Step 2–Register characterization: this step consists of the characterization of the registers present in each corpus through register analysis [4]. The authors first identified the situation in which the conversations occur and then defined the prevailing linguistic features in each corpus. The analysis relied on information from the Biber's grammatical tagger [6] and the linguistic features were analyzed both individually and aggregated into five dimensions according to the text-linguistic register framework [4].

Step 3–Text modification: this step aims at producing a new, parallel corpus, named FLG_{mod}. For every answer provided by a tourist assistant in the FLG corpus, the authors produced a corresponding answer that portrays the register characteristics of $DailyDialog$. FLG and FLG_{mod} fulfill the requirement of parallel data for user studies on register differences.

Step 4–The study: finally, the authors performed a user study to evaluate the impact of register on user experience. Participants were presented with individual questions and pairs of answers (from FLG and FLG_{mod}) and, for each, were asked to choose which answer they preferred based on three measures of quality: appropriateness, credibility, and user experience. The analysis included fitting a statistical learning model to identify the linguistic features that best predict the user choices.

All the research materials related to Chaves et al.'s study are available on GitHub [10]. The following sections present how we apply this methodological approach in our replication study.

4   Data Collection

In Chaves et al. [13], the situational parameters of $DailyDialog$ have a large variability, particularly for the interlocutor's role and relationship among them. For example, $DailyDialog$ includes conversations between travelers and immigration control personnel, guests and hotel concierge, tourists and tour guides, among many others. For the replication, we want to select a corpus with less variability of situational parameters within the corpus. We chose the $Frames$ [3] dataset, which is a corpus of 1349 human-human, text-based interactions[3] within the context of booking travel packages. We followed the situational analytical framework [8] to identify the situational parameters in comparison to FLG (Table 1). The purpose of this *situational analysis* is to characterize the interactions using a conversational taxonomy based around seven parameters (Table 1). The variation in the situational parameters between *Frames* and *FLG* is mainly in the purpose and topic parameters; *Frames* focuses on pre-travel decision-making, while *FLG* focuses on en-route information search.

5   Register Characterization

We characterized the register of the *Frames* corpus as presented in [13]. In a nutshell, we submitted the conversations from *Frames* to the Biber's grammatical tagger [6], which tags and counts linguistic features. The features are also aggregated into *dimension scores* using a factor analysis algorithm [6] to reveal the prevailing characteristics of the register (i.e., the levels of personal involvement, narrative flow, contextual references, persuasion, and formality) [4].

We applied a one-way MANOVA to generate a statistical comparison of the dimension scores across corpora (*Frames* and *FLG*), where the dependent variables are the values of the five dimension scores. The independent variables are the *Frames* (control group) and the three tourist assistants from the *FLG* corpus, namely $TA1$, $TA2$, and $TA3$ (experimental groups). We considered each tourist assistant as a group to account for stylistic variation among them. The MANOVA revealed that the dimension scores for *FLG*'s tourist assistants significantly differ from the dimension scores for *Frames* ($Wilks = 0.95, F = 5.71, p < 0.0001$). We also performed a one-way univariate analysis ($df = 3, 1489$) for each of the five dimensions to identify the individual dimensions that influence the prevailing register characteristics (Table 2).

The dimension score reveals that the purpose (decision-making vs. information search) likely impacted the narrative flow (dimension 2) and the persuasion

Table 1. Situational analysis (*Frames* vs. *FLG*).

Situational parameter	Frames	FLG
Participants	Tourist and travel assistant	Tourists and tourist assistants
Relationship	Tourist assistant and tourist, the former owns the knowledge	Tourist assistant and tourist, the former owns the knowledge
Channel	Written, instant messaging tool	Written, instant messaging tool
Production	Quasi-real-time	Quasi-real-time
Setting	Private, shared time, virtually shared place	Private, shared time, virtually shared place
Purpose	Decision-making; book travel packages; user's constraints	Information search
Topic	Travel packages reservation	Local information (e.g., attractions)

---

[3] Download and more details at https://www.microsoft.com/en-us/research/project/frames-dataset/.

(dimension 4) since the tourist assistant in *Frames* focused on describing the options rather than arguing on what were the best deals. The variation within the *TA*s suggests the influence of stylistic preferences [11].

Table 2. Univariate analysis of dimension scores ($df = 3, 1489$). For each dimension, the table shows the estimated dimension score $\pm$ the standard error per group (*Frames*, *TA*1, *TA*2, *TA*3), and the corresponding F- and p-values.

	Frames	TA1	TA2	TA3	F	p-value
Dim. 1: Involvement	13.18 ± 0.68	14.73 ± 3.62	5.69 ± 3.66	-5.02 ± 3.48	10.07	<0.0001
Dim. 2: Narrative flow	-4.94 ± 0.04	-4.45 ± 0.20	-4.31 ± 0.21	-4.79 ± 0.20	4.47	0.0040
Dim. 3: Contextual ref	-1.06 ± 0.16	-3.33 ± 0.87	-1.75 ± 0.88	-2.65 ± 0.83	3.42	0.0166
Dim. 4: Persuasion	-0.09 ± 0.15	1.98 ± 0.81	-0.02 ± 0.82	1.93 ± 0.78	4.12	0.0064
Dim. 5: Formality	-0.49 ± 0.14	-0.81 ± 0.74	-1.70 ± 0.75	-2.10 ± 0.71	2.42	0.0642

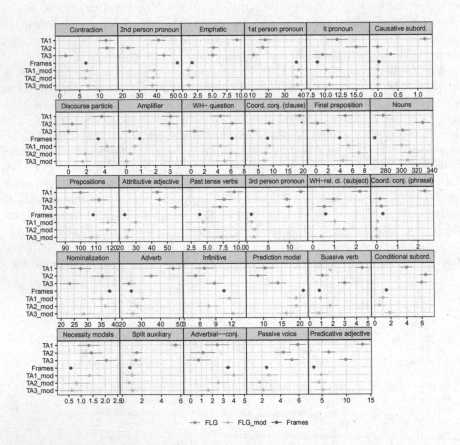

Fig. 1. Visualization of ANOVA results for individual features (Color figure online)

Figure 1 depicts the linguistic features that vary significantly between the two corpora (*FLG* and *Frames*), as revealed by the ANOVA analysis per feature.

The figure shows the estimates for *Frames* (control group, in blue) and each tourist assistant in *FLG* ($TA1$, $TA2$, and $TA3$, in red). The horizontal line represents the standard error. We found that 29 out of 48 linguistic features were significantly different across corpora. The next step was to modify the conversations to produce another parallel corpus.

6   Text Modification

Text modification process followed the same procedures as described in [13]. Firstly, we cloned the *FLG* corpus to create the initial FLG_{mod_2}. Then, we inspected the *Frames* corpus to understand how one particular feature is used in *Frames*. Then, we reproduced the use in FLG_{mod2} using a Python script (see [10]). Figure 1 shows the comparison between *Frames* and FLG_{mod_2} after performing a sufficient number of modifications to substantially reduce the F-values. The figure shows the estimates for *Frames* (control group, in blue) and each tourist assistant in *FLG* ($TA1_{mod}$, $TA2_{mod}$, and $TA3_{mod}$, in green). The horizontal line represents the standard error. Table 3 shows an example of a modified answer, where modified words are highlighted in bold, and the tags attributed to the words are between square brackets.

Table 3. Example of a modified answer (*FLG* vs. FLG_{mod_2}).

Original answer (*FLG* **corpora**)	Modified answer (FLG_{mod_2} **corpora**)
There is a self-guided Rte 66 tour that starts in the **Historic Train** *[attributive adjective]* Center on 1 E. Rte. 66. In the visitor's center there is a **self-guided map** *[attributive adjective]* that shows the original alignment through the redeveloped Southside Historic District and passes by **classic drive-in** *[attributive adjective]* motels and **Flagstaff** *[noun]* landmarks of old. Let me know **if** *[conditional subordination]* you have further questions	**We** *[first person pronoun]* **offer** *[present verb]* a self-guided Rte 66 tour **for you** *[preposition, second person pronoun]* that starts in the Train Center on 1 E. Rte. 66. In **our** *[first person pronoun]* visitor center, a map **has** *[present verb]* the original alignment through the redeveloped Southside Historic District and passes by motels and landmarks of old. Tell me your other questions

Once the FLG_{mod_2} parallel corpus was developed, we perform the user study on the impact of linguistic register on user perceptions.

7   User Perceptions Study

Following the procedures described in [13], we ranked the question-answer pairs in our parallel corpora based on the Levenshtein distance [32] between the pairs of original (*FLG*) and modified answers (FLG_{mod2}), and selected the top 10% (54 question-answer pairs) for evaluation.

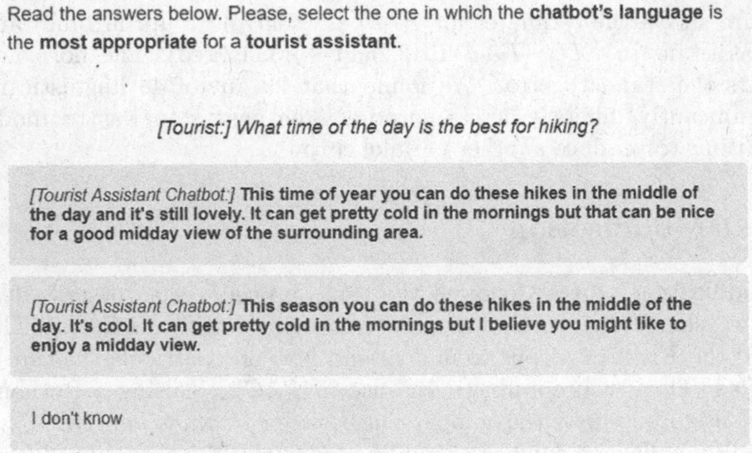

Read the answers below. Please, select the one in which the **chatbot's language** is the **most appropriate** for a **tourist assistant**.

[Tourist:] What time of the day is the best for hiking?

> *[Tourist Assistant Chatbot:]* **This time of year you can do these hikes in the middle of the day and it's still lovely. It can get pretty cold in the mornings but that can be nice for a good midday view of the surrounding area.**

> *[Tourist Assistant Chatbot:]* **This season you can do these hikes in the middle of the day. It's cool. It can get pretty cold in the mornings but I believe you might like to enjoy a midday view.**

> I don't know

Fig. 2. Example of a question. The participant was invited to select the answer that portrays the most appropriate language.

We recruited participants to answer an online questionnaire, where they chose, given a question, which answer would better represent a tourist assistant chatbot. For each tourist's question, presented on the screen one at a time, participants could choose one out of three options: the original answer (from FLG), the modified version (from FLG_{mod2}), or "I don't know" (see an example in Fig. 2). Original and modified answers were presented in a randomized order. In total, participants answered 27 questions, nine for each of the constructs (perceived language appropriateness, perceived credibility, and user experience).

7.1 Participants

Participants were recruited through Prolific[4] in September 2020. We received a total of 174 submissions, 29 of which were discarded due to either technical issues in the data collection or failure to answer the attention checks ($N = 145$). All the participants claimed English as their first language and were located in the USA. Additionally, we configured Prolific to recruit only participants who did not participate in the previous study, to avoid biases in the data collection. Most participants had a four-year bachelor's degree (49) or some college, but no degree (42). Twenty participants graduated from high school, and 17 had Master's degrees. Common educational backgrounds were STEM (34), Arts and Humanities (28), and others (29). Three participants had non-binary gender; 70 declared themselves as female, and 72 as male. The age range is 18–60 ($\mu = 30.77$ years-old, $\sigma = 10.32$).

---

[4] https://www.prolific.co.

7.2 Analysis of the Linguistic Features

We fitted the generalized linear model (GLM), using the *glmnet* package in R [21], using the same cross-validation algorithm presented by [13][5]. For comparison purposes (to determine an upper bound on prediction accuracy), we also fitted two non-linear learning models: random forest and gradient boosting, as performed in [13]. The prediction variables include (i) the difference between original and modified counts per linguistic feature; (ii) variables representing the participant who answered the question; (iii) the participants' self-assessed social orientation; and (iV) the author of the answer in FLG ($TA1$, $TA2$, $TA3$).

The evaluation dataset started with 3,915 observations (145 participants, 27 evaluations per participant). We discarded blank answers and the "I don't know" option, resulting in a dataset with 3,858 observations. Each question-answer pair was evaluated from 22 to 26 times per construct. As in the original study [13], participants overall preferred the answers from the original corpus, although the modified version was sometimes chosen.

Figure 3 shows the prediction accuracy and AUC plots for the four fitted models. Since participants generally preferred the original FLG corpus answers, the prediction threshold is close to always predicting the most frequent class (original). The prediction accuracy of `glmnet` and `xgboost` are only slightly better than the baseline. Nevertheless, the AUC values are consistently better than the baseline. As in the original study [13], the non-linear models are not considerably more accurate than the linear model, which justify the use of the *glmnet* model.

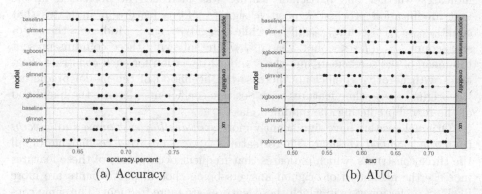

(a) Accuracy   (b) AUC

Fig. 3. Accuracy (a) and AUC (b) results per model for each construct (appropriateness, credibility, and user experience). The baseline represents a model that always predicts the most frequent class (original).

Table 4 presents the coefficients of the linguistic features selected in six or more folds. The first and second columns indicate, respectively, the linguistic feature of interest and the sign of original − modified calculation, which

---

[5] The R code and datasets are available on GitHub [10].

Table 4. Coefficients and standard deviation of the non-zero variables per construct. The dots indicate that the corresponding feature was not selected for that particular construct.

Linguistic features	orig. − mod.	Mean of coefficients ± Std. Deviation		
		Appropriateness	Credibility	User experience
Split auxiliary	(+)	−0.010 ± 0.003	−0.027 ± 0.004	−0.017 ± 0.007
Adverbs	(+)	−0.009 ± 0.001	−0.002 ± 0.001	−0.005 ± 0.001
Nouns	(+)	−0.001 ± 0.000	−0.003 ± 0.001	-0.001 ± 0.001
Contractions	(+)	−0.003 ± 0.001	·	−0.007 ± 0.002
Causative subordination	(+)	−0.011 ± 0.012	·	·
Predicative adjective	(+)	·	−0.003 ± 0.001	·
Agentless passive	(+)	0.002 ± 0.001	0.006 ± 0.001	0.005 ± 0.003
Third-person pronoun	(+)	0.006 ± 0.001	0.005 ± 0.000	0.005 ± 0.001
"It" pronoun	(+)	0.004 ± 0.002	0.003 ± 0.001	·
Conditional subordination	(+)	·	0.002 ± 0.002	0.004 ± 0.002
Attributive adjective	(+)	·	0.006 ± 0.001	0.001 ± 0.001
Emphatic	(+)	·	·	0.007 ± 0.004
Preposition	(−)	−0.003 ± 0.000	−0.001 ± 0.001	−0.002 ± 0.001
Infinitive	(−)	−0.002 ± 0.001	−0.012 ± 0.001	·
Nominalization	(−)	·	−0.003 ± 0.001	−0.003 ± 0.002
Prediction modal	(−)	0.008 ± 0.002	0.008 ± 0.002	0.014 ± 0.002
Adverbial−conjuncts	(−)	·	0.004 ± 0.004	·

indicates whether one particular feature was increased or decreased in the text modification process. A positive sign (+) for a feature f_i indicates that $\text{count}_{\text{original}}(f_i) > \text{count}_{\text{modified}}(f_i)$, while a negative sign (−) indicates the opposite ($\text{count}_{\text{original}}(f_i) < \text{count}_{\text{modified}}(f_i)$). The following three columns present the mean of the coefficients and the standard deviation for each construct. Features with negative coefficients increase the likelihood of the model predicting the original class, while features with positive coefficients increase the likelihood of the model predicting the modified class.

Original answers have significantly more *split auxiliaries*, *nouns*, and *adverbs* than the modified versions. These features have a negative coefficient for all the three constructs, which indicates that frequent occurrences of these features increase the likelihood of original answers being chosen; participants are more likely to prefer answers in which these features are more frequent. The same conclusion applies to *contractions*, *causative subordinations*, and *predicative adjectives*, although *contractions* show up as relevant for appropriateness and user experience only, *causative subordinations* are relevant only for the appropriateness construct, and *predicative adjective* predicts credibility only.

Original answers also have significantly more *agentless passives* and *third-person pronouns*. These features have a positive coefficient for all three constructs, indicating that frequent occurrences of these features increase the likelihood of modified answers being chosen. This outcome suggests that participants are more likely to prefer answers in which these features are less frequent. The same conclusion applies to *"it"* pronouns, *conditional subordinations*, *attributive adjectives*, and *emphatics*, but these features are not relevant for all constructs. *"It"* pronouns did not show up as relevant for user experience, *conditional subordinations* and *attributive adjectives* did not influence appropriateness, and *emphatics* show up as relevant only for user experience.

Modifications have significantly more *prepositions* than the original answers. This feature has a negative coefficient for all three constructs, which indicates that frequent occurrences of *prepositions* increase the likelihood of original answers being chosen. This outcome suggests that participants are more likely to prefer answers in which these features are less frequent. The same inference applies to *infinitives* and *nominalizations*, although *infinitives* did not show up as a relevant feature for user experience, and *nominalizations* did not predict the appropriateness. Modifications also have a larger number of *prediction modals*. This feature has a positive coefficient for all three constructs, which indicates that increasing their occurrences increased the likelihood of modified answers being chosen. This outcome highlights the preferences for answers in which these features are more consistently present. The same conclusion applies to *adverbial–conjuncts*, although this feature shows up as relevant only for credibility. Noticeably, when we aggregate the estimate to the standard deviation for this feature, it sums up to zero, suggesting that this outcome may be noise.

In summary, the outcomes confirm the association between the use of register-specific language and the user perceptions of appropriateness, credibility, and user experience. In accordance with the original study's outcomes, linguistic features are stronger predictors than variables that indicate individual characteristics of either participants or assistants, suggesting that adopting the expected register influence positively the user perceptions of the interaction.

7.3   Discussion

Chaves et al. from [13] showed that using language that fits to a particular context, i.e., that is register-specific, has a significant impact on user perceptions of their interaction with chatbots. In this study, we replicate that study's methodology to investigate whether this conclusion is supported if FLG is compared to a different corpus. Our results supported the insights from the original study. The study strengthens the conclusion that the chatbot's language–characterized under the lens of register–can impact the user perceptions, which, ultimately, may result in increased quality, acceptance, and adoption [19,29,39].

Secondly, the analysis of individual linguistic features supports the previous inferences for at least four linguistic features, namely *preposition, causative subordination, third-person pronoun*, and *conditional subordination*. In this replication study, *preposition* was selected for all the constructs, and participants preferred answers in which this feature is less frequent. Prepositions (e.g., *at, in, of*, etc.) in our study were often used to provide an extra piece of information (e.g., *in Flagstaff, at 4am*). Many occurrences of this feature may reduce the efficiency, violating the maxim of quantity that states that a sentence in a conversation should have just the right amount of content [28].

Conditional subordination is negatively associated with credibility in both studies, which supports the inference that when the chatbot gives options, it sounds as it is not confident about the information provided [13]. Using less conditional subordination requires more personalization so that the chatbot is assertive when offering a suggestion or recommendation, instead of offering a list of options (i.e., *if you like hiking, then check [...]; otherwise, check [...]*).

Regarding *causative subordination* (e.g., *because*), participants are more likely to prefer answers in which this feature occurs. Noticeably, this feature is a fairly uncommon feature (mean of 1 per 1,000 words [4]) when compared to others such as *nouns* (mean of 180 per 1,000 words [4]). Our result indicates that, when this feature occurs, it is preferred over receiving the information without the subordination. This preference can be associated with human-likeness since the absence of the *causative subordination* results in a broken discourse, which is associated with robotic sounding (e.g., *[...] it was used as a major trading hub, **because** there are artifacts that were found there [...]* vs. *[...] it was used as a major trading hub. There are artifacts that were found there [...]*).

Participants preferred less frequent occurrences of *third-person pronouns* in all three constructs in the current study. *Third-person pronouns* are used in *FLG* to add details about business or attractions (e.g., "*they* have public restrooms"), which may reduce efficiency. Additionally, by using *third-person pronouns*, the assistant provides the information from an external standpoint, which results in a more impersonal tone [9] (e.g., "**they** *[the museum community]* have musical performances" vs. "**we** *[the assistant as part of the museum community]* have musical performances"). These results suggest that reinforcing the tourist assistant chatbot as a representative of its social category by using (plural) first-person pronouns would be preferable over the impersonal third-person pronoun.

On the other hand, this study shows conflicting outcomes regarding the levels of *prediction modals* and *contractions*. In [13], participants preferred lower levels of these features, whereas the current study indicates a preference for higher levels of these features in all the three constructs. This dissonance can be explained by the differences in how *Frames* and *DailyDialog* use these features. In *DailyDialog*, *would* is the most common *prediction modal*, which mostly co-occurred with first-person pronouns (i.e., "*I would*", "*I'd*"). As discussed in [13], the co-occurrences with first-person pronouns may have influenced the outcomes for prediction modals and contractions, as these co-occurrences cause uncanny effects due to excessive personification. In contrast, *Frames* has more frequent occurrences of other forms of *prediction modals*, such as *shall* and *will*. *Will* is the most frequent modal and it often co-occurs with *nouns* (e.g., "*campgrounds will open*" or "*downtown will have vegetarian options*") instead of personal pronouns. As a consequence, the negative effect was flattened and the frequent occurrences of *prediction modals* and *contractions* resulted in a positive effect.

This study allowed us to observe inferences about features not manipulated in the original study. *Split auxiliaries* are likely influenced by the preferences for frequent occurrences of *adverbs*, as split auxiliaries occur when adverbs are placed between auxiliaries and their main verb [4] (e.g., *"will **obviously** limit"*). Many *adverbs* are used in *FLG* to indicate the tourist assistant's stance (e.g., *"Absolutely!"* and *"there are definitely some,"* which indicate assurance, or *"you'd probably be fine,"* which indicates uncertainty). These features emphasize the level of confidence that the assistant has about the information, which positively affects the user perceptions of all the evaluated constructs. The same conclusions apply to *predicative adjectives*, which is also frequently used for marking stance [4]. This feature was selected as a predictor of credibility, which clearly relates to the ability to express opinion (e.g., *"That would **be difficult**." "the sandwiches **are delicious**," "the restaurant **is good**"*).

In contrast, results show that participants are more likely to prefer answers in which the occurrences of *agentless passives, infinitives, nominalizations* are less frequent. These features are, in general, uncommon in conversations [4,9], which may justify the user's negative impressions about higher frequencies of these features. *Emphatics* and *"it" pronouns* are rather frequent in conversations. However, *emphatics* are characteristic of informal, colloquial discourse, whereas "it" pronouns indicate limited informational content [4]. In this research, the tourist assistant chatbots are representatives of a professional category specialized in providing information, which may increase the user's expectations for formal and specialized discourse. This results contradicts the results presented by [37], which showed that customers may not assign different roles to chatbots as communication partner in a human-chatbot customer service setting.

Contributions and Implications. The results presented in this paper, combined with the findings from [13], emphasize that there is more to chatbot language variation than the dichotomy of formal vs. informal language. Previous literature that focuses on the spectrum of formality has found inconsistent results about whether chatbot language should sound (in)formal (see, e.g., [37]). [37] even suggested that different perceptions of formality may have been influenced by the function which some linguistic features perform in the utterances. Our results reinforced that disregarding register may overshadow language variation's nuances and result in an overly simplified model for chatbot language. Research on sociolinguistics has long stressed the role of register in predicting language variation in human-human conversations [7]. Our findings demonstrate that this role can be stretched to include human-chatbot conversations and that register analysis is a powerful tool for characterizing the patterns of language that a chatbot would be expected to use within a particular domain.

Additionally, this paper brings insights on the user expectations about chatbots' language use in the context of tourism information search. Firstly, it reinforces the need for language efficiency; as the authors point out in [13], efficiency is crucial in information search scenarios, which makes detailed descriptions unnecessary in many cases. Thus, filling words or expressions, and additional pieces of information should be avoided. Secondly, it provides understanding on possible linguistic features that (overly) convey human-likeness. The study showed that users prefer fluid, connected sentences ("and", "or", "because") rather than several simple utterances; and that positioning the chatbot as part of a social group (e.g. using "*we*", but not overusing "I") is preferred over impersonal tone and external standpoint ("they", "there are"). Finally, it is important that the chatbot has the ability to express opinion by using predicative adjectives (e.g. "is good") and make it clear the level of confidence about the information (even when the assistant is not so sure), which can be expressed with specific adverbs (e.g. "absolutely", "probably".).

8   Conclusions

This paper presented a methodological replication study that aims at demonstrating the reproducibility of the methodology proposed by Chaves et al. [13] to characterize the register of chatbot discourse. Additionally, this replication helps understand the effect of corpus selection in previous findings. Our results confirmed the influence of using register-specific language in user perceptions of their interactions with chatbots and reinforced the need to consider register when designing chatbot language. Since we performed a methodological replication, the limitations discussed in [13] also applies to this study, including the subjectivity introduced by the semi-manual text modification and the choice of the linguistic features submitted to the *glmnet* model for feature selection. Additionally, we emphasize that the conversations in the *Frames* corpus were collected in a lab setting, so the language expressed in the corpus reproduces the expectations of the users regarding the tourist assistant's patterns of language.

Our findings open a wide range of new research opportunities in chatbot language design. Given the identified relevance of linguistic register for user experience, the next natural step is to walk toward building computational models to perform register adaptation, enabling the future development of chatbot conversational engines both tailored to the target context and able to adapt register to the specific communicative purpose dynamically. Additionally, we need to develop efficient frameworks to automate the steps of this methodology to facilitate the register characterization and linguistic feature selection for particular contexts. We invite the research community to embrace these challenges to increase chatbots' acceptance as online service providers and improve user experiences with this technology.

References

1. Araujo, T.: Living up to the chatbot hype: the influence of anthropomorphic design cues and communicative agency framing on conversational agent and company perceptions. Comput. Hum. Behav. **85**, 183–189 (2018)
2. Argamon, S.: Register in computational language research. Regist. Stud. **1**(1), 100–135 (2019)
3. Asri, L.E., et al.: Frames: a corpus for adding memory to goal-oriented dialogue systems. In: Proceedings of the SIGDIAL 2017 Conference, pp. 207–219. Association for Computational Linguistics, Saarbrucken(2017)

4. Biber, D.: Variation Across Speech and Writing. Cambridge University Press, Cambridge, UK (1988)
5. Biber, D.: Register as a predictor of linguistic variation. Corpus Linguist. Ling. Theory 8(1), 9–37 (2012)
6. Biber, D.: Mat-multidimensional analysis tagger (2017). https://goo.gl/u7h9gb
7. Biber, D.: Text-linguistic approaches to register variation. Regist. Stud. 1(1), 42–75 (2019)
8. Biber, D., Conrad, S.: Register, Genre, and Style, 2nd edn. Cambridge University Press, New York (2019)
9. Biber, D., Johansson, S., Leech, G., Conrad, S., Finegan, E., Quirk, R.: Longman Grammar of Spoken and Written English, vol. 2. Pearson Longman, London (1999)
10. Chaves, A.P.: Github Repository (2020). https://github.com/chavesana/chatbots-register
11. Chaves, A.P., Doerry, E., Egbert, J., Gerosa, M.: It's how you say it: identifying appropriate register for chatbot language design. In: Proceedings of the 7th International Conference on Human-Agent Interaction (HAI 2019). p. 8. ACM, New York, October 2019. https://doi.org/10.1145/3349537.3351901
12. Chaves, A.P., Egbert, J., Gerosa, M.A.: Chatting like a robot: the relationship between linguistic choices and users' experiences. In: ACM CHI 2019 Workshop on Conversational Agents: Acting on the Wave of Research and Development. p. 8. Glasgow (2019). https://convagents.org/
13. Chaves, A.P., Egbert, J., Hocking, T., Doerry, E., Gerosa, M.A.: Chatbots language design: the influence of language variation on user experience. ACM Trans. Comput.-Hum. Inter. (to appear Author's version at arXiv:210111089)
14. Chaves, A.P., Gerosa, M.A.: How should my chatbot interact? A survey on social characteristics in human-chatbot interaction design. Int. J. Hum.-Comput. Interact. 37, 1–30 (2020)
15. Conrad, S., Biber, D.: Multi-dimensional Studies of Register Variation in English. Routledge, New York (2014)
16. Dennis, A.R., Valacich, J.S.: A replication manifesto. AIS Trans. Replic. Res. 1(1), 1 (2015)
17. Elsholz, E., Chamberlain, J., Kruschwitz, U.: Exploring language style in chatbots to increase perceived product value and user engagement. In: Proceedings of the 2019 Conference on Human Information Interaction and Retrieval, pp. 301–305. ACM, New York (2019)
18. Fogg, B.: Computers as persuasive social actors. In: Fogg, B. (ed.) Persuasive Technology, Chap. 5, pp. 89–120. Interactive Technologies, Morgan Kaufmann, San Francisco (2003)
19. Følstad, A., Brandtzaeg, P.B.: Users' experiences with chatbots: findings from a questionnaire study. Qual. User Exp. 5(1), 1–14 (2020). https://doi.org/10.1007/s41233-020-00033-2
20. Følstad, A., Nordheim, C.B., Bjørkli, C.A.: What makes users trust a chatbot for customer service? An exploratory interview study. In: Bodrunova, S.S. (ed.) INSCI 2018. LNCS, vol. 11193, pp. 194–208. Springer, Cham (2018). https://doi.org/10.1007/978-3-030-01437-7_16
21. Friedman, J., Hastie, T., Tibshirani, R.: Regularization paths for generalized linear models via coordinate descent. J. Stat. Softw. Articles 33(1), 1–22 (2010). https://doi.org/10.18637/jss.v033.i01, https://www.jstatsoft.org/v033/i01

22. Gnewuch, U., Morana, S., Maedche, A.: Towards designing cooperative and social conversational agents for customer service. In: Proceedings of the International Conference on Information Systems 2017, vol. 1. Association for Information Systems, South Korea (2017)

23. Go, E., Sundar, S.S.: Humanizing chatbots: the effects of visual, identity and conversational cues on humanness perceptions. Comput. Hum. Behav. **97**, 304–316 (2019)

24. Google Developers: Conversation design by google (2021). https://developers. google.com/assistant/conversation-design/what-is-conversation-design.https:// developers.google.com/assistant/conversation-design/what-is-conversation-design. Accessed 3 Mar 2021

25. Grudin, J., Jacques, R.: Chatbots, humbots, and the quest for artificial general intelligence. In: Proceedings of the 2019 CHI Conference on Human Factors in Computing Systems, pp. 1–11. ACM, New York (2019)

26. Hill, J., Ford, W.R., Farreras, I.G.: Real conversations with artificial intelligence: a comparison between human-human online conversations and human-chatbot conversations. Comput. Hum. Behav. **49**, 245–250 (2015)

27. Hwang, S., Kim, B., Lee, K.: A data-driven design framework for customer service chatbot. In: Marcus, A., Wang, W. (eds.) HCII 2019. LNCS, vol. 11583, pp. 222–236. Springer, Cham (2019). https://doi.org/10.1007/978-3-030-23570-3_17

28. Jacquet, B., Hullin, A., Baratgin, J., Jamet, F.: The impact of the Gricean maxims of quality, quantity and manner in chatbots. In: 2019 International Conference on Information and Digital Technologies (IDT), pp. 180–189. IEEE (2019)

29. Jakic, A., Wagner, M.O., Meyer, A.: The impact of language style accommodation during social media interactions on brand trust. J. Serv. Manag. **28**(3), 418–441 (2017)

30. Jenkins, M.-C., Churchill, R., Cox, S., Smith, D.: Analysis of user interaction with service oriented chatbot systems. In: Jacko, J.A. (ed.) HCI 2007. LNCS, vol. 4552, pp. 76–83. Springer, Heidelberg (2007). https://doi.org/10.1007/978-3-540-73110-8_9

31. Jiang, R.E., Banchs, R.: Towards improving the performance of chat oriented dialogue system. In: 2017 International Conference on Asian Language Processing (IALP), pp. 23–26. IEEE, New York (2017)

32. Kessler, B.: Computational dialectology in Irish Gaelic. In: Proceedings of the Seventh Conference on European Chapter of the Association for Computational Linguistics, EACL 1995, pp. 60–66. Morgan Kaufmann Publishers Inc., San Francisco (1995). https://doi.org/10.3115/976973.976983, https://doi.org/10.3115/976973.976983

33. Kirakowski, J., et al.: Establishing the hallmarks of a convincing chatbot-human dialogue. In: Human-Computer Interaction. InTech, London (2009)

34. Laranjo, I., et al.: Conversational agents in healthcare: a systematic review. J. Am. Med. Inf. Assoc. **25**(9), 1248–1258 (2018)

35. Li, J., Galley, M., Brockett, C., Spithourakis, G.P., Gao, J., Dolan, B.: A persona-based neural conversation model. arXiv preprint arXiv:1603.06155 (2016)

36. Li, Y., Su, H., Shen, X., Li, W., Cao, Z., Niu, S.: Dailydialog: a manually labelled multi-turn dialogue dataset. In: International Joint Conference on Natural Language Processing (IJCNLP), pp. 986–995. Asian Federation of Natural Language Processing, Taipei, Taiwan (2017)

37. Liebrecht, C., Sander, L., van Hooijdonk, C.: Too informal? how a chatbot's communication style affects brand attitude and quality of interaction. In: Conversations 2020: 4th International Workshop on Chatbot Research (2020)

38. Maslowski, I., Lagarde, D., Clavel, C.: In-the-wild chatbot corpus: from opinion analysis to interaction problem detection. In: International Conference on Natural Language. Signal and Speech Processing, pp. 115–120. International Science and General Applications, Marocco (2017)

39. Morrissey, K., Kirakowski, J.: 'Realness' in chatbots: establishing quantifiable criteria. In: Kurosu, M. (ed.) HCI 2013. LNCS, vol. 8007, pp. 87–96. Springer, Heidelberg (2013). https://doi.org/10.1007/978-3-642-39330-3_10

40. Nass, C., Steuer, J., Tauber, E.R.: Computers are social actors. In: Proceedings of the SIGCHI Conference on Human Factors in Computing Systems, pp. 72–78. ACM, New York (1994)

41. Nevill, C., Bell, T.: Compression of parallel texts. Inf. Process. Manag. **28**(6), 781–793 (1992)

42. Pillai, R., Sivathanu, B.: Adoption of AI-based chatbots for hospitality and tourism. Int. J. Contemp. Hosp. Manag. **32**(10), 3199–3226 (2020)

43. Resendez, V.: A very formal agent: how culture, mode of dressing and linguistic style influence the perceptions toward an Embodied Conversational Agent? Master's thesis, University of Twente (2020)

44. Svenningsson, N., Faraon, M.: Artificial intelligence in conversational agents: a study of factors related to perceived humanness in chatbots. In: Proceedings of the 2019 2nd Artificial Intelligence and Cloud Computing Conference on ZZZ, pp. 151–161 (2019)

45. Tariverdiyeva, G.: Chatbots' perceived usability in information retrieval tasks: an exploratory analysis. Master's thesis, University of Twente (2019)

46. Tegos, S., Demetriadis, S., Tsiatsos, T.: An investigation of conversational agent interventions supporting historical reasoning in primary education. In: Micarelli, A., Stamper, J., Panourgia, K. (eds.) International Conference on Intelligent Tutoring Systems, pp. 260–266. Springer International Publishing, Cham (2016)

Conversational Agent Voting Advice Applications: A Comparison Between a Structured, Semi-structured, and Non-structured Chatbot Design for Communicating with Voters About Political Issues

Naomi Kamoen(✉) [iD], Tessa McCartan, and Christine Liebrecht [iD]

Tilburg School of Humanities and Digital Sciences, Department of Communication and Cognition, Tilburg University, Tilburg, The Netherlands
{N.Kamoen,C.C.Liebrecht}@tilburguniversity.edu

Abstract. Voting Advice Applications (VAAs) are online survey tools that inform voters about political parties and their standpoints. Recent research shows that these tools may be improved by integrating a chatbot function that can provide on demand background information about the political issues. This new goal-oriented tool for information-seeking tasks is called a Conversational Agent Voting Advice Application (CAVAA). In an experimental study ($N = 185$) during the Dutch national elections of 17 March 2021, three CAVAA designs (a structured design with buttons, a non-structured design with a text field, and a semi-structured design with buttons and a text field) have been compared on tool evaluation measures (ease of use, usefulness, and playfulness), and political measures (perceived political knowledge and voting intention). Also, a comparison has been made between users with a high or a low educational level. Results show that the structured design is perceived to be more playful than the non-structured design. Moreover, lower educated users rate the structured and the semi-structured design as easier to use than the non-structured design. Finally, lower educated users also report higher levels of political knowledge after using a CAVAA than higher educated users. This suggests that CAVAAs can be a valuable tool to inform voters.

Keywords: Voting Advice Applications · Conversational agents · Chatbot design · Usefulness · Ease of use · Playfulness · Voting intention · Political knowledge

1 Introduction

In times of the national elections, citizens face the difficulty of deciding which political party to vote for. Over the years, the number of political parties and candidates to choose from has increased in many European countries, making it more difficult for voters to stay informed about the political parties and their standpoints (see [11, 26]). In the

A. Følstad et al. (Eds.): CONVERSATIONS 2021, LNCS 13171, pp. 160–175, 2022.
https://doi.org/10.1007/978-3-030-94890-0_10

Netherlands, for example, voters had no less than 37 political parties to choose from during the last national elections of March 2021 [21].

While voters struggle to make choices, Voting Advice Applications (VAAs) offer a possible solution. VAAs are survey-like tools in which voters can state their opinion on a set of political attitude statements (e.g., 'Dog tax should be increased'). Their answers are then compared to the political viewpoints of the parties running in the elections, and, based on this comparison, a personal voting advice is generated [7]. In many European countries VAAs attract a large audience [11]. In the Netherlands, for example, where VAAs find their origins, the two most popular VAAs were consulted more than 10 million times during the Dutch Parliamentary Elections of 2021 [30].

Not only do VAAs attract a wide audience, research also shows that VAAs have many beneficial effects: they increase their user's political interest [25, 27] and political knowledge [17, 32], leading to a higher turn-out at the ballots [10, 12]. While this sounds promising, research shows at the same time that VAA users frequently experience comprehension problems when responding to the political attitude statements, as no less than one in every five VAA statements causes a comprehension problem [16]. These problems are sometimes related to a user's lack of semantic knowledge about, for example, the political jargon used in the questions (e.g., 'What is dog tax?'), or they may relate to users lacking pragmatic knowledge about the current state of affairs with respect to the political issue (e.g., 'How high is the dog tax currently?').

While one might expect that VAA users would make an effort to solve their comprehension problems so as to receive a valid voting advice, research shows that only a small portion of VAA users (about 1.4%) search the internet to find information to resolve their comprehension problems [16]. Users hence seem to expose satisficing behavior (see [22–24]), which means that they make only a very minimal effort to respond to the statements in the tool. Instead of looking up information on the internet (e.g., via a search engine), users have been shown to make assumptions about the meaning of the terms in the statement and to provide an answer based on these assumptions [16]. This obviously hampers the validity of the voting advice, which is based on the answers to the attitude statements.

An earlier study [18] suggested that implementing a chatbot into a Voting Advice Application is a promising way to provide users with relevant additional information when responding to political attitude statements in a VAA. Chatbots (or conversational agents) are helpful tools that may provide assistance in performing information-seeking tasks through interaction with users in everyday language [28]. In a VAA designed as a chatbot (hereafter referred to as a CAVAA, which is an abbreviation for Conversational Agent Voting Advice Application), users can request additional political information on demand when responding to a political attitude statement. It is exactly this "on demand" aspect (see [28]) that makes a chatbot-functionality a promising way to provide information in a VAA context where users only make a minimal effort to solve their comprehension problems. One advantage of a CAVAA is that users do not have to switch between channels (e.g., the VAA and a search engine) to look up information. Second, a CAVAA can tailor the information to the specific needs of the user, while general search engines such as Google provide information that is not structured to meet the users' demands, which means that users have to extract information from a larger document themselves. Third, the conversational nature of chatbots enables users to ask multiple questions about one political statement (e.g., both semantic and pragmatic information), while at the same time users that do not require any additional information are not confronted with additional ballast when responding to a political statement. Consequently, these characteristics of chatbots reduce the effort VAA users have to make to inform themselves. Therefore, a CAVAA seems to respond well to the processing mode of low elaboration users are in.

In an experimental study [18], a comparison between a CAVAA and a regular VAA showed that indeed the CAVAA performed better with respect to a broad measure for tool evaluation. Moreover, users of the CAVAA were also able to answer more questions about political issues at hand correctly. A second experimental study reported in [18] focused on the specific CAVAA design, comparing a structured version where users could access additional information via buttons, a non-structured version in which users could access information by typing their questions themselves, and a semi-structured version that combined these functionalities. Results show that users experienced the structured version more positively than the non-structured version. Moreover, users answered more knowledge questions about politics correctly when they had worked with the semi-structured version rather than the fully structured version, but no differences were observed with respect to the perceptual knowledge indicators.

While these results provide first evidence that chatbots have potential for information retrieval in a political context, there is a need for a further understanding of what specific chatbot design is most suitable. To the best of our knowledge, there is only one study on this specific topic [18], and a drawback of that study was its limit ecological validity as is was conducted outside of a real-life election context. Moreover, the respondents were always higher educated, whereas lower educated voters are most in need of additional information about politics [34]. Within the broader domain of chatbot research, efficiency effects were found for button designs [15], but there is still a general call for more systematic research about how specific chatbot designs affect users' chatbot experience [28]. The current study therefore set out to examine the effect of the three CAVAA designs (structured, semi-structured, and non-structured) again, but this time amongst both higher and lower educated voters, and during a real-life political election: the Dutch national elections of 17 March 2021. Moreover, the current study used an improved version of the chatbots used in [18] to avoid miscommunication with the non-structured bot as alternative explanation for the findings. Finally, the current study investigated the effects of the three chatbot designs on a broader range of dependent variables as compared to [18], as in the current study the three CAVAA designs are compared with respect to three specific tool evaluation measures (perceived usefulness [6], ease of use [6] and playfulness [1]), as well as two political measures (perceived political knowledge and voting intention). In this way, the current study will not only add to knowledge about the design of CAVAAs specifically, but it will also contribute to the larger field of chatbot research as there is a clear need (see [9]) for studies in specific real-life user contexts, focusing on a broad range of user experience measures and a varied sample of participants.

2 Related Research

2.1 Effects of the Chatbot Design

Perceived Ease of Use. If people are confronted with a new technology, such as a CAVAA, there are several factors that affect the decision as to whether the technology will be used again. The Technology Acceptance Model (TAM; [6]) describes two such factors: perceived ease of use and perceived usefulness.

Perceived ease of use refers to the extent to which users perceive working with a tool as simple and intuitive [6]. In a chatbot-context this measure has been frequently applied, as these tools are usually employed to offer specific information in an efficient and productive manner [3].

A chatbot's interface can stimulate the ease of use of a chatbot application. In a survey study, it has been shown that an interface with controlled conversation elements, like the presence of buttons in a structured design, is easy to use, and, at the same time, removes the limitations, such as miscommunication, that might play a role in a non-structured chatbot interface [20]. What is more, buttons in chatbots are considered as natural and efficient [15]. Because of the presence of buttons, a structured or a semi-structured chatbot design may therefore be perceived as easier to use than a non-structured design.

In the specific context of CAVAAs, it has indeed been shown that a structured CAVAA is experienced to be more user-friendly than the other two CAVAA designs [18]. In that study, however, a broad measure for user experience was reported instead of distinguishing between the TAM [6] sub dimensions of perceived ease of use and perceived usefulness. In the current research, we will investigate these aspects separately. Based on the literature discussed, the hypothesis to be tested with respect to perceived ease of use is:

H1: A structured and a semi-structured CAVAA lead to a higher ease of use evaluation than a non-structured CAVAA design.

Perceived Usefulness. Perceived usefulness describes the degree to which users practically benefit from working with a tool [6]. This evaluation is oftentimes related to enhancing or improving one's job performance [4], which can be translated to the context of CAVAAs as the extent to which the tool helps them to obtain relevant political information necessary for making a vote choice.

The chatbot's design could impact on users' evaluation of perceived usefulness. On the one hand, according to earlier research [28], a structured design could result into users losing awareness of alternative information and develop a narrow understanding of the topic. In the case of a CAVAA, this would imply that users will gather more useful information from the non-structured design, which gives them the absolute freedom to ask any question they like.

On the other hand, one could also argue that users probably gain more useful information when working with a structured CAVAA that – because of its button structure – drives users down the path of clicking on additional information [28]. Given the low elaboration mode VAA users are generally in [16], one could reason that guiding users to request additional information helps them to actually access additional information in the tool. In case users are confronted with a non-structured CAVAA, they could more easily decide to not request information at all, and simply answer the VAAs attitude statements without any additional information. This behavior could result into lower perceptions of the tool's usefulness, compared to a CAVAA design with clickable buttons. This line of reasoning is in accordance with [3], who state that chatbots that help to obtain information in an effective and efficient manner will be perceived as more useful as users consult the tool with a productivity goal.

Considering the above arguments, the semi-structured CAVAA is expected to contribute most to the perceived usefulness, as this design both contains predefined buttons that match with the users' need for an effortless processing of information, and a text entry-functionality that enables them to obtain more information than the information that is available via the predefined buttons. It is therefore expected that:

H2: A semi-structured CAVAA leads to higher perceived usefulness than a structured or a non-structured CAVAA design.

Perceived Playfulness. Over the years, several constructs have been suggested that could also predict the usage and adoption of new technologies (e.g., [14]), in addition to ease of use and usefulness described in the TAM [6]. One of these factors is related to experiential and hedonic aspects of technology and called perceived playfulness of the new technology. Playfulness is defined as "a short-term system-specific trait or state, because an individual can feel more or less playful at various times during his or her visit" ([1]: p. 267). This construct is relevant in the context of VAAs, as research has demonstrated that many VAA users use the tool for entertainment purposes [33]. Also in chatbot research, "entertainment" appeared to be one of the key motivations to use these interactive tools [3].

With regard to the chatbot's design, chatbot research shows that the entertainment value of a chatbot is high if a chatbot meets the expectations of users and people expect they can ask their questions to a chatbot themselves [13]. Moreover, getting a suitable answer to a self-formulated question is also more personal, which people also enjoy more in a conversation [3]. Therefore, one may expect that the non-structured version and the semi-structured version would score higher on perceived playfulness than the fully structured version.

Contrary to this expectation based on the literature, however, it has been observed that the structured CAVAA design was perceived as more, rather than less, playful compared to the other two designs [18]. The authors formulated two explanations for this unexpected difference. First, it could be that the structured design was more entertaining because miscommunication between the user and the bot could have been occurred more frequently in the other versions (this is a risk of an open chat function, see [20]). In the prior CAVAA study [18], however, the chatbot conversations themselves were not analyzed and therefore there is no empirical evidence available about the functioning of the bots. Another explanation for the unexpected difference is that the structured version is found more playful because it gives people a direction about the type of questions that can be asked.

Although we are uncertain about the reason for the observed differences for perceived playfulness in earlier research, we will formulate our hypothesis based on the findings in [18], since any other research of chatbots in the field of VAAs is lacking:

H3: A structured CAVAA design leads to a higher playfulness evaluation than a semi- and a non-structured CAVAA design.

Perceived Political Knowledge. Like a regular VAA [32], a CAVAA in general is expected to have a positive influence on increasing political understanding. Research shows that a VAA is used as a quick-and-dirty aid in the sense that users are only willing to make a little effort [16]. Because users are in a mode of low elaboration, a structured CAVAA design may be most beneficial for increasing the user's political knowledge, as this design requires the lowest effort; people just have to click a button to access relevant information. On the other hand, a non-structured design has more information programmed, so one could also argue that this design allows users to ask a broader range of questions and consequently obtain more political knowledge. The prior CAVAA study [18] compared the three designs with respect to perceived political knowledge and found no differences. As no differences were observed there, and, based on the literature, an argument can be made for two contrasting hypotheses, we will set out to explore the differences between the three designs with respect to this measure.

Voting Intention. Since the current study was conducted during real-life elections, it is relevant to examine whether the three CAVAA designs impact users' voting intentions too. Previous research [5] states that people who possess more political knowledge, are more likely to vote. Hence, one can say that if the political knowledge of voters increases, their intention to vote goes up too. As our hypotheses for the differences between designs for perceived knowledge lacks a direction, and as voting intention was not measured in a previous comparison of the three designs [18], we will also just explore the differences between the three conditions for voting intention.

2.2   The Users' Level of Education

VAAs are used by different 'types' of users, for instance people with a high or low level of education [33]. Generally, voters with a lower level of education have less political knowledge, and have a lower political interest than VAA users with a high level of education [19]. In addition, the low-educated have more difficulty understanding politics and are less involved and less interested in politics than the highly educated. As the 2017 Dutch National Election Survey suggests [34], a well-designed VAA could therefore, in addition to being of great importance for all VAA users, be even more important for VAA users with a lower educational level. Therefore, the current study examines the effects of the three CAVAA designs for users with a higher and lower level of education separately.

Since users can request political information in different ways for each CAVAA design, the effects of the three CAVAA versions may be different for people with a high or low level of education. Dual process models of information processing (e.g., [22, 31]) state that people who have higher cognitive capacities (for example, the higher educated) tend to process information about that subject more deeply. Moreover, it has been shown that people who have a lower level of education experience more difficulty expressing themselves in clear words [8]. Therefore, formulating correct questions in a non-structured CAVAA can be challenging for this particular group. Finally there is research indicating that lower-educated find templated webpages more user-friendly [2]. In light of these findings, we expect that:

H4: The differences as they were formulated in H1, H2 and H3 will be larger for lower than for higher educated users.

3   Method

3.1   Design

To test the hypotheses, an experiment has been conducted with a 3 (CAVAA design: structured, semi-structured, or non-structured) $\times$ 2 (level of education: high or low) between-subject design. Each participant has been randomly assigned to one of the three CAVAA designs; the level of education was operationalized as a quasi-experimental variable. In a subsequent questionnaire, participants assessed the dependent variables of this study: ease of use, usefulness, and playfulness of the CAVAA, as well as their perceived political knowledge, and voting intention. This study has been approved by the Research Ethics and Data Management Committee of Tilburg University, REDC 2021.9. All experimental materials can be accessed via Dataverse (https://doi.org/10. 34894/49FZYF).

3.2   Participants

A total of 185 participants completed the full study, of which 62 men (33.5%) and 123 women (66.5%). Their age ranged between 17 and 62 years, with a mean age of 21.53 years ($SD = 5.27$).

It was checked whether the participants in the three CAVAA conditions were comparable with regard to gender, age, level of education and whether the current election was the first time they could express their vote. Since no significant differences were observed between the three groups (gender ($\chi 2\ (2) = 3.40, p = .183$), age ($F(2, 182) = 0.79, p = .454$), level of education ($\chi 2\ (10) = 16.76, p = .080$), and first time voting ($\chi 2\ (2) = .07, p = .964$)), there is no reason to assume that there were *a priori* differences between the three conditions.

To distinguish between lower and higher educated users, we made a classification in two groups on the basis of a question about educational level (see https://doi.org/10. 34894/49FZYF for the exact question asked). A total of 77 participants were categorized as lower educated (senior secondary vocational education level, or lower) and 104 as higher educated (higher vocational, i.e., HBO or university level). We checked whether there were *a priori* differences between the group of higher and lower educated users. While no differences were observed for gender ($\chi 2\ (1) = 1.45, p = .229$), the higher educated appeared to be older on average age ($F(1, 183) = 10.71, p < .001$), and (hence) they also indicated more frequently that the upcoming elections were not the first that they could express their vote in ($\chi 2\ (1) = 56.52, p < .001$). To account for these differences, we performed all main analyses twice: once without any corrections and once with age and first time voting as covariates.

3.3 Materials

Political Statements. A structured, semi-structured and a non-structured version of a CAVAA for the Dutch National Elections of 17 March 2021 were developed to test the hypotheses. At the heart of these three tools was a set of 20 political attitude statements that users had to answer in order to receive a voting advice. These 20 political statements were based on statements in existing Dutch VAAs (*Kieskompas* and *Stemwijzer*) and already used in an earlier CAVAA study [18].

Statements were deliberately selected that could cause comprehension problems, such as 'The scheme for the deduction of mortgage interest should be abolished' and 'The Netherlands must allow the cultivation of genetically modified crops (GMOs)'. The terms 'mortgage interest deduction' and 'GMOs' are terms for which CAVAA users can experience comprehension problems [16].

In total, 18 out of the 20 statements were taken from [18]; 2 statements from that study were no longer topic of the debate at the time we developed the materials for the current research and these statements were therefore replaced with new statements about the Corona crisis.

CAVAA Versions. To develop the three CAVAA versions, we started out from the CAVAAs used in [18]. These chatbots have been developed using software from Flow.ai (see www.flow.ai). Before using these bots again for the purposes of the current study, we first conducted a qualitative content analysis of 90 conversations (with a user responding to 20 political attitude statements in each conversation). In this qualitative study, we coded, among other things, (a) whether the user terminated the conversation early, (b) whether miscommunication between the user and the bot occurred, and if so, (c) the cause for the miscommunication. Results showed that miscommunication between the chatbot and the user hardly ever appeared. When miscommunication did occur, it happened mostly in the open design because the bot was not trained for certain concepts (e.g., 'mortgage interest reduction' instead of 'deduction'), or because it did not recognize certain ways of asking for the advantages of a policy change (e.g., what is an advantage of X). On the basis of these observations, we improved the existing chatbots by adding more relevant words and synonyms to the intent recognition module. Below we will discuss the three CAVAA versions in more detail.

Structured CAVAA. The structured CAVAA displayed three buttons below each statement. The first button was labelled as 'What does X mean?', in which X was replaced for a specific term in the statement. Clicking this button would lead the user to semantic information. The second button was displayed as: 'What is the current state of affairs?', and this button lead to pragmatic background information about the political issue in the statement. With the third button ('I have no need for additional information'), users could indicate that they had no need for information.

When users clicked on the semantic button to access the explanation of a term in the statement, the two remaining buttons with the current state of affairs and the choice not to obtain more information were displayed again, and the other way around for when users clicked on the pragmatic button.

Non-structured CAVAA. In the non-structured design, users only had the option to type in questions themselves, without the presence of buttons. The CAVAA was trained on the meaning of difficult words in the statements (i.e., semantic information), questions about the current state of affairs (i.e., pragmatic information), and about the advantages and disadvantages of the policy in the statement (i.e., other information). Instead of displaying three buttons for each political statement, the CAVAA displayed after each political statement: 'You can ask me a question about this statement, but you can also answer the statement directly' followed by the button 'I want to answer the statement'. This way, it was made explicit that users were allowed to ask a question themselves, but that they could also answer the statement immediately. In order to avoid irritating repetition in the CAVAA, from the fourth statement onwards only a button was added to the statement with 'I have no question about this statement', which enabled users to directly answer the statement.

Semi-structured CAVAA. In the semi-structured design, the functionalities of the structured and non-structured design were combined. As in the structured design, users could use the three buttons offered, and the CAVAA was also trained to answer user questions, so that users could also type in a question themselves. Figure 1 shows an example of the semi-structured version of the chatbot and via this link https://doi.org/10.34894/49FZYF an mp4-clip can be accessed in which the functionalities of the chatbot are demonstrated.

3.4 Instrumentation and Procedure

The study has been conducted online between 3 and 17 March 2021 (Election Day). Participants were contacted partially through the Human Subject Pool of Tilburg University and partially through the researchers' own networks. Participants were asked to open a link to Qualtrics, which automatically led to one of the three CAVAA versions. In each version, participants were given an introduction to the topic and an instruction on how to use the CAVAA. After this introduction, the participants were asked to provide informed consent. The text stated that participation in the study was completely voluntary and anonymous, that participants could stop at any time, and that the study had been approved by the Research Ethics and Data Management Committee of the university.

As soon as the participants had given informed consent, a number of questions about the demographic characteristics of the participants followed. Next, participants could click on a link that directed them to one of the three CAVAA versions. After having answered all 20 political statements in the CAVAA, the user obtained a voting advice. Thereafter, the user was redirected to the survey in Qualtrics to evaluate the CAVAA with respect to the five dependent variables.

Ease of Use. Ease of use was operationalized with 5 items based on [1] and adapted to fit the purposes of the current study. An example of this is: 'It is easy for me to use the chatbot voting aid. Disagree 0 0 0 0 0 0 0 Agree'. The scale had a good reliability ($\alpha = .73, M = 5.39, SD = 1.55$).

Usefulness. Usefulness was operationalized with 5 items also based on [1] and adapted to fit the purposes of the current study. An item example is: "By using a chatbot voting

Fig. 1. Example of the semi-structured CAVAA showing the first question (*We will start with statement 1. There should be a binding referendum with which citizens can stop laws being implemented*), three buttons (*What is a binding referendum, What is the current state of affairs,* and *I do not need additional information*), and a text-entry functionality to request specific information.

aid, I can answer the statements more easily than in a regular voting aid. Disagree 0 0 0 0 0 0 0 Agree". The reliability of the scale was good ($\alpha = .87$, $M = 4.62$, $SD = 1.72$).

Playfulness. Playfulness was measured with 5 items based on [29]. An example is: 'The chatbot voting aid gave me pleasure filling in the voting aid. Disagree 0 0 0 0 0 0 0 Agree'. Again, questions were adapted to fit the current context. The scale showed a good reliability ($\alpha = .88$, $M = 5.32$, $SD = 1.43$).

Political Knowledge. Perceived political knowledge was measured with 3 items based on [27]. An item example of this is: 'By using a chatbot voting aid, I gain more insight into the positions of political parties. Disagree 0 0 0 0 0 0 0 Agree'. The scale had a good reliability ($\alpha = .78$, $M = 4.39$, $SD = 1.73$).

Voting Intention. Voting intention was measured by one question, asking participants whether they had the intention to vote during the upcoming national elections of 17 March 2021. Participants answered this question by indicating either 'yes', 'no' or 'I do not know yet'. For the analysis of voting intention, the latter two categories were grouped together. Hence, we evaluated the proportion of voters who would certainly vote in the upcoming elections relative to the proportion of voters who were either not sure or indicated they were unlikely to go voting.

4 Results[1]

Participants evaluated the CAVAA on its ease of use, usefulness and playfulness, and they indicated whether they believed they had obtained more political knowledge by using the tool, as well as whether they were likely to vote in the upcoming elections. The means and standard deviations of all dependent variables can be found in Table 1. For each dependent variable, a Factorial ANOVA was conducted to examine whether these perception scores were affected by the CAVAA design and participants' education level.

Ease of Use. For perceived ease of use a main effect of educational level was observed $(F(1, 179) = 39.70, p < .001, \eta2 = .18)$, showing that the higher educated found all three CAVAA versions easier to use as compared to the lower educated. In addition, both a main effect of CAVAA version $(F(2, 172) = 6.36, p = .002)$, and an interaction effect between educational level and CAVAA version $(F(2, 172) = 4.05, p = .019, \eta2 = .04)$ were found. These results can be interpreted such that for the higher educated there are no clear differences in ease of use depending on the CAVAA version $(F(2, 105) = 0.31, p = .738)$, whereas for the lower educated a difference can be found $(F(2, 74) = .243 \ p = .003)$. For the lower educated, the structured version is evaluated better with respect to the ease of use than the non-structured version $(p = .002)$ and also the semi-structured version receives marginally better evaluations than the non-structured version $(p = .063)$. Hence, a structured or semi-structured design is evaluated better in terms of ease of use, but this only holds true for the lower educated.

Usefulness. For perceived usefulness results show no main effect of level of education $(F (1, 179) = .47, p = .496)$, no main effect of CAVAA version $(F(2, 179) = 1.32, p = .270)$ and also no interaction effect $(F(2, 179) = 1.26, p = .286)$.

Playfulness. As was the case for ease of use, the results for playfulness show a main effect of the level of education but this time lower educated perceived all three CAVAA designs to be more entertaining than the higher educated $(F (1, 179) = 27.33, p < .001, \eta2 = .13)$. The analysis also showed a main effect of CAVAA version $(F(2, 179) = 4.90, p = .008)$. Post-hoc analyses indicate that the structured version receives higher playfulness evaluations than the non-structured version $(p = .015)$, but that no differences are observed between the other versions (semi-structured versus structured: $p = .75$; semi-structured versus non-structured: $p = .29$). The interaction between the level of education and CAVAA version was not significant $(F(2, 179) = .90, p = .409, \eta2 = .01)$.

Political Knowledge. Similar to the results for playfulness, a significant main effect of level of education was observed for perceived political knowledge $(F(1, 179) = 19.67, p < .001, \eta2 = .09)$: lower educated users indicated to have obtained more political knowledge than higher educated users. The analysis showed no significant main effect of the CAVAA version $(F(2, 179) = 2.56, p = .080)$, nor an interaction effect between CAVAA version and level of education $(F(2, 179) = .20, p = .823)$.

---

[1] All analyses were ran a second time with age and first time voting as covariates. For none of the DVs did this change the interpretation of the results. Hence, results are robust for correction on initial differences with respect to these variables.

Table 1. Means (*M*) and standard deviations (*SD*) between brackets per dependent variable and per experimental condition.

	Educ. level	Ease of use	Usefulness	Playfulness	Pol. knowledge	Voting intention
Structured	High	5.86 (0.85)	4.70 (1.51)	5.16 (1.08)	4.23 (1.49)	.86 (0.34)
	Low	5.37 (0.80)	4.98 (0.85)	6.25 (0.71)	5.19 (0.87)	.71 (0.46)
	Total	5.67 (0.86)	4.81 (1.29)	5.59 (1.09)	4.61 (1.35)	.80 (0.40)
Semi structured	High	5.74 (0.87)	4.39 (1.36)	4.96 (1.17)	4.02 (1.39)	.91 (0.29)
	Low	4.99 (1.06)	4.85 (1.35)	5.87 (1.28)	5.05 (1.16)	.59 (0.50)
	Total	5.40 (1.02)	4.59 (1.36)	5.36 (1.29)	4.48 (1.38)	.77 (0.42)
Non-structured	High	5.72 (0.78)	4.58 (1.45)	4.80 (1.00)	3.79 (1.45)	.86 (0.35)
	Low	4.27 (1.36)	4.27 (1.63)	5.36 (1.20)	4.53 (1.61)	.50 (0.51)
	Total	5.12 (1.27)	4.45 (1.52)	5.03 (1.12)	4.10 (1.55)	.71 (0.46)
Total	High	5.77 (0.83)	4.56 (1.44)	4.97 (1.08)	4.02 (1.44)	.88 (0.33)
	Low	4.86 (1.18)	4.69 (1.34)	5.82 (1.15)	4.92 (1.27)	.60 (0.49)
	Total	5.39 (1.08)	4.62 (1.40)	5.32 (1.18)	4.39 (1.44)	.76 (0.43)

Note. All dependent variables were measured on a 7-point Likert scale, with the exception of voting intention (which was coded as 0 or 1).

Voting Intention. Yet again a main effect of level of education was found for voting intention ($F(1, 179) = 21.47, p < .001$): higher educated respondents indicated more frequently that they had the intention to go voting in the upcoming elections. No main effect of CAVAA design was observed ($F(2, 179) = 1.03, p = .359$), and also the interaction between CAVAA version and educational level failed to reach significance ($F(2, 179) = 1.08, p = .341$).

5 Conclusion

Since VAA users frequently experience comprehension problems when answering political attitude statements and only a very small portion of them search for additional information on the internet to resolve these problems [16], chatbot technology has been implemented to create Conversation Agent Voting Advice Applications (CAVAAs) that can provide additional political information on demand [18]. This study aimed to examine the influence of three CAVAA designs (structured, semi-structured, or non-structured) on tool evaluation measures (perceived usefulness, ease of use, and playfulness), and political measures (political knowledge and voting intention), for both higher and lower educated users.

Results show that the CAVAA design influences both the playfulness and the ease of use of the tool. First, a structured design is perceived to be more playful than a non-structured design. Second, both the structured and the semi-structured design are evaluated better in terms of ease of use than a non-structured design, but this only holds true for the lower educated users. In addition, results show that regardless its design, differences between higher and lower educated users are observed. After using a CAVAA, lower educated participants assessed the tool's playfulness more positively than higher educated participants, they indicated to have obtained more political knowledge, but, at the same time, they were less likely to go voting in the upcoming elections.

6   Discussion

Ease of Use and Usefulness. In the earlier study [18], one broad measure of user friendliness was reported, combining aspects related to the simplicity of the design (ease of use) and the practical benefit of the tool (usefulness). In that study, the structured design scored better on this overall measure of user friendliness as compared to both other versions. In the current research, we separately analyzed two sub dimensions of user friendliness according to the Technology Acceptance Model (TAM, [6]; also see [1]): ease of use and usefulness. Results for ease of use are somewhat comparable with the earlier findings [18], as the structured version received the highest scores, but this effect was only observed for lower educated users. By contrast, in the current study no differences between CAVAA designs were observed for usefulness. This implies that the primary added value of a structured or semi-structured design lies in its simplicity, rather than in its practical benefit. The finding that the structured version scored better on ease of use for lower educated users, matches with research showing that an interface with buttons is simpler than an open interface with a type function [20].

Perceived Playfulness. While previous chatbot research from other domains demonstrated that users find a non-structured chatbot design more playful [3, 13], the study in [18] reported the highest playfulness scores for the structured CAVAA version. The current study observed a similar effect with the structured version being rated higher on playfulness compared to the non-structured CAVAA. We think that this finding is due to the fact that in a VAA setting users are in such a mode of low elaboration [16] that they only experience joy in playing with the CAVAA if is offers easily accessible information via buttons. It would be interesting to test this explanation further in a qualitative think-aloud study; such a study can provide an insight into how users use a tool and why they evaluate it positively or negatively.

Political Knowledge. The present study showed no differences between the CAVAA designs for perceived political knowledge. This is in line with the findings of [18], where also no differences for that measure were observed. In the current study, as well as in [18], perceived knowledge was only measured after working with the CAVAA. For a future study it would be interesting to measure the same perceptions both beforehand and afterwards so that a difference score can be calculated and compared between versions. Moreover, it would be interesting to include a factual measure of political knowledge and compare that between versions (compare [18]); perhaps such an indicator would be more sensitive of demonstrating knowledge differences related to the design of a CAVAA.

Voting Intention. No differences were found between the three CAVAA versions for the intention to go voting in the Dutch national elections that were upcoming at time of conducting the experiment. There is no comparison to be made between this finding and the earlier study on CAVAAs [18], as in that study voting intention was not measured. In the current study, the overall percentage of voters that indicated that they would probably go voting was 76%. Interestingly, this percentage comes very close to the overall actual turn-out rate in the Dutch 2021 national elections (78%; see [35]). Therefore, overreporting is unlikely to be the cause of the results obtained. To better understand the results for voting intention, it would be interesting to measure voting intention both before and after tool usage and compare that between CAVAA versions; such a delta score might be a more sensitive indicator of possible differences caused by CAVAA design.

Level of Education. Only for one of our dependent variables, ease of use, did we observe an interaction between CAVAA version and the user's level of education. This interaction was in the expected direction such that the differences between CAVAA versions were larger for the lower educated than for the higher educated users. This illustrates the usefulness of investigating CAVAA effects for different sub groups (also see [9]) and to include sub groups that are in special need of additional information about political issues.

Besides this interaction effect, quite some main effects of educational level were shown: the lower educated value a CAVAA's playfulness more positively, they indicated to have obtained more political knowledge, but, at the same time, they were less likely to go voting in the upcoming elections. These findings illustrate that a CAVAA as a new election tool could really be beneficial for lower educated voters, potentially contributing to a decrease of the knowledge gap.

As for the specific design of a CAVAA, and arguably also other chatbots that provide assistance in information-seeking tasks, we recommend chatbot developers and clients to use a structured set-up of the chatbot. A structured chatbot with only buttons scores better on ease of use (for lower educated users) and playfulness (both lower and higher educated users). This is probably because the design gives a hint about what kind of information can be accessed, and also because this version better responds to the processing mode of low elaboration users are in. A structured chatbot design thus enables both lower and higher educated users to inform themselves about complex topics in a fun and rather effortless way.

References

1. Ahn, T., Ryu, S., Ahn, T., Ryu, S., Han, I.: The impact of Web quality and playfulness on user acceptance of online retailing. Inf. Manage. **44**(3), 263–275 (2007). https://doi.org/10.1016/j.im.2006.12.008
2. Almahamid, S., Mcadams, A.C., Al Kalaldeh, T., Al-Sa'Eed, M.: The relationship between perceived usefulness, perceived ease of use, perceived information quality, and intention to use E-Government. J. Theoret. Appl. Inf. Technol. **11**(1), 30–44 (2010)
3. Brandtzaeg, P.B., Følstad, A.: Why people use chatbots. In: Kompatsiaris, I., et al. (eds.) INSCI 2017. LNCS, vol. 10673, pp. 377–392. Springer, Cham (2017). https://doi.org/10.1007/978-3-319-70284-1_30
4. Davis, F.D.: User acceptance of information technology: system characteristics, user perceptions and behavioral impacts. Int. J. Man Mach. Stud. **38**(3), 475–487 (1993)
5. Delli Carpini, M.X., Keeter, S.: What Americans Know about Politics and Why it Matters CT. Yale University Press, New Haven (1996)
6. Davis, F.D.: Perceived usefulness, perceived ease of use, and user acceptance of information technology. MIS Q. **13**(3), 319–340 (1989). https://doi.org/10.2307/249008
7. De Graaf, J.: The irresistible rise of Stemwijzer. In: Cedroni, L., Garzia, D. (eds.) Voting Advice Applications in Europe: The State of the Art, pp. 35–46. Scriptaweb, Napoli (2010)
8. Elling, S., Lentz, L., De Jong, M.: Users' abilities to review web site pages. J. Bus. Tech. Commun. **26**(2), 171–201 (2012). https://doi.org/10.1177/1050651911429920
9. Følstad, A., et al.: Future directions for chatbot research: an interdisciplinary research agenda. Computing **103**(12), 2915–2942 (2021). https://doi.org/10.1007/s00607-021-01016-7
10. Garzia, D., De Angelis, A., Pianzola, J.: The effect of voting advice applications on electoral participation. In: Garzia, D., Marschall S. (eds.) Voters with Parties and Candidates. Voting Advice Applications in a Comparative Perspective, pp. 105–114. ECPR Press (2014)
11. Garzia, D., Marschall, S.: Voting Advice Applications under review: the state of research. Int. J. Electron. Gov. **5**(3–4), 203–222 (2012)
12. Gemenis, K., Rosema, M.: Voting Advice Applications and electoral turnout. Elect. Stud. **36**, 281–289 (2014). https://doi.org/10.1016/j.electstud.2014.06.010
13. Hedberg, S.R.: Is AI going mainstream as last? A look inside Microsoft Research. IEEE **13**(2), 21–25 (1998). https://doi.org/10.1109/5254.671087
14. Hornbæk, K., Hertzum, M.: Technology Acceptance and user experience. ACM Trans. Comput.-Hum. Interact. **24**(5), 1–30 (2017). https://doi.org/10.1145/3127358
15. Jain, M., Kumar, P., Kota, R., Patel, S.N.: Evaluating and informing the design of chatbots. In: Proceedings of the 2018 Designing Interactive Systems Conference, pp. 895–906. ACM, New York (2018)
16. Kamoen, N., Holleman, B.: I don't get it. Response difficulties in answering political attitude statements in Voting Advice Applications. Surv. Res. Meth. **11**(2), 125–140 (2017). https://doi.org/10.18148/srm/2017.v11i2.6728
17. Kamoen, N., Holleman, B., Krouwel, A., Van de Pol, J., De Vreese, C.: The effect of voting advice applications on political knowledge and vote choice. Ir. Political Stud. **30**(4), 595–618 (2015). https://doi.org/10.1080/07907184.2015.1099096
18. Kamoen, N., Liebrecht, C., Mekel, P., Van Limpt, S.: Stemhulp-chatbots: Politieke informatie op maat. Tekstblad **26**(4), 12–15 (2020)
19. Kleinnijenhuis, J., et al.: Nederland vijfstromenland: De rol van de media en stemwijzers bij de verkiezingen van 2006. Bert Bakker, Amsterdam (2007)
20. Klopfenstein, C.U.N.O., Delpriori, S., Malatini, S., Bogliolo, A.: The rise of bots: a survey of conversational interfaces, patterns, and paradigms. In: Proceedings of the 2017 Conference on Designing Interactive Systems, pp. 555–565. ACM, New York (2017)

21. Kiesraad: 37 Partijen nemen deel aan de Tweede Kamerverkiezingen. https://www.kiesraad.nl/actueel/nieuws/2021/02/05/37-partijen-nemen-deel-aan-tweede-kamerverkiezing

22. Krosnick, J.A.: Response strategies for coping with the cognitive demands of attitude measures in surveys. Appl. Cogn. Psychol. **5**(3), 213–236 (1991). https://doi.org/10.1002/acp.2350050305

23. Krosnick, J.A.: The threat of satisficing in surveys: the shortcuts respondents take in answering questions. Surv. Meth. Newsl. **20**, 4–8 (2000)

24. Krosnick, J.A., Narayan, S.S., Smith, W.R.: Satisficing in surveys: initial evidence. In: Braverman, M.T., Slater, J.K. (eds.) Advances in Survey Research, pp. 29–44. Jossey Bass, San Francisco (1996)

25. Krouwel, A., Holleman, B., Kamoen, N., Van de Pol, J., De Vreese, C.: Effecten van online stemhulpen. In: Peters, K. (eds.) Griffiers Jaarboek, pp. 19–28 (2018)

26. Krouwel, A., Vitiello, T., Wall, M.: The practicalities of issuing vote advice: a new methodology for profiling and matching. Int. J. Electron. Gov. **5**(3–4), 223–243 (2012)

27. Ladner, A.: Voting advice applications: impact on voting decisions in the 2011 Swiss national elections. Paper presented at the 62nd Political Studies Association Annual International Conference, 3–5 April, Belfast (2012). https://serval.unil.ch/resource/serval:BIB_9019E7F44D1A.P001/REF.pdf

28. Liao, Q.V., Geyer, W., Muller, M., Khazaen, Y.: Conversational interfaces for information search. In: Fu, W.T., vanOostendorp, H. (eds.) Understanding and Improving Information Search. HIS, pp. 267–287. Springer, Cham (2020). https://doi.org/10.1007/978-3-030-38825-6_13

29. Moon, J.W., Kim, Y.G.: Extending the TAM for a World-Wide-Web context. Inf. Manage. **38**(4), 217–230 (2001)

30. NRC Handelsblad: Recordgebruik online stemhulpen, in totaal meer dan 10 miljoen keer geraadpleegd. Nrc.nl, 17 March 2021. https://www.nrc.nl/nieuws/2021/03/17/recordgebruik-online-stemhulpen-in-totaal-meer-dan-10-miljoen-keer-geraadpleegd-a4036166. Consulted on 7 Nov 2021

31. Petty, R., Cacioppo, J.T.: From Communication and Persuasion: Central and Peripheral Routes to Attitude Change. Springer, New York (1986)

32. Schultze, M.: Effects of voting advice applications (VAAs) on political knowledge about party positions. Policy Internet **6**(1), 46–68 (2014). https://doi.org/10.1002/1944-2866.POI352

33. Van de Pol, J., Holleman, B., Kamoen, N., Krouwel, A., De Vreese, C.: Beyond young, highly educated males: a typology of VAA users. J. Inf. Technol. Politics **11**(4), 397–411 (2014). https://doi.org/10.1080/19331681.2014.958794

34. Van der Meer, T., Van der Kolk, H., Rekker, R.: Aanhoudend wisselvallig: Nationaal Kiezersonderzoek (2017). https://kennisopenbaarbestuur.nl/media/256288/aanhoudend-wisselvallig-nko-2017.pdf

35. Wikipedia: Tweede kamerverkiezingen (2021). https://nl.wikipedia.org/wiki/Tweede_Kamerverkiezingen_2021

Social Research with Gender-Neutral Voices in Chatbots – The Generation and Evaluation of Artificial Gender-Neutral Voices with Praat and Google WaveNet

Sandra Mooshammer(✉) ⓘ and Katrin Etzrodt ⓘ

TU Dresden, 01069 Dresden, Germany
sandra.mooshammer@mailbox.tu-dresden.de

Abstract. Artificial voice generation enables the creation of gender-neutral voice-based chatbots, such as "Q", and with this, new possibilities for social scientists to investigate effects of gender in chatbots on users. However, for this research, gender-neutral and matching male and female voices are necessary. This paper aims to match this need by providing a method for the creation of acoustically gender-neutral voices which can serve as a base for further investigation. The method requires less technical knowledge than most other approaches while, at the same time, theoretical assumptions about gender perception and neutrality can be modeled into the voices. Specifically, fundamental frequency and formant frequencies are outlined as major influences and subsequently included in voice production. In addition, an efficient two-step test for assessing gender perception is demonstrated. Applied to the produced voices, the test proved to be successful in determining gender-neutral variants. In sum, the paper shows that the production method and underlying theory are suited to create gender-neutral voices as well as matching male and female variants.

Keywords: Voice-based chatbots · Gender neutrality · Voice production

1 Introduction

To this day, voices in voice-based chatbots are predominantly female. Sey and Fesalbon found that out of 70 different voice-based chatbots, 68% solely had a female voice, 13% sounded exclusively male, and another 13% offered different genders as options to choose from [1]. Among those offering different genders are also the most widely spread voice-based chatbots, such as Siri, Amazon Alexa, or Google Home. However, in addition to standard male and female voices, other possibilities are being explored. For example, in 2019, a cooperation of Danish organizations produced "Q," an attempt to create a gender-neutral chatbot voice [2]. Q's fundamental frequency is located between 145 and 175 Hz (Hz), a region between typical male and female frequencies [2]. About 50% of the participants found the voice to be gender-neutral, while the other 50% perceived the voice as male or female in equal proportions [3].

© Springer Nature Switzerland AG 2022
A. Følstad et al. (Eds.): CONVERSATIONS 2021, LNCS 13171, pp. 176–191, 2022.
https://doi.org/10.1007/978-3-030-94890-0_11

A crucial issue concerning "genderless" voices in chatbots is their impact on the users. The effect of *gender* in computer systems has been researched extensively, with fundamental works stemming from the research group around Clifford Nass and Byron Reeves (e.g., [4–6]), who demonstrated that computers and technical systems sometimes are perceived as social actors. Thus, also gender in technical systems may elicit social (and often stereotype-driven) responses. The creation of *gender-neutral* voices adds new questions: How is the voice perceived? Under which circumstances does the perception change? Are social roles and gender stereotypes applied? And how does neutrality affect the users' attitude towards the technical system?

Some attempts have been made to hypothesize about the perception of such voices and their effects [7, 8]. It is clear, however, that in continuation of theoretical discussions, these questions and their derivatives can only be investigated by using an actual gender-neutral voice. Moreover, to make reasonable inferences, the neutral voice should be compared to male and female voices in the analysis. These should also be, apart from their gender, as similar as possible to the investigated neutral voice.

This paper aims to enable investigations on phenomena that may arise from artificial gender-neutral voices by providing an approach for social scientists to generate gendered and gender-neutral voices – which fulfill the conditions mentioned above – economically and without becoming computer scientists. Hence, it becomes possible to comparatively investigate gender effects exclusively due to acoustic parameters and not to other linguistic properties that can, for example, occur when using different human speakers. For this purpose, we will first elaborate on the primary characteristics of gender-neutral and gendered voices from a theoretical and practical perspective. Second, we will describe the production and evaluation of these voices. Subsequently, we will discuss the approach for its applicability to social sciences.

2 Literature Review

2.1 Perception and Properties of Gender-Specific Voices

Gender is usually assigned intuitively to a voice. Whether a voice is perceived as male or female is based on the combination of various physical acoustic parameters determined by the vocal tract as well as psychological and social aspects. Gender neutrality, however, has received less attention in research. The basics of gender perception will be examined in the following.

The Fundamental Frequency "F0". The sound of speech is produced in the vocal tract by forcing air through the *vocal folds* so that they begin to vibrate, which is specified in the unit Hz (Hertz), referring to the number of vibrations of the vocal folds per second. Male vocal folds are, on average, thicker and vibrate slower than those of women. As a result, the fundamental frequency of the voice (F0) differs between men and women. According to Simpson [9] and related studies [10–12], F0 is on average between 100 and 120 Hz in men and between 200 and 220 Hz in women, whereby the use of pure vowels tends to elicit higher F0 in contrast to connected speech [10] and the length and nature of speech samples also has an impact [12]. However, this is only true for the languages studied in each case (German, English); In other languages, for example in Asian ones,

F0 differs less significantly, which suggests that differences between male and female F0 could be partly culturally learned [9]. In addition, Berg, Fuchs et al. [13] indicate that F0 of women in German and English has decreased compared to older studies; they found a new mean value of 168.5 Hz for women, whereas men remained within the known range at 111.9 Hz. Furthermore, F0 is often lower for older than younger women and can rise slightly for older men [12, 14].

The Formant Frequencies "FF". Another difference is the *length* of the vocal tract, referring to the space from vocal folds to lips. The average is 14 to 14.5 cm for females compared to 17 to 18 cm for males [9]. In vowel production, resonances, called formant frequencies (FF), occur in this area. Vowels have several formants with an individual ratio for each vowel (the first "e" in "ever" is linguistically described as [e] and has a slightly different formant ratio from the second "e"; this sound is the vowel [ə] in linguistic terms) [15]. Usually, the lowest two or three formants are regarded in research. Due to the greater length of the vocal tract, FF are deeper in male than female voices. Even similarly sized males and females differ in formant height [11].

Studies by Hillenbrand et al. [16] and Peterson and Barney [17] on the English language indicate that formants of males and females differ by factors of 1.17 ([17], own calculation) or 1.15 ([16], own calculation – other studies report differences of factors from 1.17 to 1.2 [18]). However, the average over the first three formants (F1, F2, F3) for individual vowels differs between the two studies of [16, 17], sometimes by more than 100 Hz, and the values for the individual formants differ even more. Furthermore, no ranges or standard deviations are given. Meanwhile, although males and females differ significantly, the formants of both genders show an overlap: The highest formants [11] or quartiles [19] for F1, F2, and F3 in male speaker groups are mostly higher than the lowest corresponding formants/quartiles in female groups.

However, vowel formants may differ between languages. Thus, the previous findings may not be easily transferred to the German language, which also uses more different vowels than English [20]. Pätzold and Simpson [19] examined 19 (out of 24) German vowels and umlauts in their study. Their findings indicate that German vowels may have lower values than the English ones for both genders; namely a primary difference of 100 Hz for men and 200 Hz for women in comparison to the results described above. However, these results have to be relativized. The researchers reported the median (whereas the other studies used the arithmetic mean), and measured spoken sentences instead of vowels, which makes the differences difficult to interpret. If F0 differs between vowels and connected speech (see above), it is possible that this effect also occurs for formants. Hence, the difference that [19] found may not be due to the investigated language but the used sentences and the different reporting.

Since there is a lack of further studies, we can only conclude that there is a difference in the fundamental frequency between genders, but it remains uncertain which exact formants are typical for men and women. Evidence only exists for a significant difference and its approximate magnitude.

Influences of F0 and FF on Gender Perception. The majority of existing studies identified F0 as the primary parameter for gender assignment in *isolated vowels and syllables* [21–24]. If F0 of a vowel or syllable is raised from masculine to feminine while the masculine formants remain constant, a feminine voice is predominantly recognized, and vice versa. In *connected speech*, FF become more influential [11, 22]. However, additional criteria which are only present in connected language may also play a role [11]. Assmann et al. [25] demonstrated that sentences initially spoken by a man and then raised to a medium level of F0 and FF tended to be perceived as more masculine than a woman's sentences raised to the same level. This suggests that other factors besides F0 and FF have an effect on gender perception. Skuk and Schweinber-ger, for example, verified that the gendered perception of a voice could be achieved by combining changes in FF and spectrum level [23]. Furthermore, men tend to have a creakier and less breathy voice quality than women [9] – possible gender indicators.

Nonetheless, the simultaneous manipulation of F0 and FF of a voice, while neglecting other parameters, is sufficient for a convincing change in the perceived male or female gender of a voice [11, 23]. As a result, the intended gender is correctly identified with a minimal probability of 80% after the change [22, 24].

2.2 Gender Neutrality

As shown above, there are ranges in both F0 and FF in which male and female voices average. Between these ranges lies a span where high male and low female values overlap. Here, the gender is less clear and harder to assign. Gallena et al. identified pitches between 156 and 165 Hz as the neutral range of F0 [15]. Gelfer and Bennett found a similar ambiguous middle range between 145 and 165 Hz [11]. The state of research on formants and their gender-neutral ranges is less clear, yet it can be assumed that such a range exists because formants differ for males and females and overlap in a middle range as described above. Therefore, it can be considered acoustically ambiguous if a voice lies within the middle ranges in both parameters.

However, whether and to what extent voices are attributed gender neutrality cannot be clearly answered on the basis of previous research. In the gender-neutral range of F0 and FF, other acoustic parameters like the ones described above, which are otherwise masked by the effect of the two large factors, could contribute more to gender identi-fication. Also, the *match or mismatch* of F0 and FF may be influential for perceiving ambiguity. Whereas a match – if F0 and FF lie within a gender-typical range – results in a voice perceived as more natural and gendered, a mismatch leads to a less clear gender assignment of the voice, i.e., it is perceived as more gender-neutral [25]. Apart from acoustic parameters, identifying perceived gender neutrality in a voice by hearing (in comparison to classifying a distinct gender) is influenced by the way of measurement and becomes complex by additional influences like the naturalness of the voice, other cues such as embodiment, or social and cultural norms.

How gender is *measured* has a tremendous impact on the detection of neutrality. Mullennix et al. [26] indicated that the gender perception of voices is not fundamen-tally categorical, but runs along a continuum that depends on the level of F0 and FF. Vowels located in a gender-neutral region were also ranked in the middle region of a scale representing a continuum between male and female. However, a second study in the same article [26] demonstrated that the same voices are predominantly classi-fied as male or female when the three categories "male," "female," and "other" are given. Hence, from the designation of the categories, people may not have assumed that "other" was intended as an intermediate level between the two genders. Although the study is 26 years old, and nowadays, "other" may be recognized as an intermediate level, it demonstrates socio-cultural influences on the measurable recognition of gender and neutrality. Another example for measurement effects occurred in a study concerning transgender people who received voice training to change from a masculine to a feminine voice [27]. Participants were asked to classify the voices as male or female and to rate their masculinity/femininity in relation to the chosen gender on a 7-point scale. The authors identified a F0 of 150–160 Hz that they considered a threshold for a consistently female rather than male perception. However, the *lack of a category* for neutrality forced people into the two gender categories, which prevents inferences about the classification as distinctly male or female. The non-gradual measurement neglected that voices categorized as male but very feminine (or vice versa) could also be (but are not automatically!) gender-neutral, resulting in possible overestimations of masculinity/femininity. This assumption is supported by results of Bralley et al. [28], who used a seven-point scale from masculine to feminine. They found that a trans-gender person scored 3.7 before and 4.6 after voice training. Both scores are close to the scale midpoint, which can be interpreted as neutrality, but a change into the feminine direction was made visible – Gelfer and Schofield's [27] approach would not display this nuance adequately. Subsequent studies with transgender persons have confirmed that ambiguous voices may well be rated as approximately neutral [29, 30].

However, whether and to what extent gender neutrality is attributed to voices depends on further factors. For *natural* speech, the perception of gender neutrality mainly occurs when acoustic parameters are ambivalent. For example, single acoustically gender-neutral vowels may well be explicitly perceived as gender-neutral [15, 26]. In the context of *artificially* generated speech, Behrens et al. [31] incidentally recognized that three out of six participants perceived a robot that had either a male or a female voice as genderless. It is possible that this happened due to the use of a text-to-speech software which (deliberately, according to the researchers,) produced a very mechanical-sounding voice. Some studies with Pepper [32, 33] confirm this sensitivity to the voice type. Although the robot has an androgynous [34] (or possibly slightly more female [35]) appearance and was equipped with a gender-neutral voice by the researchers, it was primarily rated male in these studies, whereas only one third assessed it as "neither male nor female." Thus, gender assignment in artificial voices may work differently than in natural ones. However, it is possible that this voice was not entirely neutral: The authors explained that Pepper's voice was generated using different F0 values (which they did not explicitly define). Yet, they ignored that formants and other acoustic parameters can play a role in gender identification with a neutral fundamental frequency. But even if these aspects are considered in an artificial, disembodied voice, gender-neutrality is not assigned consistently. Although the chatbot "Q" appears gender-neutral, only 50% of 4500 subjects explicitly judged it as neutral on a five-point scale with male and female poles, with the other half evenly split between an attribution to both genders [3]. In this respect, the acoustical gender-neutrality of a voice does not guarantee a gender-neutral classification.

The aforementioned issues bring social and psychological factors to the fore. Sutton lists three possible influences on the gender perception of neutral voices: "This categorisation may be influenced by other gendering elements of the design such as, but not limited to, the physical appearance of the product and product branding, specific pronunciations in the speech rather than the overall voice quality, and the activity or activity related topic that the VUI is performing" [7]. As these factors might be influential, they were considered for the gender-neutral voice-based chatbot of the paper at hand. Details are addressed in the "Method" section when applicable.

3   Method

3.1   Choice of Production Methods

The first commercially oriented gender-neutral voice-based chatbot was Q. At first, the developers had planned to create Q by recording the voices of "24 people who identified as male, female, transgender, and gender fluid, and attempted to layer their voices, and then find an average" [3]. Due to technical difficulties, however, the voice was finally created from one base voice with a fundamental frequency in a neutral range where various parameters, such as the pronunciation of the consonant "s," were modified [3]. Further details were not specified – neither the specific parameter values nor the used parameters per se – making the process irreplicable.

Scientific research uses approaches that range from the mere manipulation of F0 [32, 33] to the artificial vocoder generation of spoken syllables and their manipulation on a F0 and FF continuum [23] to the application of "novel heterodyning along with formant band shaping filters" on prerecorded generic human voices [15]. However, while the majority of studies stem from linguistics and regard the contribution of acoustic factors to gender perception, only a few can be located in the area of social science due to a focus on the effects on gender-neutral voices (e.g., [32, 33]). Moreover, whereas linguistic studies are characterized by high technical knowledge and detailed work (a short overview of methods used in such studies is provided by [15]), research with a social scientific focus relies on more basic production techniques.

However, the study at hand aimed at a straightforward approach that is at the same time easy to use and able to manipulate more parameters than just F0, but in contrast refine the voice's fundamental and formant frequencies. Thus, following Gelfer and Bennett [11] the Praat program (www.praat.org) from Paul Boersma and David Weenink was chosen for analysis and manipulations of voices. Praat is openly accessible, provides numerous commands for the analysis and editing of sound samples, is well documented, and its use does not require an elaborated technical knowledge.

3.2   Production of the Voices

Specification of Acoustical Parameters and Generating the Root Voice. Since F0, FF, and their interplay were identified as the key parameters for the perceived gender of a voice, only these two factors were manipulated. Because aspects of spoken language such as vocal range, accents, intonation, loudness, and speed can enter into the perception of voices and their personality [6, 36], which could influence ratings of the voices in later use cases, these parameters had to be kept comparable. To achieve this, an audio file of an artificial, approximately neutral root voice was produced using Google's WaveNet technology, which generated an audio file from written text. All manipulated voices were derived only from this audio file (all voices can be accessed at our OSF repository[1]). Google WaveNet employs a technology that generates artificial voices based on real voice recordings and is therefore perceived as more natural than other text-to-speech systems [37]. Since Gelfer and Bennett [11] demonstrated that artificial gender-related changes of a voice are more convincing if the root voice is male, "de-DE-Wavenet B" – the highest of the male German voice profiles offered – was chosen as the basis for the present study. By using the highest available option, the female frequencies were reached with less loss of quality.

First, the desired *level of F0* was determined. For men who speak English or German, this is on average between 100 and 120 Hz, for women between 200 and 220 Hz [9]. Therefore, the male voice was given a F0 of 110 Hz, the female a F0 of 220 Hz, setting the perceived frequency exactly an octave apart. With higher Hz values, a greater difference between the frequencies is needed to perceive a change, so the neutral voices could not be calculated as the mean between $F0_{male}$ and $F0_{female}$. (For example, the distance between 110 and 220 Hz is perceived by the ear the same as the distance between 220 and 440 Hz. Therefore, other units (e.g., logarithmic scales like the semitone scale) are often used to better represent the perceived change [9].) Voices that are artificially averaged on the Hertz scale between masculine and feminine F0 tend to be perceived as feminine, whereas slightly lower ones tend to be perceived as androgynous [23]. Thus, the perceived mean between $F0_{male}$ and $F0_{female}$ differs from a computed mean and must be calculated as follows, using a logarithmic approach:

$$e^{(ln(110)+ln(220))*0,5} \approx 156 \text{ Hz} \tag{1}$$

156 Hz is, thus, the perceived average between the typical male and female frequencies. However, as this procedure has not been scientifically documented before, several variants of possible gender-neutral voices with different F0 values should be tested against each other to find the "most neutral" voice. Considering this, three neutral variants were produced with an F0 of 140, 156 and 172 Hz, respectively.

To create the voices, (1) the text read by "de-DE-Wavenet B" was recorded and (2) its fundamental frequency was fine-tuned with the Praat program to reach the predetermined 156 Hz. (3) A formant analysis in Praat on the processed voice identified the formants (F1, F2 and F3) for every vowel occurring in the text, with formants being analyzed at the center of the vowels. From this, the median values for each vowel were calculated to control for outliers and the results were compared with previous formant analyses of male and female voices [16, 17], and [19]. Although we mentioned that an exact range for the genders cannot be determined for formants and with this no exact mean value between such ranges, we found that the formants were neither significantly below the male nor significantly above the known female formants, but in most cases in a middle range. The exact values can be found in the OSF (A1). Compared with

---

[1] https://doi.org/10.17605/OSF.IO/5UC8Z.

the values reported in [17] and [16], F1 is lower than the average male voice, but the effect balances out over the height of the other formants. In relation to [19], some vowel formants are slightly lower than the reported male values and others are slightly higher than the female values, but the effect also balances out. The comparisons proved that the formants of the produced voice can be considered approximately gender-neutral, so this voice was subsequently used as a neutral basis for the production of all other voices.

Manipulation of Fundamental Frequency and Formant Frequencies. For voice manipulation, the Praat "Change gender" function was used. With this function, F0 of a voice can be determined by entering the desired Hertz value and the formants can be changed by a factor which is freely specifiable [38]. Using this function, the remaining voices were generated: F0 values as specified above were combined with the desired factors. For the difference between male and female formants, average factors of about 1.15 to 1.20 are given (see above). Since the neutral voice should represent a middle value and the formants of the other voices should be clearly assignable, the formants from the neutral to the male voice were changed by a factor of 0.9, to the female voice by a factor of 1.1. With the latter, however, undesirable distortions in the sound appeared, which could be controlled by using the factor 1.08 as the highest possible change. The difference between male and female formants was thus ultimately exactly 1.2. The formants for the neutral voices were initially not altered.

The voices created by this method (one male "M2", one female "F2", three neutral "N2", "N5", and "N8") were further manipulated in their formants to obtain three formant heights for each F0 value. In contrast to F0, less is known about the typical FF ranges for male, female and neutral voices. Thus, this step was necessary to create a higher number of variants for the subsequent determination of the optimal voices via a more elaborated analysis. For this purpose, a lower (factor 0.95) as well as a higher version (factor 1.05) with the same F0 was generated from each source voice. This way, three female, three male, and nine neutral voices were produced (Table 1).

Table 1. Acoustic parameters of the generated voices

Voice	M1	M2	M3		Voice	F1	F2	F3
F0	110	110	110		F0	220	220	220
FF	0.855	0.9	0.945		FF	1.026	1.08	1.134

Voice	N1	N2	N3	N4	N5	N6	N7	N8	N9
F0	140	140	140	156	156	156	172	172	172
FF	0.95	1	1.05	0.95	1	1.05	0.95	1	1.05

Notes: Fundamental frequencies (F0) and formants (FF) of all generated voices are shown. All data of the fundamental frequency are in Hertz (Hz). FF are shown in relation to the voice N5, since this is the root for all other voices and FF of the other voices were manipulated by means of the respective factor. Male voices are denoted by M, neutral ones by N, female ones by F.

3.3   Evaluation of the Voices

Design. The voices were tested in an online quasi-experiment. Participants did not hear all the voices – partly to avoid lengthening the survey, and partly because small differences might be missed due to a large number of voices in a row. To ensure nevertheless sufficiently different assessments for each voice, eight out of the 15 variants were randomly assigned to the participants. All voices presented a 30-s stimulus text about a gender-neutral topic to exclude possible context effects. Various papers address stereotypical connections of topics [6], hobbies or occupations [39–42] with a certain gender. Additionally, context has been shown to have effects on the perception of other neutral or ambiguous things and persons [43, 44] Moreover, children speak in higher or lower voices when they are asked to talk like a gender-stereotypic profession, e.g., "nurses" or "mechanics", which shows an unconscious connection between stereotypical occupations and associated voices [45]. In sum, these findings indicate that the context impacts gender perception. Especially with ambiguous stimuli, other information might unconsciously be considered in order to sort the stimulus into pre-existing categories. Thus, the topic about which the voice-based chatbot talked about had to be chosen carefully. Occupations such as author, journalist, accountant or various nature sciences are mainly perceived as gender neutral [39–42] (although they may still be assigned to a gender subconsciously [42]). Corresponding to the occupation "biologist", an informative text about penguins was used (see OSF – A2).

The voices were presented via a grey audio player on the survey page. The simple design was chosen to eliminate influences of visual stimuli: Explicit elements such as hairstyles [46], but also body posture, or ratio of chest, waist and hip [47] can be crucial in gender assignment to robots. This effect extends to simple shapes, when round, slender objects and curved lines are perceived more female than edged, bulky ones with straight lines [48–50]. Furthermore, aspects like texture [50] and color ("blue vs. pink") [51, 52] may affect an object's gender assignment.

According to the before mentioned graduality of a voice's gender classification, participants rated each voice on a 7-point scale from "male" (1) to "female" (7). The middle category (4) was labeled "neither/I cannot judge". In addition, they assessed the sound characteristics 'naturalness' and 'pleasantness' on a 5-point Likert scale: Technologies perceived as "technical" are rated differently than those containing more natural, "human-like" characteristics, which becomes visible, e.g., in trust measurement [53, 54]. As shown above, naturalness can also have an impact on neutrality perception. Moreover, it is conceivable that the question of how pleasant a voice sounds contributes to their perception and rating. Thus, it is important to choose similarly pleasant voices to prevent the disapproval of a single voice in later investigations, which would distort results. Finally, participants' open-ended comments and socio-demographic data (gender, age, nationality, level of education, and field of occupation) were taken into account when interpreting the ratings and choosing the most suitable and comparable voices.

Gender perception of the three ultimately selected voices was controlled in a follow-up study which served as a second testing step. Participants were randomly assigned one voice and after a short greeting by the voice, they heard one of three different texts (stereotypically male and female ones about airplanes and love were added to the penguin text). Next, they rated gender perception on a scale from 1 (male) to 5 (female). Again, comments and socio-demographic data were recorded.

Sample. A total of 31 participants completed the quasi-experiment. The sample was young ($M = 29.33$, $SD = 11.96$), predominantly female (55%) and inhabited a high level of education (32% had a high school degree, 42% a Bachelor's degree). Nine persons were from a field associated with humanities, six were from nature and computer sciences. The rest of the participants stemmed from various other occupational backgrounds. The sample mainly consisted of Germans, with the exception of two US-Americans and an Italian. As these persons reported fluency in German and were all living in Germany, they were considered experienced enough with the language and thus included in the study.

The sample of the follow-up study was bigger ($N = 343$), but otherwise similar: Participants were young ($M = 30.04$, $SD = 11.84$), female (58%) and highly educated (36% owned a high school degree, 52% a university degree). They worked or studied in the fields of commerce (22%), social and health occupations (20%), humanities (18%) or nature and computer science (15%) and were mostly German (97%). For a visual overview of the testing process, see our OSF (A3).

4 Results

4.1 Gender Perception

The evaluation of the perceived gender revealed two voices as predominantly male (in the range of 1 and 2), two were rated in the distinct gender-neutral/ambiguous range (3.5–4.5), and six were perceived as clearly female (6–7, Table 2). This imbalance can be explained by the greater manifoldness of the female voice: Older women tend to have a lower F0 than younger ones and F0 in female speaking voices has generally been decreasing for decades [12–14]. Therefore, some of the voice variants intended to be neutral also possibly fell into a range that could be interpreted as female due to high formants and fundamental frequency.

Additionally, ANOVAs were conducted to compare gender assessments (see OSF – A4). These analyses uncovered that the formants had a visible influence on gender perception of neutral voices. For those with a constant F0, increasing heights of FF increased the perception of femaleness (see Table 2). The perception at the low and high formants differed by more than one scale point each, and the differences between the voices were significant (for N1–N3: $F(2, 47) = 5.64$, $p = .006$; for N4–N6: $F(2, 44) = 20.87$, $p < .001$; for N7–N9: $F(2, 45) = 8.37$, $p < .001$). Although similar effects appeared in the male voices, they were not significant ($F(2, 46) = 0.84$, $p = .437$) and even the highest male voice M3 was still perceived as "rather masculine". The female voices were not affected by the formants either. This result confirms the findings of the studies reviewed above: If F0 can be clearly assigned to a gender, formants have less influence on gender perception than in the case of ambiguous values of F0.

Table 2. Evaluations of the voices

Voice	Number of evaluations	Perceived gender		Naturalness		Pleasantness	
		M	SD	M	SD	M	SD
M1	**17**	**1.65**	**0.86**	**3.82**	**1.74**	**4.82**	**1.59**
M2	16	1.88	1.02	5.19	1.72	5.63	1.02
M3	16	2.13	1.26	4.25	1.77	4.19	2.07
N1	17	4.12	0.99	3.76	1.79	4.00	1.41
N2	16	4.69	1.45	3.88	2.00	4.38	1.45
N3	17	5.53	1.23	3.65	1.62	4.35	1.46
N4	**15**	**3.73**	**1.03**	**4.53**	**1.36**	**4.60**	**1.30**
N5	16	5.00	1.26	4.38	1.36	5.25	1.34
N6	16	6.13	0.72	4.00	1.71	4.69	1.35
N7	16	4.88	1.09	3.31	1.74	3.81	1.47
N8	16	6.00	0.97	4.25	1.61	4.94	1.12
N9	16	6.31	1.08	4.50	1.83	4.87	1.25
F1	17	6.71	0.59	2.71	1.79	3.23	1.71
F2	**15**	**6.86**	**1.06**	**3.6**	**1.92**	**4.07**	**1.49**
F3	18	6.22	0.94	2.11	1.37	2.22	1.22

White = not usable as the perceived gender does not lie between 1-2, 3.5-4.5 or 6-7
Light gray = Gender perception in a suitable range
Medium gray = Gender perception in a suitable range, F0 according to theory
Dark gray, bold = Gender perception in a suitable range, F0 according to theory, finally selected voices

4.2 Naturalness and Pleasantness of the Voices

Interestingly, all female voices were below the neutral and male voices in terms of naturalness and pleasantness (Table 2). This may be caused by the originally male root voice, which had to be altered more to achieve the desired female pitch than for the neutral and male voices. This may have resulted in stronger sound distortions.

It should therefore be noted that with regard to naturalness and pleasantness, there are in part considerable differences between the three selected voices. However, since the voices that will be used in an experimental setting should only differ in their gender, male, neutral, and female voice had to be as close as possible to each other in these assessments. Therefore, M1, N4, and W2 were selected: W2 had the most positive ratings of the female voices and was therefore closest to the appropriate male and neutral voices. M1, in turn, was closer to the female voice than M2. Finally, N4 and N1 were almost equally good fitting, but N4's gender neutrality was better grounded in theory: F0 was exactly at the 156 Hz level originally assumed to be gender neutral. (To keep the neutral F0 between male and female ones (as predicted based on theory), voices that were perceived as female but had been produced as neutral versions were excluded from the final choice).

4.3 Confirmation of the Assessments

In the follow-up study described above, randomly using one of the chosen voices W2, M1, and N4 in the same form of presentation, and one out of three texts, gender perception was confirmed on a 5-point scale with 3 as the ambiguous rating. M1 was perceived as male with a rating of 1.22 ($SD = 0.69$, $n = 112$), N4 as mainly neutral with 2.82 ($SD = 1.27$, $n = 113$) and F2 as female with 4.9 ($SD = 0.34$, $n = 118$). To control for possible distortions in the ratings which could be caused by the stereotypically male and female texts, the rates were analyzed again, solely for the neutral text. The results of the present study were confirmed again: The gender of M1 was perceived as 1.18 ($SD = 0.76$, $n = 38$), N4 as 3.05 ($SD = 1.26$, $n = 38$), and F2 as 4.93 ($SD = 0.36$, $n = 42$). Thus, gender assignment and especially gender neutrality of N4 could be confirmed in two studies, albeit with a larger standard deviation in the second study, indicating the participants' higher uncertainty regarding their perception of the acoustically neutral voice. The difference might be due to the larger number of participants in the second study and the assessment of only one voice instead of eight.

5 Discussion and Conclusion

The paper has three methodological contributions. *First*, we provide a gender-neutral voice and matching male and female variants for social scientists. The presented voices proved to fit theoretically and empirically to known perceptions of voice gender: Drawing on F0 ranges and FF difference factors from linguistic literature while controlling for psychological and social influences suggested in social science research, we succeeded in creating voices respectively perceived as male, female and neutral. Hence, they are suitable for investigating the perception of gender-neutral approaches as well as the effects of gender neutrality in voice-based chatbots compared to distinctly gendered voices. *Second*, the paper enables social scientists to design similar voices with the Open Access program Praat. The main advantage of the presented method is its simplicity. Once a root voice is available, desired variants can be derived without much technical knowledge. However, whereas a high male voice would conceivably be a good root voice, it seems crucial to conduct a formant analysis on the voice first to enable researchers to apply standardized, scientifically grounded formant ratios as shown above. *Third*, the two-step evaluation process allowed in the first step to efficiently identify the most suiting variants and eliminated context effects of multiple previously presented voices in the second step. The small sample of the first step appeared to be sufficient, regarding the confirmation in the larger sample. In future research, more control variables can be regarded in addition to pleasantness and naturalness, depending on the specific aspects in which comparability is desired.

Moreover, we *substantially contributed* to the research on gender-neutral voices by uncovering that the proposed changes of F0 and FF are sufficient to evoke convincing changes in perceived gender and to enable the creation of variants which are perceived as gender-neutral. This is in line with linguistic research on gender-specific properties of voices as we discussed in Sect. 2, as well as with the conclusions about neutrality that we drew from these results. We confirmed that gender perception in voices is variable enough to be measured on a continuum instead of using gender categories, as Mullennix et al. [26] proposed, and that neutral voices are indeed in the realm of the perceived mean which is slightly lower than the calculated mean on the Hertz scale. Moreover, we confirmed formants' importance for gender assignment.

In sum, the presented method offers the opportunity to create comparable voices for further investigation of gender effects. Predominantly, it requires less technical knowledge than most other approaches, while, at the same time, more theoretical assumptions beyond the difference of F0 can be modeled into the voices. We demonstrated an efficient two-step test for the produced voices, which accounted for the known effect, yet unknown ranges of differing male and female formants. Finally, we demonstrated that without testing the created voices, gender perception may be skewed even when F0 and FF are at a theoretically gender-neutral level.

References

1. Sey, A., Fesalbon, L.: OK Google: is AI gendered? In: Sey, A., Hafkin, N. (eds.) Taking Stock. Data and Evidence on Gender Equality in Digital Access, Skills and Leadership, pp. 144–145. United Nations University Institute on Computing and Society/International Telecommunications Union, Macau (2019)
2. genderlessvoice: Meet Q. The First Genderless Voice (2020). www.genderlessvoice.com
3. MacLellan, L.: This AI voice is gender-neutral, unlike Siri and Alexa (2019). https://qz.com/work/1577597/this-ai-voice-is-gender-neutral-unlike-siri-and-alexa/
4. Nass, C., Steuer, J., Tauber, E.R.: Computers are social actors. In: Adelson, B., Dumais, S., Olson, J. (eds.) Proceedings of the SIGCHI Conference on Human Factors in Computing Systems Celebrating Interdependence - CHI 1994, pp. 72–78. ACM Press, New York (1994). https://doi.org/10.1145/191666.191703
5. Reeves, B., Nass, C.: The Media Equation: How People Treat Computers, Televisions, and New Media Like Real People and Places. CSLI Publications, Stanford (1996)
6. Nass, C., Brave, S.: Wired for Speech: How Voice Activates and Advances the Human-Computer Relationship. MIT Press, Cambridge (2005)
7. Sutton, S.J.: Gender ambiguous, not genderless. In: Torres, M.I., Schlögl, S., Clark, L., Porcheron, M. (eds.) Proceedings of the 2nd Conference on Conversational User Interfaces, pp. 1–8. ACM, New York (2020). https://doi.org/10.1145/3405755.3406123
8. Danielescu, A.: Eschewing gender stereotypes in voice assistants to promote inclusion. In: Torres, M.I., Schlögl, S., Clark, L., Porcheron, M. (eds.) Proceedings of the 2nd Conference on Conversational User Interfaces, pp. 1–3. ACM, New York (2020). https://doi.org/10.1145/3405755.3406151
9. Simpson, A.P.: Phonetic differences between male and female speech. Lang. Linguist. Compass 3, 621–640 (2009). https://doi.org/10.1111/j.1749-818X.2009.00125.x
10. Fitch, J.L.: Consistency of fundamental frequency and perturbation in repeated phonations of sustained vowels, reading, and connected speech. J. Speech Hear. Disord. 55, 360–363 (1990). https://doi.org/10.1044/jshd.5502.360
11. Gelfer, M.P., Bennett, Q.E.: Speaking fundamental frequency and vowel formant frequencies. Effects on perception of gender. J. Voice 27, 556–566 (2013). https://doi.org/10.1016/j.jvoice.2012.11.008
12. Ma, E.P.-M., Love, A.L.: Electroglottographic evaluation of age and gender effects during sustained phonation and connected speech. J. Voice 24, 146–152 (2010). https://doi.org/10.1016/j.jvoice.2008.08.004

13. Berg, M., Fuchs, M., Wirkner, K., Loeffler, M., Engel, C., Berger, T.: The speaking voice in the general population: normative data and associations to sociodemographic and lifestyle factors. J. Voice **31**, 257.e13-257.e24 (2017). https://doi.org/10.1016/j.jvoice.2016.06.001

14. D'haeseleer, E., Depypere, H., Claeys, S., Wuyts, F.L., Baudonck, N., van Lierde, K.M.: Vocal characteristics of middle-aged premenopausal women. J. Voice **25**, 360–366 (2011). https://doi.org/10.1016/j.jvoice.2009.10.016

15. Gallena, S.J.K., Stickels, B., Stickels, E.: Gender perception after raising vowel fundamental and formant frequencies. Considerations for oral resonance research. J. Voice **32**, 592–601 (2018). https://doi.org/10.1016/j.jvoice.2017.06.023

16. Hillenbrand, J.M., Getty, L.A., Clark, M.J., Wheeler, K.: Acoustic characteristics of American English vowels. J. Acoust. Soc. Am. **97**, 3099–3111 (1995). https://doi.org/10.1121/1.411872

17. Peterson, G.E., Barney, H.L.: Control methods used in a study of the vowels. J. Acoust. Soc. Am. **24**, 175–184 (1952). https://doi.org/10.1121/1.1906875

18. Wu, K., Childers, D.G.: Gender recognition from speech. Part I: coarse analysis. J. Acoust. Soc. Am. **90**, 1828–1840 (1991). https://doi.org/10.1121/1.401663

19. Pätzold, M., Simpson, A.P.: Acoustic analysis of German vowels in the Kiel Corpus of read speech. Arbeitsberichte des Instituts für Phonetik und digitale Sprachverarbeitung Universität Kiel, pp. 215–247 (1997)

20. Strange, W., Bohn, O.-S., Trent, S.A., Nishi, K.: Acoustic and perceptual similarity of North German and American English vowels. J. Acoust. Soc. Am. **115**, 1791–1807 (2004). https://doi.org/10.1121/1.1687832

21. Gelfer, M.P., Mikos, V.A.: The relative contributions of speaking fundamental frequency and formant frequencies to gender identification based on isolated vowels. J. Voice **19**, 544–554 (2005). https://doi.org/10.1016/j.jvoice.2004.10.006

22. Hillenbrand, J.M., Clark, M.J.: The role of f_0 and formant frequencies in distinguishing the voices of men and women. Atten. Percept. Psychophys. **71**, 1150–1166 (2009). https://doi.org/10.3758/APP.71.5.1150

23. Skuk, V.G., Schweinberger, S.R.: Influences of fundamental frequency, formant frequencies, aperiodicity, and spectrum level on the perception of voice gender. J Speech Lang. Hear. Res. **57**, 285–296 (2014). https://doi.org/10.1044/1092-4388(2013/12-0314)

24. Whiteside, S.P.: The identification of a speaker's sex from synthesized vowels. Percept. Mot. Skills **87**, 595–600 (1998). https://doi.org/10.2466/pms.1998.87.2.595

25. Assmann, P.F., Nearey, T.M., Dembling, S.: Effects of frequency shifts on perceived naturalness and gender information in speech. In: INTERSPEECH-2006 - ICSLP, Ninth International Conference on Spoken Language Processing, pp. 889–892 (2006)

26. Mullennix, J.W., Johnson, K.A., Topcu-Durgun, M., Farnsworth, L.M.: The perceptual representation of voice gender. J. Acoust. Soc. Am. **98**, 3080–3095 (1995). https://doi.org/10.1121/1.413832

27. Gelfer, M.P., Schofield, K.J.: Comparison of acoustic and perceptual measures of voice in male-to-female transsexuals perceived as female versus those perceived as male. J. Voice **14**, 22–33 (2000). https://doi.org/10.1016/S0892-1997(00)80092-2

28. Bralley, R.C., Bull, G.L., Gore, C.H., Edgerton, M.T.: Evaluation of vocal pitch in male transsexuals. J. Commun. Disord. **11**, 443–449 (1978). https://doi.org/10.1016/0021-9924(78)90037-0

29. Hancock, A.B., Colton, L., Douglas, F.: Intonation and gender perception: applications for transgender speakers. J. Voice **28**, 203–209 (2014). https://doi.org/10.1016/j.jvoice.2013.08.009

30. van Borsel, J., de Pot, K., de Cuypere, G.: Voice and physical appearance in female-to-male transsexuals. J. Voice **23**, 494–497 (2009). https://doi.org/10.1016/j.jvoice.2007.10.018

31. Behrens, S.I., Egsvang, A.K.K., Hansen, M., Møllegård-Schroll, A.M.: Gendered robot voices and their influence on trust. In: Kanda, T., Šabanović, S., Hoffman, G., Tapus, A. (eds.) HRI 2018 Companion, 5–8 March 2018, Chicago, IL, USA, pp. 63–64. ACM Press, New York (2018). https://doi.org/10.1145/3173386.3177009.
32. Bryant, D., Borenstein, J., Howard, A.: Why should we gender? In: Belpaeme, T., Young, J., Gunes, H., Riek, L. (eds.) Proceedings of the 2020 ACM/IEEE International Conference on Human-Robot Interaction, pp. 13–21. ACM, New York (2020). https://doi.org/10.1145/331 9502.3374778
33. Rogers, K., Bryant, D., Howard, A.: Robot gendering: influences on trust, occupational competency, and preference of robot over human. In: Bernhaupt, R., et al. (eds.) Extended Abstracts of the 2020 CHI Conference on Human Factors in Computing Systems, pp. 1–7. ACM, New York (2020). https://doi.org/10.1145/3334480.3382930
34. Pandey, A.K., Gelin, R.: A mass-produced sociable humanoid robot: Pepper: the first machine of its kind. IEEE Robot. Autom. Mag. 25, 40–48 (2018). https://doi.org/10.1109/MRA.2018. 2833157
35. McGinn, C., Torre, I.: Can you tell the robot by the voice? An exploratory study on the role of voice in the perception of robots. In: HRI 2019 - The 14th ACMIEEE International Conference on Human-Robot Interaction, 11–14 March 2019, Daegu, South Korea, pp. 211–221. IEEE, Piscataway (2019)
36. Apple, W., Streeter, L.A., Krauss, R.M.: Effects of pitch and speech rate on personal attributions. J. Pers. Soc. Psychol. 37, 715–727 (1979). https://doi.org/10.1037/0022-3514.37. 5.715
37. van den Oord, A., et al.: WaveNet: a generative model for raw audio (2016)
38. Praat: Sound: Change gender (2020). https://www.fon.hum.uva.nl/praat/manual/Sound__Cha nge_gender___.html
39. Couch, J.V., Sigler, J.N.: Gender perception of professional occupations. Psychol. Rep. 88, 693–698 (2001). https://doi.org/10.2466/pr0.2001.88.3.693
40. Glick, P.: Trait-based and sex-based discrimination in occupational prestige, occupational salary, and hiring. Sex Roles 25, 351–378 (1991). https://doi.org/10.1007/BF00289761
41. Teig, S., Susskind, J.E.: Truck driver or nurse? The impact of gender roles and occupational status on children's occupational preferences. Sex Roles 58, 848–863 (2008). https://doi.org/ 10.1007/s11199-008-9410-x
42. White, M.J., White, G.B.: Implicit and explicit occupational gender stereotypes. Sex Roles 55, 259–266 (2006). https://doi.org/10.1007/s11199-006-9078-z
43. Higgins, E.T., Bargh, J.A., Lombardi, W.J.: Nature of priming effects on categorization. J. Exp. Psychol. Learn. Mem. Cogn. 11, 59–69 (1985). https://doi.org/10.1037/0278-7393.11. 1.59
44. Freeman, J.B., Ma, Y., Han, S., Ambady, N.: Influences of culture and visual context on real-time social categorization. J. Exp. Soc. Psychol. 49, 206–210 (2013). https://doi.org/10. 1016/j.jesp.2012.10.015
45. Cartei, V., Oakhill, J., Garnham, A., Banerjee, R., Reby, D.: "This is what a mechanic sounds like": children's vocal control reveals implicit occupational stereotypes. Psychol. Sci. 31, 957–967 (2020). https://doi.org/10.1177/0956797620929297
46. Eyssel, F., Hegel, F.: (S)he's got the look: gender stereotyping of robots. J. Appl. Soc. Psychol. 42(9), 2213–2230 (2012). https://doi.org/10.1111/J.1559-1816.2012.00937.X
47. Trovato, G., Lucho, C., Paredes, R.: She's electric—the influence of body proportions on perceived gender of robots across cultures. Robotics 7, 1–13 (2018). https://doi.org/10.3390/ robotics7030050
48. Fagot, B.I., Leinbach, M.D., Hort, B.E., Strayer, J.: Qualities underlying the definitions of gender. Sex Roles 37, 1–18 (1997). https://doi.org/10.1023/A:1025614618546

49. Lieven, T., Grohmann, B., Herrmann, A., Landwehr, J.R., van Tilburg, M.: The effect of brand design on brand gender perceptions and brand preference. Eur. J. Mark. **49**, 146–169 (2015). https://doi.org/10.1108/EJM-08-2012-0456

50. Tilburg, M., Lieven, T., Herrmann, A., Townsend, C.: Beyond "pink it and shrink it" perceived product gender, aesthetics, and product evaluation. Psychol. Mark. **32**, 422–437 (2015). https://doi.org/10.1002/mar.20789

51. Cunningham, S.J., Macrae, C.N.: The colour of gender stereotyping. Br. J. Psychol. **102**, 598–614 (2011). https://doi.org/10.1111/j.2044-8295.2011.02023.x

52. Hess, A.C., Melnyk, V.: Pink or blue? The impact of gender cues on brand perceptions. Eur. J. Mark. **50**, 1550–1574 (2016). https://doi.org/10.1108/EJM-11-2014-0723

53. Lankton, N., McKnight, D.H., Tripp, J.: Technology, humanness, and trust: rethinking trust in technology. JAIS **16**, 880–918 (2015). https://doi.org/10.17705/1jais.00411

54. Califf, C.B., Brooks, S., Longstreet, P.: Human-like and system-like trust in the sharing economy: the role of context and humanness. Technol. Forecast. Soc. Chang. **154**, 119968 (2020). https://doi.org/10.1016/j.techfore.2020.119968

Design Matters! How Visual Gendered Anthropomorphic Design Cues Moderate the Determinants of the Behavioral Intention Towards Using Chatbots

V. Phoebe Pawlik[(✉)] [iD]

Technical University of Munich, 80333 Munich, Germany
phoebe.pawlik@tum.de

Abstract. The design cue gendered anthropomorphism plays an important role in tailoring chatbots towards customers' design preferences. Yet, it still remains unexplored if this design cue affects the determinants of the behavioral intention towards using chatbots as moderating variable. Therefore, this paper investigates the moderating influence of gendered anthropomorphic design cues on the key determinants of the behavioral intention that are defined by the Unified Theory of Acceptance and Use of Technology (UTAUT). For this purpose, three chatbot design groups have been created and compared: a female and a male designed chatbot with gendered anthropomorphic design cues, as well as one chatbot without gendered anthropomorphic design cues. A sample of 209 participants is randomly assigned to each design group. The PLS-SEM multigroup analysis shows gendered anthropomorphic chatbot design cues yield significant positive impact of the performance expectancy towards the behavioral intention to use chatbots. This was not the case for the design group without gendered anthropomorphic design cues. Also, in contrast to the male anthropomorphic chatbot design, the female anthropomorphic chatbot design yields significant positive impact of social influence on the behavioral intention.

Keywords: Chatbot · Anthropomorphism · Gender · Design cues · Behavioral intention · UTAUT · Post-purchase customer service

1 Introduction

Whenever the potential of artificial intelligence or automation in customer service is discussed, chatbots are usually talked about in the same breath [e.g. 3, 24, 40, 48]. Chatbots are virtual interfaces that interact with users in natural language [12]. This characteristic makes them valuable for a wide range of applications at different stages of customer service [23, 40]. In the pre-purchase stage, chatbots are e.g. useful information providers for customers [40]. In the purchase stage, chatbots are predicted to become a negotiation counterpart to the customer and obtain e.g. digital pricing functions [23]. Such functions might be especially useful in industries with dynamic demand and supply changes, such

© Springer Nature Switzerland AG 2022
A. Følstad et al. (Eds.): CONVERSATIONS 2021, LNCS 13171, pp. 192–208, 2022.
https://doi.org/10.1007/978-3-030-94890-0_12

as mobility services (e.g. Uber) [23]. In the post-purchase stage, chatbots are considered to take over customer recommendation and follow-up tasks [23]. Correctly deployed, chatbot applications in customer service cannot only increase customer-brand connection [11] and personalized customer interaction, but also improve company finances [42]. According to a recent report, $11 billions of cost savings are expected through chatbot deployments in the three main application areas of health care, banking and retail by 2023 [25].

However, the critical issue is not the deployment of chatbots in customer service, rather the behavioral intention of customers to use them [41]. Without customer's intention to use chatbots, they cannot provide value, neither for the customer, nor for the company [37]. Determinants define the behavioral intention towards using a chatbot [37, 47]. Previous studies investigated the impact of design cues as direct influence on the behavioral intention [e.g. 35, 41]. Technology acceptance research has investigated the impact of design cues as influences of the determinants of the behavioral intention [13]. Remaining unexplored is an investigation of design cues as moderators of the behavioral intention [46].

Therefore, the objective of this paper is to investigate how visual design of chatbots act as moderators and affect the determinants of the behavioral intention to use chatbots. For this purpose, gendered anthropomorphism in its three categories female, male and absent is identified as relevant visual design cue. These are applied on the key determinants of the behavioral intention of the Unified Theory of Acceptance and Use of Technology (UTAUT). The key UTAUT determinants serve as basis for this study's investigation because the UTAUT is a highly validated and popular model used for behavioral intention assessments [49]. Also, following a recent call of Venkatesh [46], the first author of the UTAUT, it requires validation in the field of AI-based technologies. For achieving the objective of this study, a vignette survey has been chosen as ideal study design to eliminate bias occurring from errors of actual chatbot interactions. The vignette has been created for an advanced post-purchase customer service situation in form of three design groups: female, male (gendered anthropomorphic), as well as non-gendered anthropomorphic and compared. The survey data is analyzed using partial least squares structural equation modelling (PLS-SEM).

As a result, multiple contributions are provided by this paper: First, the moderating impact of gendered anthropomorphism as design cue on the determinants of the behavioral intention, performance expectancy, effort expectancy and social influence, derived from the key UTAUT determinants, is investigated. The results provide an empirical contribution to chatbot acceptance research in the gap of post-purchase customer service. Second, this is an early study investigating the UTAUT in the field of AI-based technologies and proposes an extension of the UTAUT through the moderating impact of gendered anthropomorphic design cues. Finally, practical implications for suitable chatbot design in post-purchase customer service settings that match customer expectations are derived.

2 Theoretical Background and Hypotheses Development

2.1 Chatbot Acceptance Research and Definition of the Key UTAUT Determinants

The major stream of chatbot acceptance research stems from the profound field of technology acceptance research that is motivated by understanding users' perceptions of new technologies and subsequently proposes validations or extensions of existing technology acceptance models [29]. Grounded in the Theory of Planned Behavior [2] multiple technology acceptance models have been derived [29]. Among them, the Unified Theory of Acceptance and Use of Technology (UTAUT) by Venkatesh et al. [47] is regarded as robust and popular acceptance model [49]. The UTAUT [47] explains three key variables that contribute towards the behavioral intention to use a technology: the performance expectancy, the effort expectancy and the social influence. The performance expectancy refers to "the degree to which an individual believes that using the system will help him or her to attain gains in job performance" [47, p. 447]. The effort expectancy describes the physical or mental effort that a person believes to require for using the technology. The social influence explains the impact that other people want a potential user to use the technology. Thereby, only people who are important to the potential user are relevant.

These key variables have been tested using different technology acceptance models in various chatbot application contexts [29]. A qualitative study of Amelia et al. [4], structured according to the UTAUT and the service robot acceptance model (SRAM) [50], found indication that the three key variables are impacting the behavioral intention to use chatbots in the field of retail baking. However, Sugumar and Chandra's [43] quantitative application of the UTAUT2 [45] found no proof for significant impact of the factors effort expectancy and social influence in the field of financial service chatbots. For a chatbot application in the pre-purchase customer service of an online shopping setting, the variable performance expectancy was found to be a strong indicator towards the behavioral intention to use chatbots [37]. This was tested using the technology acceptance model (TAM) [13]. As these findings show, the determinants explaining the behavioral intention to use chatbots are not consistent across different application contexts. Rese et al. [37] even highlighted potential differences resulting from different application stages of customer service which leads to the conclusion that each context has to be investigated individually in order to derive accurate results.

This research provides a chatbot acceptance validation in the field of post-purchase customer service. Also, due to a missing quantitative validation of the UTAUT on an elaborated, AI-based chatbot, the key UTAUT variables are chosen for investigation. Therefore, the following hypotheses for the AI-based chatbot application context of post-purchase customer service are derived:

H1: *The behavioral intention to use chatbots in the post-purchase customer service phase is positively impacted by a) performance expectancy, b) effort expectancy and c) social influence.*

2.2 The Role of Gendered Anthropomorphic Chatbot Design Cues

As stated in the Computers are Social Actors paradigm (CASA) [31, 32], humans interact with chatbots in a similar way they interact with humans if the chatbot applies attributes that are perceived to be human-like [5, 16]. Thus, human-like chatbot design cues yield higher levels of anthropomorphism [5]. Adam et al. [1] observed that participants were more likely to accept a request made by a chatbot if anthropomorphic design cues were applied. Also, Rhim et al. [38] revealed significantly higher satisfaction rates in the context of survey chatbots that resulted from the application of anthropomorphic design cues. In line with these findings, anthropomorphism has found to have a direct positive influence on the behavioral intention towards using chatbots, as Sheehan et al. [41] and Blut et al. [7] derived. Sheehan et al. [41] found that miscommunication in a human-chatbot interaction leads to lower levels of anthropomorphism and subsequently to lower behavioral intentions towards using chatbots in customer service. However, in the field of financial service chatbots, Sugumar and Chandra [43] could not find anthropomorphism to have a significant influence on the behavioral intention to use chatbots. Besides different chatbot application contexts, differences regarding the exact type of influence anthropomorphic design cues have on the behavioral intention to use chatbots could account for such research finding differences. Venkatesh [46] provides a conceptual argumentation that explains technology design characteristics to act as moderators, rather than direct influences on the behavioral intention to use AI-based technologies. This study builds on previous research that proved anthropomorphic design cues to be a driver of the behavioral intention to use chatbots and the yet unconfirmed concept that anthropomorphic design cues serve as moderator in determining the behavioral intention. Therefore, the hypothesis that anthropomorphic design cues act as moderator of the behavioral intention determinants is investigated.

The discussion of the impact of anthropomorphic chatbot design also addresses the role of gender as subcategory of anthropomorphic design cues [9]. In the decisive study of Nass and Moon [32] that derived the CASA paradigm, also gendered anthropomorphic design cues were applied onto the computers. They then showed that participants assigned stereotypes they have regarding a certain gender to the computer that they interacted with. Grounded on this finding, Brahnam and De Angeli [9] replicated the study with chatbots and validated this relationship between gendered anthropomorphic design cues and the assignment of stereotypes. Also, Dingler et al. [14] further emphasized that biased chatbot design impacts human perception. Ultimately, different types of gendered anthropomorphic design cues show different effects on the behavioral intention towards using chatbots [7, 8]. Blut et al. [7] revealed that female chatbot design positively moderates the effect of the factor anthropomorphism on the behavioral intention. Borau et al. [8] highlighted higher behavioral intentions if female chatbots are applied. One can argue that these relationships hold true for the context of post-purchase customer service. Therefore, in order to include the assessment of the effects of gendered anthropomorphic design cues, this study is designed as an investigation of the variable anthropomorphic design cues in all three categories relevant in related research: female, male (gendered anthropomorphism) and absent gendered anthropomorphic design cues.

H2: *Gendered anthropomorphic design cues moderate the relationship between performance expectancy, effort expectancy and social influence on the behavioral intention to use chatbots.*

Figure 1 shows the resulting research model. As methodical related work shows [e.g. 6, 18, 51], the assessment of moderating effects of a categorical variable requires an analysis for each defined category: female, male and absent.

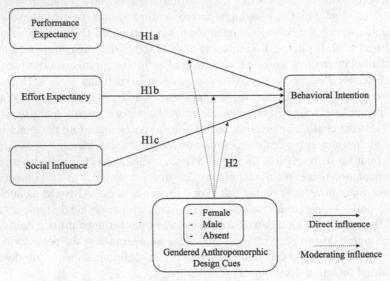

Fig. 1. Research model

3 Research Design and Data Collection

The data was collected via a vignette survey for multiple reasons. In the critical post-purchase stage of customer service in which effective customer support yields customer engagement, intelligent and elaborated chatbots that are capable of taking over service tasks are expected [23]. Despite "[...] fast-paced advances in artificial intelligence, conversations with text-based chatbots often reach their limits and do so relatively quickly." [37, p. 11]. Since currently available chatbots show limited capabilities of intelligence, previous research investigating the behavioral intention of chatbots used experimental conditions [e.g. 41]. This option leads to experimental investigations of chatbots in very narrow use cases that lack the generalizability towards complex service scenarios [41]. A vignette study enables to overcome this obstacle and to observe customers' behavioral intention towards using intelligent chatbots in a rather complex service interaction. Further, vignette studies have been found to be a valid study approach for observing customer perceptions and intentions in the context of chatbots in the field of finance, pre-customer service of luxury products and social media [11, 16, 33]. Applying a vignette survey design to the context of a post-purchase customer service setting provides a further validation of this approach. Additionally, vignette studies contribute to the internal validity of the results [16].

The participants in this study received a survey in which they first read a short text introducing them into a customer service situation in which they use a chatbot in order to fulfill a customer service task in the post-purchase context (Fig. 2). They then saw a screenshot of the chatbot conversation. The screenshot contained either non-gendered anthropomorphic design cues, as shown in Fig. 2 or the screenshot contained gendered anthropomorphic design cues. These gendered anthropomorphic design cues were either female (Fig. 3) or male (Fig. 4). The content of the conversation in the screenshot was the same across all design groups. Afterwards, they answered the questions of the survey (Table 1).

The aim was to create a post-purchase customer service situation the participants can relate to. Therefore, the customer requests about product availability and delivery time were derived from the FAQ section of a German drug store [15]. In addition, the disinfectant was chosen because due to the COVID-19 pandemic, this is a basic product almost everyone can relate to. Since the goal was to test an advanced chatbot, the chatbot was designed to be intelligent. In the conversation screenshot the user asks if there is still disinfectant left and the chatbot recognizes that the customer just placed an order. The chatbot then assumes that the customer might want to add the item they just asked the availability for.

Also, this research focuses on visual chatbot design cues. As anthropomorphic design cues, the visual cues of Araujo's [5] and Go and Sundar's [19] studies have been applied. In Araujo, the anthropomorphic chatbot was given a human-like name. Accordingly, the anthropomorphic chatbots of this study received human-like names. Also, in order to measure differences between differently gendered anthropomorphic chatbots, the male chatbot was called Daniel and the female chatbot was called Daniela. The name similarity was chosen in order to avoid bias. The chatbot without gendered anthropomorphic design was called Chatbot. In Go and Sundar [19], a picture of a human was used as visual design cue for the anthropomorphic chatbot and no picture for the non-anthropomorphic one. Accordingly, a picture of a woman was taken from the license free platform Pixabay [36] and applied onto the female anthropomorphic designed chatbot of this study. In order to avoid bias triggered through different attractivity of the pictures, the picture for the male anthropomorphic chatbot was created through the gender swap function of FaceApp. This approach to avoid attractivity bias through applying gender swap was taken from Toader et al. [44].

A five points Likert scale ranging from strongly agree to strongly disagree was included for the answer of each survey question. The survey questions are modifications, adapted from Brauer [10]. The questions for the construct behavioral intention were derived from Venkatesh et al. [47]. In order to avoid repetitive, redundant questions that mislead the actual measurement of the construct behavioral intention due to survey fatigue [18] of the participants, the first indicator question for behavioral intention (BI1) was formulated in a more general way. This approach has been adapted from a related vignette study [11] in which it was used for the factor communication competence.

You have just placed a large order online at a drugstore and noticed that you have forgotten the disinfectant. Since the order has exceeded the minimum order value, you would like to add the forgotten disinfectant. There is a chatbot on the customer service website of the drugstore. You contact the chatbot with your request and the following conversation ensues:

Fig. 2. Survey design for the group with absent gendered anthropomorphic design cues

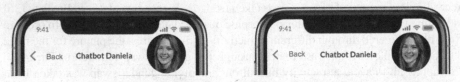

Fig. 3. Female anthropomorphic chatbot design

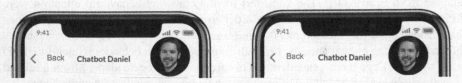

Fig. 4. Male anthropomorphic chatbot design

Table 1. Questionnaire

Performance Expectancy
(PE1) With this chatbot, I could do my online shopping faster.
(PE2) I find the chatbot useful to assist me with customer service concerns.
Effort Expectancy
(EE1) Having a conversation with the chatbot is intuitive.
(EE2) I would not need any help to use the chatbot.
(EE3) Customers have enough basic technical knowledge to conduct this chat with the chatbot.
Social Influence
(SI1) My family/friends/environment use chatbots regularly.
(SI2) Chatbots have a good reputation in my environment.
Behavioral Intention
(BI1) It will be impossible to avoid using chatbots in customer service in the next 6 months.
(BI2) I intend to use chatbots in customer service in the next 6 months.

Also, the indicator question EE3 was address towards the effort expectation of customer perceptions in general. Since the participants, however, were assigned into a customer role through the vignette description, they were indirectly intended to infer about their of own perception and subsequently create a more reliable construct of effort expectancy.

Altogether, 209 persons from Germany participated in the survey. 86 participants saw the chatbot with the female anthropomorphic design, 60 the male anthropomorphic chatbot design and 63 the non-gendered anthropomorphic chatbot design. The participants were recruited via network sampling [28] through Facebook and Survey Circle. The dataset was collected as part of the author's Master's Thesis [34] that distinctively focused on the UTAUT application, but not on the moderating effect of gendered anthropomorphic design cues. The participants were randomly assigned to one chatbot design group. The statistical power of each group was validated with G*Power and higher than the threshold of 0.8 (alpha $= 0.05$, $f^2 = 0.2$). To be precise, the statistical power of the male chatbot group was 0.81, the one of the female chatbot group was 0.94 and the one of the non-anthropomorphic chatbot group was 0.83. 56% of the overall participants were women and 44% men. Most of the participants, 85.2%, were in the age group between 20–35 years and can therefore be assigned to the generation millennials [30]. The precise gender and age distribution of the participants in each group is shown in Table 2. As in related studies [e.g. 43, 47], this study controls the effect of the variables gender and age on the decisive construct behavioral intention.

Table 2. Gender and age distribution of survey participants

Gendered anthropomorphic design cues group	Gender of participants		Age distribution				
	Female	Male	<20	20-25	26-35	36-45	>45
Female	32.6%	67.4%	0%	59.3%	27.9%	8.1%	4.7%
Male	76.7%	23.3%	13.3%	58.3%	21.7%	0%	6.7%
Absent	68.3%	31.7%	3.2%	50.8%	36.5%	9.5%	0%

4 Results

For testing H1a, H1b and H1c of the research model, partial least squares structural equation modelling (PLS-SEM) has been applied to each chatbot design group. PLS-SEM is especially suitable for the assessment of latent constructs, such as performance expectancy, effort expectancy, social influence and behavioral intention [20]. Due to the robustness of PLS-SEM towards relatively small sample sizes and the ability to evaluate complex relationship models, its application became quite famous over the last years [21]. For evaluating H2, the analysis proceeds with a multigroup analysis (MGA). The software SmartPLS 3.3.3 [39] was used for the calculations.

The impact of the control variable age on the decisive factor behavioral intention was found to be insignificant across all chatbot design groups: $\beta = -0.083$; $p = 0.210$ for the female anthropomorphic design group, $\beta = -0.073$, $p = 0.265$ for the male anthropomorphic design group and $\beta = 0.040$, $p = 0.362$ for the non-anthropomorphic chatbot design group. The impact of gender was also insignificant for the female anthropomorphic chatbot design group ($\beta = -0.058$, $p = 0.262$) and for the male anthropomorphic chatbot design group ($\beta = -0.1$, $p = 0.162$). For the non-anthropomorphic design group the effect of gender was significant ($\beta = 0.272$, $p < 0.01$), but the effect size was weak at $f^2 = 0.128$. Due to the insignificant effects of age on the behavioral intention and the merely small effect of gender in the non-anthropomorphic design group, the effects of the control variables can be neglected. Thus, they are not part of the further evaluation.

PLS-SEM requires an evaluation of the outer model in order to assess the reliability of the construct measurements and the assessment of the inner model which reveals the significance between the construct relationships [20]. The inner research model, the impact of performance expectancy, effort expectancy and social influence on the behavioral intention, is described as formative construct, whereas each latent variable is reflectively measured. As elaborated in Hair et al. [20], the evaluation of the reflectively measured outer model requires the investigation of the internal-consistency reliability, convergence validity, as well as the discriminant validity.

The internal-consistency reliability is measured through the composite reliability which is above the threshold 0.7 for all constructs. The convergence validity is assured through the assessment of the average variance extracted which is above 0.5 in all cases (Table 3). Also, the indicator loadings should be regarded in order to assess the convergence validity (Table 4). With one exception of the factor loading of SI2 with the value of 0.412, all loadings are above 0.6. Since 0.4 is regarded to be the minimum acceptable threshold for the indicator loadings [21], convergence validity is ensured. The Heterotrait-Monotrait (HTMT) criterion is recommended as measure for the assessment of the discriminant validity [20]. All of the HTMT criteria of the three models are below the strict threshold of 0.85 (Table 5). Thus, discriminant validity is proven.

For the evaluation of the inner, structural model, the value inflation factor (VIF) is regarded first. Table 5 also shows the VIF values for each chatbot design group. Since all of the VIFs are above the minimum threshold of 0.2 and below the threshold of five, no collinearity problems exist for the structural model. Therefore, the structural model provides a valid basis for testing the hypotheses through the path coefficients.

Table 3. Internal-consistency reliability and convergence validity

Latent construct	Composite reliability > 0.7			Average Variance Extracted > 0.5		
	Female	Male	Absent	Female	Male	Absent
Performance Expectancy	0.918	0.796	0.860	0.848	0.666	0.758
Effort Expectancy	0.811	0.784	0.804	0.589	0.552	0.578
Social Influence	0.810	0.701	0.849	0.681	0.579	0.740
Behavioral Intention	0.880	0.870	0.892	0.787	0.771	0.804

Table 4. Indicator loadings

Construct indicator	Indicator loadings > 0.4		
	Female	Male	Absent
Performance Expectancy			
PE1	0.931	0.924	0.964
PE2	0.911	0.691	0.765
Effort Expectancy			
EE1	0.793	0.825	0.795
EE2	0.748	0.605	0.719
EE3	0.761	0.780	0.766
Social Influence			
SI1	0.811	0.994	0.953
SI2	0.839	0.412	0.756
Behavioral Intention			
BI1	0.863	0.871	0.897
BI2	0.910	0.885	0.897

Table 5. Discriminant validity and value inflation factor

Latent construct	HTMT < 0.85				VIF < 5
	1	2	3	4	1
Female					
1 Behavioral Intention					
2 Effort Expectancy	0.422				1.519
3 Performance Expectancy	0.510	0.762			1.559
4 Social Influence	0.775	0.245	0.325		1.051
Male					
1 Behavioral Intention					
2 Effort Expectancy	0.514				1.358
3 Performance Expectancy	0.759	0.719			1.296
4 Social Influence	0.468	0.549	0.631		1.192
Absent					
1 Behavioral Intention					
2 Effort Expectancy	0.455				1.070
3 Performance Expectancy	0.231	0.354			1.083
4 Social Influence	0.661	0.231	0.300		1.027

For evaluating the significances of the path coefficients, the data for each chatbot group has been bootstrapped 5.000 times (one-tailed t-test, p < 0.01). The path coefficient of performance expectancy on the behavioral intention is significant at p = 0.01 for the female anthropomorphic designed chatbot group, as well as for the male anthropomorphic designed chatbot group at p < 0.001. Thus, H1a is accepted for the female and male anthropomorphic design group. For the non-anthropomorphic designed chatbot group the performance expectancy path coefficient does not significantly impact the behavioral intention, therefore, H1a has to be rejected for the group with absent anthropomorphic design.

Both path coefficients for the effort expectancy on the behavioral intention in the female and male anthropomorphic designed group are not significant which leads to a rejection of H1b for those two design groups. In contrast, in the non-anthropomorphic designed group, the influence of the effort expectancy on the behavioral intention is significant at p < 0.01. Therefore, H1b can be accepted for the non-anthropomorphic designed chatbot group.

Also, the path coefficient of the social influence on the behavioral intention is significant (p < 0.01) for the female anthropomorphic designed and the non-anthropomorphic designed chatbot group (p < 0.001). Therefore, H1c is accepted for the group with female and absent gendered anthropomorphic design. For the male anthropomorphic designed group, H1c has to be rejected because no significant impact of the social influence on the behavioral intention was found. Figure 5 summarizes the path coefficient values and their significances at each design group.

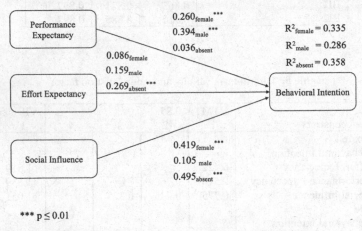

*** p ≤ 0.01

Fig. 5. Path coefficients and determination coefficients

Q^2 for the behavioral intention of the female chatbot model is 0.195. For the male chatbot model Q^2 is 0.264 and for the non-anthropomorphic chatbot model Q^2 is 0.224. These Q^2 values are calculated using blindfolding with an omission distance of eight and indicate that all of the models have a prognostic relevance [21].

As structured in Table 6, the MGA shows that the performance expectancy coefficient of the female and the non-gendered anthropomorphic design group show a difference of 0.224 which is significant at $p < 0.1$. A significant path difference of 0.358 is also found between the male anthropomorphic chatbot and the non-gendered anthropomorphic chatbot group at $p < 0.01$. Therefore, both gendered anthropomorphic chatbot design groups significantly differ from the non-anthropomorphic design group which indicates a moderating influence of the variable gendered anthropomorphic design cues. The MGA shows no significant differences across the design groups regarding the impact of the effort expectancy on the behavioral intention. However, the social influence which the structural model found to be significant for the female and non-anthropomorphic group, significantly differs from the path coefficient of the male design group. These results show that the different categories of the variable gendered anthropomorphism yield significant differences on the determinants of the behavioral intention. Therefore, gendered anthropomorphic design cues moderate their impact and H2 can be accepted.

Table 6. Multigroup analysis result

	Female	Male	Diff. (Female vs. Male)
PE -> BI	0.260***	0.394***	-0.134
EE -> BI	0.086	0.159	-0.073
SI -> BI	0.419***	0.105	0.313**

	Female	Absent	Diff. (Female vs. Absent)
PE -> BI	0.260***	0.036	0.224*
EE -> BI	0.086	0.269***	-0.183
SI -> BI	0.419***	0.495***	-0.079

	Male	Absent	Diff. (Male vs. Absent)
PE -> BI	0.394***	0.036	0.358***
EE -> BI	0.159	0.269***	-0.110
SI -> BI	0.105	0.495***	-0.392**

Diff. = difference, *$p < 0.1$, **$p < 0.05$, ***$p < 0.01$

5   Discussion

The results show that performance expectancy influences the behavioral intention towards using chatbots only for the gendered anthropomorphic designed chatbot groups. This relationship is significant, regardless if the designed type of gender is female or male. This result implies that people who face a visually gendered anthropomorphic designed chatbot might be influenced by the performance they expect from using the chatbot in the post-purchase stage of customer service. This finding is in line with the CASA paradigm [32] that highlights the positive effects of human-like attributes on how humans perceive chatbots [27].

Second, social influence has been found to have a significantly positive impact on the behavioral intention to use chatbots in the female anthropomorphic designed chatbot group, but not in the male anthropomorphic designed chatbot group. This adds to prior research that found female chatbot design to be superior in customer's perception

[8, 44]. This might be one reason why female chatbot design is predominant in practice [17]. Therefore, if people talk with their social network about chatbots which creates social influence towards using chatbots, they might talk about chatbots in their female anthropomorphic design associations. To give an example, the chatbot of Zalando is called "Emma" or the chatbot of Lufthansa is called "Mildred" [26].

Third, this paper provides a contribution to the call for applications of the UTAUT for AI-based technologies [46]. The three key UTAUT variables explain approximately 30% of the variance of the behavioral intention. This is an adequate explanation for an early-stage behavioral investigation [21]. Also, the simplicity of the model, describing the behavioral intention through three variables, already makes it possible to reveal significant differences in the determinants of the behavioral intention triggered by differently gendered anthropomorphic chatbot design cues. However, this study also shows that the UTAUT should be applied under the consideration of gendered anthropomorphic design cues as moderators. Therefore, an extension of gendered anthropomorphic design influences in the investigation context of chatbots is recommended.

Finally, these findings generate design implications useful for practice in the field of post-purchase customer service. Since companies applying chatbots usually aim high chatbot usage, the determinants of the behavioral intention should be regarded under considerations of moderating gendered anthropomorphic design effects. If companies apply a chatbot that's performance is not very elaborated yet (e.g. for testing reasons), it could be advisable to apply a chatbot with absent gendered anthropomorphic design because the findings suggest that for absent gendered chatbots, performance expectations will be less determining for behavioral intention than for gendered chatbots.

However, if the chatbot performance is more elaborated and even able to perform service tasks, as it was the case in this study, gendered anthropomorphic designed chatbots might be the right choice. In order to additionally reach customers that are impacted by their network, companies should stick to the currently predominant choice of designing their chatbot with female gendered anthropomorphic design cues.

6   Limitations and Further Research Implications

This study does not come without limitations. As emphasized in the study design section, the vignette study design was reasonable for assessing existing moderating effects of gendered anthropomorphic design cues on the behavioral intention determinants. However, future research should address the limitations of vignette studies. Vignette studies are suitable to reveal existing user attitudes, but these results need to be verified through observations of actual chatbot interactions [11, 16]. While chatbots are gradually becoming more advanced in their communication capabilities, it can be assumed that as soon as an actual chatbot exists in a post-purchase customer service setting that's capabilities are on the same level as the ones mocked in the vignette of this research, similar results are expected. Thus, replicating this study in such an actual chatbot setting would be of interest. Also, while the participants of this study mostly consisted of millennials, the results should only be used for behavioral generalizations among millennials. Further studies that target an older age group cannot only achieve higher generalizability but might also find additional variables that are affected by the moderating impact of gendered anthropomorphic design. Since elder people were found to be particularly influenced by their perceived enjoyment regarding their behavioral intention to use robots [22], the moderating effect of gendered anthropomorphic chatbot design might affect this additional variable as well. Furthermore, the results of this study hold for an intelligent chatbot applied in the post-purchase customer service context. Applications of intelligent chatbots in other contexts, such as the purchase phase, might conclude different results because the customers might have e.g. different performance expectations towards a chatbot at this stage. Finally, practical implications derived from chatbot design studies stress the need for investigating ethical topics around chatbot design [8].

7 Conclusion

To utilize the huge potential of chatbots in customer service automation, companies are in need to assess their customer's behavioral intention to use chatbots. This assessment requires the investigation of visual design influences as moderators of the behavioral intention. Especially, gendered anthropomorphic design cues impact performance expectations and social influence towards using chatbots. The UTAUT offers suitable guidance for the assessment of the behavioral intention towards using AI-based chatbots and the investigation of their moderating design influences.

References

1. Adam, M., Wessel, M., Benlian, A.: AI-based chatbots in customer service and their effects on user compliance. Electron. Mark. **31**(2), 427–445 (2020). https://doi.org/10.1007/s12525-020-00414-7
2. Ajzen, I.: From Intentions to Actions: A Theory of Planned Behavior. In: Kuhl, J., Beckmann, J. (eds.) Action Control. SSSP, pp. 11–39. Springer, Heidelberg (1985). https://doi.org/10.1007/978-3-642-69746-3_2
3. Ameen, N., Tarhini, A., Reppel, A., Anand, A.: Customer experiences in the age of artificial intelligence. Comput. Hum. Behav. **114**, 106548 (2021). https://doi.org/10.1016/j.chb.2020.106548
4. Amelia, A., Mathies, C., Patterson, P.G.: Customer acceptance of frontline service robots in retail banking: a qualitative approach. J. Serv. Manage. ahead-of-print (2021). https://doi.org/10.1108/JOSM-10-2020-0374
5. Araujo, T.: Living up to the chatbot hype: The influence of anthropomorphic design cues and communicative agency framing on conversational agent and company perceptions. Comput. Hum. Behav. **85**, 183–189 (2018). https://doi.org/10.1016/j.chb.2018.03.051
6. Basco, R., Hernández-Perlines, F., Rodríguez-García, M.: The effect of entrepreneurial orientation on firm performance: a multigroup analysis comparing China, Mexico, and Spain. J. Bus. Res. **113**, 409–421 (2020). https://doi.org/10.1016/j.jbusres.2019.09.020
7. Blut, M., Wang, C., Wünderlich, N.V., Brock, C.: Understanding anthropomorphism in service provision: a meta-analysis of physical robots, chatbots, and other AI. J. Acad. Mark. Sci. **49**(4), 632–658 (2021). https://doi.org/10.1007/s11747-020-00762-y
8. Borau, S., Otterbring, T., Laporte, S., Wamba, S.F.: The most human bot: female gendering increases humanness perceptions of bots and acceptance of AI. Psychol. Mark. **38**(7), 1052–1068 (2021). https://doi.org/10.1002/mar.21480

9. Brahnam, S., De Angeli, A.: Gender affordances of conversational agents. Interact. Comput. **24**(3), 139–153 (2012). https://doi.org/10.1016/j.intcom.2012.05.001

10. Brauer, R.R.: Akzeptanz kooperativer Roboter im industriellen Kontext. Dissertation. Universitätsverlag Chemnitz (2017)

11. Chung, M., Ko, E., Joung, H., Kim, S.J.: Chatbot e-service and customer satisfaction regarding luxury brands. J. Bus. Res. **117**, 587–595 (2020). https://doi.org/10.1016/j.jbusres.2018.10.004

12. Dale, R.: The return of the chatbots. Nat. Lang. Eng. **22**(5), 811–817 (2016). https://doi.org/10.1017/S1351324916000243

13. Davis, F.D.: A technology acceptance model for empirically testing new end-user information systems: theory and results. Ph.D. Thesis. Massachusetts Institute of Technology (1985)

14. Dingler, T., Choudhury, A., Kostakos, V.: Biased bots: conversational agents to overcome polarization. In: Proceedings of the 2018 ACM International Joint Conference and 2018 International Symposium on Pervasive and Ubiquitous Computing and Wearable Computers, pp. 1664–1668. ACM, Singapore (2018). https://doi.org/10.1145/3267305.3274189

15. Dm-drogerie markt: Wie können wir helfen? https://cs.dm.de/csp/. Accessed 28 Aug 2021

16. Edwards, C., Edwards, A., Spence, P.R., Shelton, A.K.: Is that a bot running the social media feed? Testing the differences in perceptions of communication quality for a human agent and a bot agent on Twitter. Comput. Hum. Behav. **33**, 372–376 (2014). https://doi.org/10.1016/j.chb.2013.08.013

17. Feine, J., Gnewuch, U., Morana, S., Maedche, A.: Gender bias in chatbot design. In: Følstad, A., et al. (eds.) CONVERSATIONS 2019. LNCS, vol. 11970, pp. 79–93. Springer, Cham (2020). https://doi.org/10.1007/978-3-030-39540-7_6

18. Fernandes, T., Oliveira, E.: Understanding consumers' acceptance of automated technologies in service encounters: drivers of digital voice assistants adoption. J. Bus. Res. **122**, 180–191 (2021). https://doi.org/10.1016/j.jbusres.2020.08.058

19. Go, E., Sundar, S.S.: Humanizing chatbots: the effects of visual, identity and conversational cues on humanness perceptions. Comput. Hum. Behav. **97**, 304–316 (2019). https://doi.org/10.1016/j.chb.2019.01.020

20. Hair, J.F., Hult, G.T.M., Ringle, C.M., Sarstedt, M., Richter, N.F., Hauff, S.: Partial Least Squares Strukturgleichungsmodellierung: Eine anwendungsorientierte Einführung. Verlag Franz Vahlen GmbH, Munich (2017)

21. Hair, J.F., Ringle, C.M., Sarstedt, M.: PLS-SEM: indeed a silver bullet. J. Mark. Theor. Pract. **19**(2), 139–151 (2011). https://doi.org/10.2753/MTP1069-6679190202

22. Heerink, M., Kröse, B., Wielinga, B.J., Evers, V.: Enjoyment, intention to use and actual use of a conversational robot by elderly people. In: Fong T., Dautenhahn, K. (eds.) HRI 2008: Proceedings of the third ACM/IEEE International Conference on Human-Robot Interaction, pp. 113–119. ACM (2008). https://doi.org/10.1145/1349822.1349838

23. Hoyer, W.D., Kroschke, M., Schmitt, B., Kraume, K., Shankar, V.: Transforming the customer experience through new technologies. J. Interact. Mark. **51**, 57–71 (2020). https://doi.org/10.1016/j.intmar.2020.04.001

24. Huang, M.-H., Rust, R.T.: Engaged to a robot? The role of AI in service. J. Serv. Res. **24**(1), 30–41 (2021). https://doi.org/10.1177/1094670520902266

25. Juniper Research: Chatbots to Deliver $11bn in Annual Cost Savings for Retail, Banking & Healthcare Sectors by 2023. https://www.juniperresearch.com/press/press-releases/chatbots-to-deliver-11bn-cost-savings-2023. Accessed 06 Aug 2021

26. Lanser, A.: Chatbots übernehmen den Kundenservice. https://www.event-partner.de/business/chatbots-uebernehmen-den-kundenservice/. Accessed 13 Aug 2021

27. Lei, S.I., Shen, H., Ye, S.: A comparison between chatbot and human service: customer perception and reuse intention. Int. J. Contemp. Hosp. Manag. **33**(11), 3977–3995 (2021). https://doi.org/10.1108/IJCHM-12-2020-1399

28. Liebrecht, C., Sander, L., van Hooijdonk, C.: Too informal? How a chatbot's communication style affects brand attitude and quality of interaction. In: Følstad, A., et al. (eds.) CONVERSATIONS 2020. LNCS, vol. 12604, pp. 16–31. Springer, Cham (2021). https://doi.org/10.1007/978-3-030-68288-0_2

29. Ling, E.C., Tussyadiah, I., Tuomi, A., Stienmetz, J., Ioannou, A.: Factors influencing users' adoption and use of conversational agents: a systematic review. Psychol. Mark. 38(7), 1031–1051 (2021). https://doi.org/10.1002/mar.21491

30. McDonald, N.C.: Are millennials really the "Go-Nowhere" generation? J. Am. Plann. Assoc. 81(2), 90–103 (2015). https://doi.org/10.1080/01944363.2015.1057196

31. Nass, C., Moon, Y.: Machines and mindlessness: social responses to computers. J. Soc. Issues 56(1), 81–103 (2000). https://doi.org/10.1111/0022-4537.00153

32. Nass, C., Steuer, J., Tauber, E.R.: Computers are social actors. In: Conference Companion on Human Factors in Computing Systems - CHI 1994, pp. 72–78. ACM Press, Boston, Massachusetts, United States (1994). https://doi.org/10.1145/259963.260288

33. Ng, M., Coopamootoo, K.P.L., Toreini, E., Aitken, M., Elliot, K., van Moorsel, A.: Simulating the Effects of Social Presence on Trust, Privacy Concerns and Usage Intentions in Automated Bots for Finance. arXiv:2006.15449 (2020)

34. Pawlik, V.P.: The Behavioral Intention of Intelligent Chatbots in Customer Service based on the Unified Theory of Acceptance and Use of Technology (UTAUT). Master's Thesis (unpublished). Technical University of Munich (2021)

35. Pillai, R., Sivathanu, B.: Adoption of AI-based chatbots for hospitality and tourism. Int. J. Contemp. Hosp. Manag. 32(10), 3199–3226 (2020). https://doi.org/10.1108/IJCHM-04-2020-0259

36. Pixabay. https://pixabay.com/photos/business-lady-woman-young-woman-3560916/. Accessed 28 Aug 2021

37. Rese, A., Ganster, L., Baier, D.: Chatbots in retailers' customer communication: how to measure their acceptance? J. Retail. Consum. Serv. 56, 102176 (2020). https://doi.org/10.1016/j.jretconser.2020.102176

38. Rhim, J., Kwak, M., Gong, Y., Gweon, G.: Application of humanization to survey chatbots: change in chatbot perception, interaction experience, and survey data quality. Comput. Hum. Behav. 126, 107034 (2022). https://doi.org/10.1016/j.chb.2021.107034

39. Ringle, C.M., Wende, S., Becker, J.-M.: SmartPLS 3. SmartPLS, Bönningstedt (2015)

40. Roggeveen, A.L., Sethuraman, R.: Customer-interfacing retail technologies in 2020 and beyond: an integrative framework and research directions. J. Retail. 96(3), 299–309 (2020). https://doi.org/10.1016/j.jretai.2020.08.001

41. Sheehan, B., Jin, H.S., Gottlieb, U.: Customer service chatbots: anthropomorphism and adoption. J. Bus. Res. 115, 14–24 (2020). https://doi.org/10.1016/j.jbusres.2020.04.030

42. Shumanov, M., Johnson, L.: Making conversations with chatbots more personalized. Comput. Hum. Behav. 117, 106627 (2021). https://doi.org/10.1016/j.chb.2020.106627

43. Sugumar, M., Chandra, S.: Do I desire chatbots to be like humans? exploring factors for adoption of chatbots for financial services. J. Int. Technol. Inf. Manage. 30(3), 38–77 (2021)

44. Toader, D.-C., et al.: The effect of social presence and chatbot errors on trust. Sustainability 12(1), 256 (2020). https://doi.org/10.3390/su12010256

45. Venkatesh, V., Thong, J.Y.L., Xu, X.: Consumer acceptance and use of information technology: extending the unified theory of acceptance use of technology. MIS Q. 36(1), 157–178 (2012). https://doi.org/10.2307/41410412

46. Venkatesh, V.: Adoption and use of AI tools: a research agenda grounded in UTAUT. Ann. Oper. Res. 308, 641–652 (2022). https://doi.org/10.1007/s10479-020-03918-9

47. Venkatesh, V., Morris, M.G., Davis, G.B., Davis, F.D.: User acceptance of information technology: towards a unified view. MIS Q. 27(3), 425–478 (2003). https://doi.org/10.2307/30036540

48. Wamba-Taguimdje, S.-L., Wamba, S.F., Kamdjoug, J.R.K., Wanko, C.E.T.: Influence of artificial intelligence (AI) on firm performance: the business value of AI-based transformation projects. Bus. Process. Manag. J. 26(7), 1893–1924 (2020). https://doi.org/10.1108/BPMJ-10-2019-0411

49. Williams, M.D., Rana, N.P., Dwivedi, Y.K.: The unified theory of acceptance and use of technology (UTAUT): a literature review. J. Enterp. Inf. Manag. 28(3), 443–488 (2015). https://doi.org/10.1108/JEIM-09-2014-0088

50. Wirtz, J., et al.: Brave new world: service robots in the frontline. J. Serv. Manag. 29(5), 907–931 (2018). https://doi.org/10.1108/JOSM-04-2018-0119

51. Yáñez-Araque, B., Sánchez-Infante Hernández, J.P., Gutiérrez-Broncano, S., Jiménez-Estévez, P.: Corporate social responsibility in micro-, small- and medium-sized enterprises: multigroup analysis of family vs. nonfamily firms. J. Bus. Res. 124, 581–592 (2021). https://doi.org/10.1016/j.jbusres.2020.10.023

Author Index

Printed in the United States
by Baker & Taylor Publisher Services